SITUATIONAL PREVENTION OF CHILD SEXUAL ABUSE

Richard Wortley

and

Stephen Smallbone

editors

Crime Prevention Studies
Volume 19

Criminal Justice Press
Monsey, NY, USA

Willan Publishing
Cullompton, Devon, UK

2006

ISSN (series): 1065-7029.
ISBN (cloth): 978-1-881798-60-6
ISBN (paper): 978-1-881798-61-3

Cover design (paperback edition) by Alisa Wortley.

Cover design (cloth edition) by G & H Soho, Inc.

CRIME PREVENTION STUDIES

Ronald V. Clarke, Series Editor

Crime Prevention Studies is an international book series dedicated to research on situational crime prevention and other initiatives to reduce opportunities for crime. Most volumes center on particular topics chosen by expert guest editors. The editors of each volume, in consultation with the series editor, commission the papers to be published and select peer reviewers.

*   *   *

Volume 1, edited by Ronald V. Clarke, 1993.

Volume 2, edited by Ronald V. Clarke, 1994.

Volume 3, edited by Ronald V. Clarke, 1994 (out of print).

Volume 4, *Crime and Place*, edited by John E. Eck and David Weisburd, 1995.

Volume 5, *The Politics and Practice of Situational Crime Prevention*, edited by Ross Homel, 1996.

Volume 6, *Preventing Mass Transit Crime*, edited by Ronald V. Clarke, 1996.

Volume 7, *Policing for Prevention: Reducing Crime, Public Intoxication and Injury*, edited by Ross Homel, 1997.

Volume 8, *Crime Mapping and Crime Prevention*, edited by David Weisburd and J. Thomas McEwen, 1997.

Volume 9, *Civil Remedies and Crime Prevention*, edited by Lorraine Green Mazerolle and Jan Roehl, 1998.

Volume 10, *Surveillance of Public Space: CCTV, Street Lighting and Crime Prevention*, edited by Kate Painter and Nick Tilley, 1999.

Volume 11, *Illegal Drug Markets: From Research to Prevention Policy*, edited by Mangai Natarajan and Mike Hough, 2000.

(continued)

Contents

(continued)

Contents

Introduction

by

Richard Wortley

and

Stephen Smallbone
School of Criminology and Criminal Justice, Griffith University

The impetus for this volume of *Crime Prevention Studies* grew from our many lunchroom discussions about the relevance, or otherwise, of situational crime prevention for understanding and preventing sexual offenses against children. Our common ground had been established years before. We had both, at different times and in different jurisdictions, worked as prison psychologists. However, our professional and academic careers had taken us on rather different paths. One of us (Stephen Smallbone) had maintained a keen interest in the clinical forensic assessment and treatment of offenders, particularly adolescent and adult sexual offenders. The other (Richard Wortley) had turned his attention away from offender rehabilitation and towards situational crime prevention theory and application. While we ourselves managed to resist any temptation to polarize our discussions, we were aware that our fields of work were in many ways in opposition to one another. Indeed, within the conceptual bases of these fields of work lie fundamental disagreements about how best to understand and prevent crime – the pathological versus the ordinary; the criminal versus the crime; enduring dispositions versus immediate situations; offender rehabilitation versus primary prevention.

Crime Prevention Studies, volume 19 (2006), pp. 1–5.

We were also aware that, outside our lunchroom, a much broader public and political debate about sexual offenses against children was raging. In Australia, as elsewhere, we have seen an extraordinary succession of legislative and policy reforms exclusively targeting child-sex offenders. In the last few years, we have seen campaigns to increase public awareness and reporting rates, the formation of special police taskforces, changes to rules of evidence, increased penalties and sentences, the establishment of a national offender register, reviews of community notification laws, implementation of wide-reaching employment screening programs, major investments in specialized sex offender treatment programs, a tightening of parole policies, the introduction of preventive detention legislation, and so on. All of these, of course, are designed to intervene only after sexual offenses against children have already occurred. Very little attention has been given to how these offenses might be prevented from occurring in the first place. No attention at all, it seems to us, has been given to the design and organization of physical and social environments so that the potential for these offenses to occur might be minimized.

Meanwhile, back in the lunchroom, we pondered the lack of scholarly exchange between sexual offender researchers and situational crime prevention researchers. To date neither of these fields has paid much attention to situational aspects of sexual offending against children, nor have they paid much attention to one another. Sexual offender researchers have concentrated on individual-level explanations and, perhaps in part to avoid controversies about moral responsibility, have tended to ignore the influence of immediate circumstances on specific offense incidents. Where situational factors have been considered, these have tended to be construed in offender-centered terms (e.g., a state of anxiety or anger, without reference to specific eliciting conditions). Sexual offenses against children are by definition interpersonal offenses, and typically occur in private places in circumstances where the offender and victim already know one another. Situational crime prevention researchers have, by contrast, tended to concentrate on property offenses that are committed in public places by offenders who do not know their victim. It may therefore be unsurprising that the reach of situational prevention has until now not extended to sexual offenses against children.

Our discussion led to a decision to invite prominent researchers from the sexual offender field and from the situational crime prevention field to consider, from their own perspectives, how situational crime prevention principles might be applied to sexual offenses against children. We wanted to define situational prevention broadly to include strategies ranging from primary prevention through to relapse prevention with persistent offenders. We hoped that this might result in a convergence of established expertise, and of new ideas, on the problem at hand. The aim of this volume, then, is to examine the situational bases of sexual offenses against children and, from this examination, to suggest situational strategies that might prevent these offenses.

This is, as far as we are aware, the first systematic attempt to apply a situational crime prevention rationale to understanding sexual offenses against children. We have attempted, therefore, to cover a wide variety of perspectives in order to establish some conceptual and empirical foundations.[1] The volume begins with two chapters that approach the problem from more or less opposite directions. In chapter 2, we (Wortley & Smallbone) set out a framework for applying situational prevention principles to understanding and preventing sexual offenses against children. We argue that a situational perspective involves a fundamental (and sometimes surprisingly difficult) shift in focus from the child-sex *offender* to the child-sex *offense* – to the questions of how, when, where and why these offenses take place. In chapter 3, Bill Marshall, Geris Serran and Liam Marshall provide an overview, from a clinical perspective, of dispositional and situational factors in child molestation. They remind us of the importance of understanding situational factors in terms of person-situation interactions, and they highlight one of the key challenges for situational prevention in this area – how to intervene in homes and other private places, where most sexual offenses against children occur, without diminishing the quality of trust between children and adults upon which our society so fundamentally relies.

In chapter 4, Leonore Simon and Kristen Zgoba present new U.S. National Incident-Based Reporting System (NIBRS) data on sexual offenses against children, and compare these to NIBRS data on several other personal offense types. Among other things, this work provides an important empirical foundation for population-wide targeting of prevention, legislation, and investigation. Conceptually, the work draws attention to important similarities and differences in the situational dimensions of sexual and other interpersonal offenses. In chapter 5, Keith Kaufman, Heather Mosher, Megan Carter and Laura Estes consider how the principles of situational crime prevention can be combined with knowledge of adolescent and adult sexual offender *modus operandi* to inform sexual abuse prevention policy and practice. This is a very detailed analysis, which takes account both of the variations in sexual offender modus operandi and of the practical opportunities and constraints for primary prevention. We think sexual offender modus operandi research may be one of the keys to unlocking the potential of situational prevention of sexual offenses against children.

In chapter 6, Pierre Tremblay presents results of a qualitative study of interactions among "boy lovers," and between these men and the adolescent males with whom they seek sexual and emotional connection. Tremblay's dispassionate treatment of his subject matter offers some rare and incisive insights into the personal world of these men, and the "convergence settings" to which they and their victims are drawn. In chapter 7, Max Taylor and Ethel Quayle take us to the virtual world of the Internet. They have, we think, managed to convey a great deal of technical information about how the structure and organization of the Internet can facilitate the trade, distribution and production of child abuse images, in a readily accessible way. Among the many lessons that can be taken from this work is that the responsibility for preventing sexual offenses against children cannot be limited to criminal justice agencies. Their comments about corporate responsibilities in this regard are instructive.

Returning to a clinical theme, in chapter 8 Frank Lambrick and Bill Glaser outline some of the situational elements in sexual offenses committed by intellectually disabled persons. They argue that, as we might expect, intellectually disabled sexual offenders may be especially responsive to situational interventions designed to increase perceived risk and effort. On the other hand, these authors also point to ways in which sexual offenses by this offender group may unwittingly be facilitated by their carers, for example by placing them in residential settings that give them ready access to vulnerable others. In chapter 9, Lynne Eccleston and Tony Ward take issue with the concept of opportunity reduction. Rather than designing interventions to reduce offenders' exposure to criminogenic situations, they suggest that it may be more efficacious to design interventions that *increase* offenders' exposure to prosocial situations. In effect, their argument is to add to, rather than replace, the traditional clinical focus on restrictive risk-management procedures, by assisting known sexual offenders to establish clear approach goals and ultimately to secure "primary human goods." Finally, in chapter 10, Benoit Leclerc, Julie Carpentier and Jean Proulx present empirical data on the modus operandi of adult offenders, distinguishing between offenders who employ coercive strategies (e.g., threatening the child), manipulative strategies (e.g., bribing the child) and nonpersuasive strategies (e.g., abusing a sleeping child). They argue that different modus operandi require the adoption of different prevention approaches.

We have found the task of assembling the chapters for this volume to be immensely rewarding, and it has helped us to clarify some of our own thoughts. We have also found the exercise to be a challenging one. While we have tried to provide editorial support and guidance, equally, we have tried not to be censorial. In the end, we have not always found ourselves to be in complete agreement with the other authors, nor even sometimes between ourselves. But then our aim was not so much to achieve consensus as it was to stimulate discussion and debate.

We would like to thank each of the authors for their contributions. In many cases we were asking them to move into unfamiliar territory and to consider new ways of thinking. We greatly appreciate their willingness to engage in this exercise and we believe that collectively they have made an important contribution to establishing some conceptual and empirical foundations for the situational prevention of sexual offenses against children.

NOTES

1. In common with other books on the topic of child sexual abuse, this volume deals only with male offenders. While there are cases of females who sexually abuse children, the overwhelming majority of offenders are male, and almost all available research in the area has been conducted on males.

Applying Situational Principles to Sexual Offenses against Children

by

Richard Wortley

and

Stephen Smallbone
School of Criminology and Criminal Justice,
Griffith University

Abstract: *Explanations of sexual offending against children have traditionally focused on the intrapsychic forces that are assumed to drive the offender's deviant behavior. The situational crime prevention perspective, on the other hand, examines the immediate behavioral setting to identify factors that encourage or permit sexual abuse. Empirical evidence increasingly indicates that sexual offenses against children are significantly mediated by opportunities and other environmental conditions. It is argued in this chapter that the primary prevention of the sexual abuse of children may be effected by systematically identifying and altering these problematic environmental elements.*

This chapter outlines the case for applying a situational prevention model to sexual offenses against children. It examines evidence for the situational bases of these offenses, describes a situational typology of sexual offenders against children, outlines the settings in which their offending occurs, and proposes situational strategies for preventing these offenses. Regular

Crime Prevention Studies, volume 19 (2006), pp. 7–35.

readers of the *Crime Prevention Studies* series will be familiar with the principles of situational crime prevention. However, we are hoping that this volume will attract researchers and practitioners in the sexual offender treatment field who may not normally read articles on situational crime prevention. Therefore, we will begin by briefly reviewing the key elements of situational prevention.

SITUATIONAL CRIME PREVENTION

Situational crime prevention is a relatively new applied criminological model that shifts the focus from supposed deficits of offenders to aspects of immediate environments that encourage or permit crime to occur. It is based on the premise that all behavior is the result of an interaction between the characteristics of the actor and the circumstances in which an act is performed. The immediate environment is more than a passive backdrop against which action is played out; it plays a fundamental role in initiating and shaping that action. Thus, the probability of crime varies according to both the criminal disposition of the individual and the crime-facilitating nature of the immediate setting. While most crime prevention efforts in the past have concentrated on the criminogenic risks and needs of the offender (e.g., through offender rehabilitation), crime can also be prevented by altering the criminogenic features of the potential crime scene. Situational crime prevention, then, is about creating safe environments rather than creating safe individuals.

Environmental perspectives such as situational crime prevention are classed as theories of crime rather than theories of criminality. This is a crucial distinction. Most criminological theories (and psychological theories that deal with crime) are theories of criminality. They seek to understand the societal, developmental and/or biological factors that have combined to create the criminal offender. In situational crime prevention, however, the criminal event rather than the offender becomes the unit of analysis. To implement situational principles, data are gathered to show where, when, why and how a particular crime occurs. The situational perspective recognizes and explores the fact that crime is not randomly distributed in time and space, but follows patterns. Burglaries, for example, are typically concentrated around "hot spots," and these hot spots are the logical focus for prevention efforts. Situational prevention adopts a micro-level, problem-solving approach that targets specific forms of crime in specific contexts. The desired end-point of a situational analysis is an intervention that is tailor-made to meet the conditions of the particular problem under consideration.

The situational perspective has two distinct theoretical roots. One theoretical basis is the rational choice perspective, adapted from the expected utility model found in economics and in the psychological decision-making literature (Cornish and Clarke, 1986). Underpinning the rational choice perspective is the assumption that criminal conduct is purposive and that offenders commit crime in order to derive some benefit. Offenders are portrayed as active decision makers who undertake cost-benefit analyses of the crime opportunities with which they are presented, and who make choices about whether or not to engage in criminal acts. The immediate environment provides the potential offender with relevant information about the likely rewards and success associated with a contemplated crime. The attractions of criminal behavior include money, increased status, sexual gratification, excitement, and so on. Disincentives include the difficulty involved in carrying out the behavior, the likelihood of getting caught and the anticipated guilt associated with violating personal standards of behavior. Crime occurs when the perceived benefits of offending are judged to outweigh the perceived costs. The decision an offender makes to engage in crime may well be a poor one and ultimately prove to be self-defeating, but nevertheless it represents the most desirable option at that time as the offender saw it.

Situational prevention based on the rational choice perspective involves manipulating the immediate environments of crime in order to increase the cost-benefit ratio of offending as perceived by the potential offender. This approach to prevention is often referred to as opportunity reduction (Clarke, 1995). In first-generation theorizing on situational prevention (Clarke, 1992), opportunities were reduced by manipulating three environmental dimensions – making crime more risky, increasing the effort to commit crime, and reducing the rewards of crime. Later, an additional category was added – removing excuses – that targeted the neutralizations that many offenders utilize to allow themselves to circumvent moral constraints on behavior (Clarke, 1997; Clarke and Homel, 1997).

The other basis for situational approaches derives from research in behavioral, social and environmental psychology. According to this view, there is a subtle and intimate relationship between individuals and their immediate environments. Underpinning the logic of this approach is the principle of behavioral specificity, challenging the view of personality as a cross-situationally consistent predisposition (Mischel, 1968). In fact, it is argued, the behavior of an individual may be highly variable from one situation to the next. A person who may be described by others as aggressive does not behave uniformly in an aggressive manner, but rather, aggression is displayed occasionally and only when certain "favorable" conditions are met. While people obviously differ in their propensity to commit crime, given the right circumstances most people are capable of criminal acts. Unlike the deliberative process described by rational choice theory, according to the behavioral specificity principle immediate environments may influence people at a sub-cognitive level in ways that they might not even be aware of to perform behaviors that they would not otherwise perform.

Whereas rational choice theory focuses on aspects of the environment that enable crime, this second group of theories tends to emphasize the instigating role of immediate environments. Summarizing research in this area, Wortley (2001, 1998, 1997) suggested four basic ways that environments may precipitate crime. Situations can present cues that prompt an individual to perform criminal behavior; they can exert social pressure on an individual to offend; they can weaken moral constraints and so permit potential offenders to commit illegal acts; and they can produce emotional arousal that provokes a criminal response. In addition to reducing opportunities for crime, prevention may require removal of these situational instigators. Recently, Cornish and Clarke (2003) have presented a revised model of situational prevention that incorporates some of these precipitating factors under the heading of reducing provocations.

EVIDENCE FOR THE SITUATIONAL BASES OF SEXUAL OFFENDERS AGAINST CHILDREN

The sexual offending literature has largely ignored the role of situational factors in the prevention of sexual offending against children. Sexual offenders, particularly those who have offended against children, are widely assumed to possess motivations that are pathological and long-standing and that separate them from non-sexual offenders. Their offending is largely portrayed as internally driven and, without individual-level intervention, likely to become chronic. Prevention is usually thought of in a tertiary sense, that is, in terms of treatment with known offenders. While it is true that the role of situational factors in the commission of sexual offenses has been recognized in a number of important conceptual models (Finkelhor, 1984; Marshall and Barbaree, 1990; Marshall et al., this volume;

Pithers et al., 1983), in practice many researchers and clinicians working in the sexual offending area have continued to focus attention on the personal, intrapsychic dimensions of the behavior and to overlook the contributions of immediate circumstances.

For their part, situational crime prevention writers have had very little to say about sexual offending. One suspects that there has been a tacit acceptance by many researchers of the pathology model of sexual offending and a belief that these offenses might fall outside the usual situational prevention rules. Indeed, one criticism often leveled at situational prevention is its disproportionate focus on property crime over interpersonal crime (Trasler, 1986). The thrust of this criticism is the assumption that as the offender's behavior becomes more "irrational," situational prevention has less to offer (Tunnell, 2002).

Recent research, however, has challenged the view that most sexual offenders are dedicated, serial offenders driven by irresistible sexual urges (Pritchard and Bagley, 2000; Simon, 2000, 1997; Smallbone and Wortley, 2004a, 2004b, 2001, 2000; Soothill et al., 2000; Weinrott and Saylor, 1991). For example, Smallbone and Wortley (2001, 2000) examined the official records of 323 convicted child-sex offenders, 169 of whom admitted their offenses and agreed to provide detailed self-report data on their psychosocial/psychosexual histories and offending behaviors. While offenders were not asked directly about the role of situational influences on their offending behavior, a number of findings strongly suggest that immediate environmental factors were important in many cases. These findings include:

- *A late onset of the behavior* – The mean age of offenders at the time of their first sexual contact with a child was 32.4 years and the modal age bracket (accounting for 37% of the sample) was 31 to 40 years. That many offenders were able to resist sexually abusing children for so long suggests the absence of strong sexually deviant motivations. At the same time, the early thirties is an age when many men are assuming child-care and other supervisory roles with children and their opportunities to offend are significantly expanded (Hanson, 2002).

- *A low incidence of chronic sexual offending* – Less than a quarter of the sample had previous convictions for sexual offenses, and almost half reported having restricted their offending to one victim. These findings complement other research that shows the official sexual recidivism rates for sexual offenders are much lower than have been traditionally assumed – around 13% after five years at risk (Hanson and Bussiere, 1998). Again these findings suggest the absence in many offenders of strong deviant motivations.

- *A high incidence of previous non-sexual offenses* – In contrast to the low incidence of previous sexual offending, around 60% of the sample had prior convictions for non-sexual offenses. Of those offenders with previous convictions, their first conviction was four times more likely to be non-sexual (82%) than sexual (18%). For many, sexual offending might be seen as part of a more general involvement in criminal activity (Simon, 2000, 1997). For these offenders, the problem seems to be less some special motivation to sexually abuse children than a more general problem involving the failure to inhibit urges and impulses, especially within the interpersonal domain. That is, many offenders in the sample may be better portrayed as "opportunity takers" than sexual deviants.

- *A low incidence of stranger abuse* – The vast majority of offenders (93.5%) abused their own child or a child that they already knew. Locating and grooming a previously unknown child for the purpose of sexual contact requires a high level of planning, commitment and effort. In contrast, most offenders had sexual contact with children with whom they had immediate or convenient access.

- *A low incidence of networking among offenders* – Around 8% of offenders said that they had talked to other offenders prior to their arrest, and 4% said that they were involved in an organized pedophile group. There was little evidence that offenders sought out a pedophile subculture.

- *A low incidence of child pornography use* – Around 10% admitted to using child pornography and 8% kept records of their sexual contacts with victims. Most offenders did not display the deep interest in pedophilia that one might expect from a dedicated offender.

- *A low incidence of paraphilic (sexually deviant) interests* – Apart from exhibitionism (5.4%), frotteurism (i.e., obtaining sexual gratification by rubbing up against another person, usually in public – 9.0%), and voyeurism (5.4%), fewer than 5% of offenders could have been diagnosed with a paraphilia other than pedophilia, including public masturbation (4.2%), fetishism (1.8%), sexual masochism (1.2%), transvestic fetishism (1.2%), making obscene telephone calls (1.2%), sexual sadism

(0.6%), bestiality (0.6%), and necrophilia (0%) (see also Smallbone and Wortley, 2004a).

Taken together these findings suggest that for many sexual offenders a control model might be more appropriate than a sexual deviance model. According to control theory (Gottfredson and Hirschi, 1990), the propensity to commit crime is widely distributed in the community, and the basic cause of criminal behavior is universal – an absence of restraint. Criminal behavior is intrinsically rewarding and requires no special motivation or pathology, while criminal acts themselves demand little in the way of specialized skills or experience. Offenders do not learn to commit crimes, but rather, they fail to learn not to commit them. Control theory asks you to imagine the extreme case of a child who has grown up without any restrictions being placed on his/her self-gratifying behavior. The outcome in such a scenario would be an individual who satisfies his/her urges indiscriminately. Absence of restraint can manifest in a wide range of behaviors. The offender who succumbs to the temptation to steal is also likely to exercise little restraint when presented with opportunities to rob, assault and so forth. Control theory, then, suggests that the causes of sexual offending against children may be the same as the causes of crime generally. The potential to view children as sexual objects may be more widespread than is usually assumed (e.g., see Barbaree and Marshall, 1989; Laws and Marshall, 1990; Malamuth, 1989; McConaghy, 1993; Smallbone, 2005). Most of the time such urges are kept in check by a range of personal, social and physical constraints. However, opportunity structures and environmental cues may play an important role in weakening controls and facilitating offending behavior (Hirschi, 1988).

TYPES OF OFFENDERS

It should not be inferred from the previous section that the situational perspective necessarily assumes that crime is opportunistic in the sense of being a spur-of-the-moment reaction to a chance circumstance. In fact, rational choice theory was primarily formulated to explain premeditated crime. Crime opportunities may be simply taken as they fortuitously occur, but they may also be sought out or created by the offender. Even planned crimes by highly motivated offenders involve situational considerations. The professional burglar, for example, does not steal arbitrarily. Rather, he/

she carefully selects targets that experience has shown will deliver maximum pay-off and entail minimum risks.

Cornish and Clarke (2003) have sought to clarify the various ways that offenders respond to situations. They proposed three offender types based on the strength of the offender's criminal disposition and the role that situational factors play in his/her offending. The first type is the anti-social predator, which Cornish and Clarke argue is the "default" offender category. These offenders possess ingrained criminal dispositions, and their motivations for offending derive from the intrinsically rewarding nature of the crimes they commit. They utilize situational data to make rational choices about the relative costs and benefits of criminal involvement, and will operate on the environment to increase criminal opportunities. Predators may specialize in a particular type of crime or may be criminally versatile, but in any event all will have developed "knowledge, skills and experience enough to minimize risk and effort, and maximize payoffs" (p. 57).

Applied to sexual offending against children, the antisocial predator equates to the stereotypic predatory child molester. They are high-frequency, chronic offenders. In a further analysis of the Smallbone and Wortley (2000) data[1] (Wortley and Smallbone, under review), 23% of the sample were identified as persistent sexual offenders (they had previous sexual offence convictions). This comprised 5% who were specialists (they had previous convictions only for sexual offences) and 18% who were versatile (they had previous convictions for both sexual and non-sexual offenses). Compared to other (non-persistent) offenders, persistent offenders were more likely to have been sexually abused themselves as children, to have had their first sexual contact with a child at an earlier age, to abuse male victims, and to abuse extrafamilial victims. The specialist persistent offenders tended to have more frequent and extended sexual contact with their victims than did the versatile persistent offenders, suggesting that they are more interested in forming an emotional relationship with the child. The versatile offenders tended to have an earlier contact with the criminal justice system, reflecting their more general criminality. The persistence of these offenders demonstrates an unambiguous sexual attraction to children. They will take calculated steps to obtain victims and will have developed a repertoire of skills and techniques to allow them to carry out their task. They are likely to be adept at identifying vulnerable children who will present the fewest risks of apprehension.

Cornish and Clarke's second type is the mundane offender. These offenders are ambiguous in their criminal commitment and opportunistic in their offending. They engage in occasional, low-level criminality. Their motivations for offending are the same as for predatory offenders, but they have a greater stake in conformity and are therefore subject to stronger personal and social constraints on their behavior. These constraints, however, weaken from time to time. In particular, to facilitate their engagement in morally proscribed behavior, mundane offenders may invoke neutralizations for their crimes (Sykes and Matza, 1957), especially where situational factors serve to obscure personal responsibility (Wortley, 2001, 1996). Mundane offenders vary in their vulnerability to temptation, and hence in the extent of their criminal involvement, but, over all, both the seriousness and frequency of their offending are lower than among predatory offenders.

The term mundane is an unfortunate one to apply to sexual offenders against children, since it seems to trivialize the seriousness of their offending. An alternate label suggested by Cornish and Clarke to describe these offenders – "opportunists" – seems more appropriate in this context. Opportunist sexual offenders will typically be criminally versatile but relatively infrequent in their sexual offending. Wortley and Smallbone found that 41% of their child molester sample were serving their first sentence for a sexual offense, but had previous convictions for non-sexual offenses. Compared with the persistent offenders, these offenders were less likely to have been sexually abused as a child and were more likely to have had their first sexual contact with a child at a later age, to abuse female victims, and to abuse intrafamilial victims. Like versatile persistent offenders, they tended not to maintain extended relationships with their victims, underscoring the opportunistic nature of their offending. The criminal versatility of these offenders suggests a generalized failure to inhibit self-gratifying urges, while their relative lack of persistence in sexual offending itself suggests sexual ambivalence rather than ingrained sexual deviance. They offend because they can.

The third type in Cornish and Clarke's classification is the provoked offender. Provoked offenders are reacting to a particular set of environmental circumstances – situational frustrations, irritations, social pressures and the like – that induce them to commit crimes they would not have otherwise committed. Their crimes include "crimes of violence that erupt in the heat of the moment; or impulsive ones committed by offenders overcome by temptation, or a temporary failure of self control" (Cornish and Clarke, 2003, p.70). The motivation for crime is supplied by the situation and the offence may represent an aberration in an otherwise law-abiding life.

Again the terminology employed by Cornish and Clarke is problematic when applied to sexual offenders, with "provoked" suggesting that the victim is responsible for initiating the behavior. Cornish and Clarke also describe these offenders as "situational," a term that is better suited for this offense.[2] This label has already been applied in the sexual offending treatment literature (Gupta and Cox, 1988; Johnston et al., 1997; Lanyon, 1986), although it has tended to be used to describe transitory psychological states (e.g., anger) rather than specific environmental conditions. Situational offenders will generally have no other criminal involvement, and their sexual offending will be a relatively isolated event. Wortley and Smallbone found that for 36% of their sample their current conviction was their first for any offence. These offenders were relatively old at the time of their first sexual contact with a child, they usually selected female victims, they usually offended within the family, and, while most had just one victim, they tended to abuse that victim repeatedly over an extended period of time. The picture here is of a caregiver or other authority figure who has abused a position of trust and who has ongoing access to the victim. In other respects the offender may be largely unremarkable. One can imagine that in many cases there would have been surprise and even disbelief among those who knew the offender when the abuse came to light. They generally will not possess an entrenched sexual attraction to children, or, if they do, they have been successful in avoiding hands-on offending. Their offending may have begun after some triggering event – for example, a moment of intimacy with the child that proved stimulating. Where this first offence was experienced as rewarding, subsequent offending would be reinforced. Nevertheless, their offending is not inevitable, and had the facilitating circumstances not occurred they may not have taken this first step.

The behavioral responses to the interaction between offender type and situation are shown in Table 1. The table illustrates two points. First, the importance of situations does not decrease as the criminal disposition of the offender increases. Rather, the role of the situation changes, and hence, the nature of situational prevention must also change. The stronger the individual's antisocial commitment, the more likely he/she is to be an active manipulator of – rather than a passive responder to – criminogenic situations. Accordingly, "harder" situational interventions are required as

Table 1: The Behavior of Offenders as a Function of an Interaction between the Disposition and the Situation

	Offender		
Situation	Situational	Opportunistic	Predatory
Challenging			**Manipulates**
Tempting		**Exploits**	
Precipitating	**Reacts to**		

the offender's criminal commitment increases. For predatory offenders, situational data primarily inform target selection. If necessary, they are prepared to expend considerable effort to achieve their goals, and obstacles to offending are challenges to be overcome. Predatory offenders will be the most difficult to deter, but the vulnerability of specific targets and the overall frequency of offending may be significantly reduced through situational prevention. For opportunistic offenders, situations offer temptations to be seized. Because of the moral ambivalence of the opportunistic offender, reducing temptations can be very effective in preventing abuse, with minimal danger of displacement to other targets. For the situational offender, opportunity reduction may not be necessary at all. Rather, relieving the precipitating conditions may be sufficient to remove the impetus to offend.

Second, offenders are not necessarily restricted to one type. There is a downward (but generally not upward) flow of offenders from higher to lower situational categories. For example, while predatory offenders are likely also to commit opportunistic and situational offenses, the reverse is generally not the case – opportunistic and situational offenders will not as a rule commit predatory crimes. In fact, predatory offenders may be more likely to commit opportunistic and situational offenses than opportunistic and situational offenders. This point was neatly demonstrated for general crime by Chenery et al. (1999). They found that 33% of vehicles parked in no-parking zones were owned by individuals with criminal records. That is, prolific offenders tend to offend across the situational spectrum. An implication of this is that predatory offenders will not always require "hard" interventions.

The explicit identification of offender types is a new development in situational prevention. While the situational approach is conceptually underpinned by models of human action (such as rational choice), individual differences have generally played little role in the design of prevention strategies. The offender has been treated as a constant. Bringing characteristics of the offender into the equation more accurately reflects the view of behavior as an interaction between person and situation, and offers the potential for better targeted crime prevention strategies (see Marshall et al., this volume). At the same time, crime patterns remain the central concern of situational prevention. In order to alter criminogenic environments, crucially we need to know the circumstances in which the offense takes place.

SETTINGS FOR SEXUAL OFFENSES AGAINST CHILDREN

The locations of many types of offenses are fixed and self-evident. Thefts from pay phones, for example, always occur at pay phones (although we may want to know which particular phones are most vulnerable). Situational prevention of thefts from pay phones will generally involve altering the design of the phones or changing the environment in their immediate vicinity (e.g., improving surveillance). Situational prevention is more problematic with offenses that do not take place in any one designated location. In the case of sexual offenses against children, we need to consider a number of different settings in which offending may be most likely to occur.

Using a modified version of Kaufman's Modus Operandi Questionnaire (Kaufman, 1989), Smallbone and Wortley (2000) asked their sample of convicted child molesters detailed questions about their pre-offense, offense, and post-offense behavior. Among these questions, offenders were asked where they found children for sexual contact (Table 2), strategies they employed to gain access to the children (Table 3), where the offending took place (Table 4), and strategies they used to be alone with the child (Table 5). Tables 2 and 3 exclude responses from intrafamilial offenders (n=79) since they will by definition find victims within the family home; Tables 4 and 5 include responses from all offenders (n=169). The tables indicate the percentage of offenders who nominated a particular response for at least one offense (an offender may offer multiple responses).

Table 2: Locations for Finding Children for Sexual Contact (extrafamilial only)

Location	%
At a friend's home	40.0
A close neighborhood	21.1
Baby-sitting	21.1
Through an organized activity	19.7
Offender's apartment building	17.3
Offender's place of employment	17.3
A distant neighborhood	15.8
A public toilet	13.2
Isolated or out of the way place (e.g., rivers, vacant lots)	11.8
A shopping mall	11.8
A park	10.5
A swimming pool	10.5
At church	10.5
Allowing the offender's own children to play with the child	10.5
A playground	5.3
Hitchhiking	5.3
The child baby-sat for other children at the offender's home	5.3
A video arcade	3.9
A movie theatre	2.6

Source: Smallbone and Wortley, 2000.

The settings for offending nominated by offenders may be described under three general categories – domestic, institutional and public. Domestic settings may be the home of both the victim and the perpetrator (in the case of intrafamilial offending), the home of the victim to which the perpetrator has access, or the home of the perpetrator (or a friend) where the victim has been taken. As Tables 2 and 4 show, domestic settings are by far the most common location to both access victims and commit the offences, with 69% of all offenses occurring in the home of the perpetrator. Situational and opportunistic offenders may be particularly likely to offend

Table 3: Strategies for Getting Access to Children for Sexual Contact (extrafamilial only)

Strategy	%
Spent time with the child while parent/caretaker was present	46.2
Made friends with the parent/caretaker of child	44.9
Helped parent/caretaker around the house	35.9
Offered to baby-sit victim	23.1
Asked neighbors or friends of family to join in family activities	21.5
Offered to drive/walk victim to or from school	19.2
Volunteered for child or teen organization	8.0
Established romantic relationship with a single parent	7.0

Source: Smallbone and Wortley, 2000.

Table 4: Locations for Taking Children for Sexual Contact

Location	%
Your own home	68.9
Going for a car ride	27.4
Isolated or out of the way places (e.g., vacant lot)	25.6
An out of the way place in the child's home	19.5
A friend or relative's home	17.1
The bush	15.5
A park	9.5
Public toilet	7.1
Swimming pool	5.4
Taking the child for walks	5.4
Playground	3.0
Movie theatre	2.4

Source: Smallbone and Wortley, 2000.

Table 5: Strategies for Being Alone with the Child

Strategy	%
Being at home alone – it was OK with my wife/girlfriend	46.7
Watching TV with them	41.7
Letting them sleep in your bed	36.3
Sneaking into their room at night	34.5
Baby-sitting	31.7
Going for a car ride with them	31.5
Tucking them into bed	29.8
Taking them places during the day without one of their parents	25.6
Going swimming with them	24.4
Seeing child while parents were at work	24.1
Taking a bath/shower with them	22.6
Going to isolated or out of the way places (e.g., vacant lots)	21.4
Taking them on overnight trips without one of their parents	20.8
Giving them a bath	17.9
Being together for a holiday	17.9
Letting the child stay up after the parent had gone to bed	17.3
Taking them camping	15.5
Being at a house of a friend/relative who said it was OK to be alone there	14.9
Going to a shopping mall	10.1
Seeing them on weekends (if divorced or separated)	8.9
Having sole custody	8.3
Taking them to school	7.7
Taking them to the video arcade	7.1
Taking them to a park	7.1
Taking them to the movies	6.5
Taking them out of school	6.0
Having the child baby-sit for your children	4.2
Going to a playground	3.6

Source: Smallbone and Wortley, 2000.

in domestic settings, but predatory offenders are also active here. For example, 45% of extrafamilial offenders established friendships with the parents of a child and 7% established a romantic relationship with a single mother in order to gain access to a victim, both strategies that indicate long-term planning (Table 3). As Table 5 shows, the offenses themselves often occur during normal day-to-day interaction between caregivers and children – watching television with children, bathing them, tucking them into bed and so forth. Undoubtedly, many of these situations will be deliberately engineered by the offender, but in the cases of situational and opportunistic offenders the offense may initially have occurred in response to being presented with these opportunities.

Institutional settings are places where groups of children congregate outside of the home for some formal purpose. They include day-care centers, schools, churches, youth groups, orphanages and so forth. In these settings the perpetrator will usually be an employee or volunteer who has some official role and who has authority over the children. Institutional settings accounted for a small but nevertheless significant number of offenses. For example, 20% of extrafamilial offenders said that they accessed children via an organized activity (Table 2). Note, however, that only 8% of extrafamilial offenders said that they joined a child or youth organization for the purpose of accessing children for sexual abuse (Table 3). In other words, these data suggest that in many cases the abuse occurred in response to opportunities that were made available to the offender.

Public settings are parks, public toilets, shopping malls, swimming pools and so forth. These locations are typically associated with predatory offenders. They are the locations that many parents will regard as most dangerous and are the traditional focus of "stranger danger" pubic education campaigns. In comparison to other locations, however, they are relatively infrequent places for locating children for sexual abuse (Table 2). They are somewhat more common as the location for abuse (Table 4), indicating that some offenders who already know their victims will take them to out-of-the-way places to carry out the offense.

Each of these settings presents challenges for situational prevention. Domestic settings will often be the locations for offenders with the least entrenched pedophilic interests, but they are also the most difficult locations to access for prevention. The person who ought to be a capable guardian of the child, and to whom one would look to put in place protective strategies, is often the abuser. Institutional settings, on the other hand, permit a good deal of control over the activities of employees and volunteers. However, the history of many organizations is that they are more concerned about protecting their reputation than they are in instituting prevention policies, and abuse in these settings can go undetected for many years. Public settings often offer the greatest potential for control over the environment. For example, authorities can design and operate public toilets in whatever manner they see fit. However, public locations where abuse may occur are almost limitless, and the base rates for offending in any one location are very low. In practice, it will be necessary to concentrate on the main public "hot spots" for abuse to apply prevention efforts. How situational prevention might be operationalized in each of these three settings, and for different types of offenders, is considered in the following section.

SITUATIONAL PREVENTION OF SEX OFFENSES AGAINST CHILDREN: SOME PROPOSALS

There are, as far as we are aware, no studies that have tested situational interventions with sexual offenders on a pre-test/post-test basis. This section therefore contains suggestions for situational interventions that are necessarily speculative. We draw on the general situational crime prevention strategies described by Cornish and Clarke (2003) and Wortley (2001). There is some overlap between these two models, and some strategies do not seem particularly applicable to sexual offending against children. Accordingly, we will concentrate on four strategies – increasing effort, increasing risk, controlling prompts and reducing permissibility.

Increasing Effort

All other things being equal, offenders will select targets that require the least effort and involve minimal deviation from their routine activities (Cohen and Felson, 1979). Increasing effort involves making the offending behavior more difficult or inconvenient to carry out. For sexual offending against children, this principally means making it harder for potential offenders to obtain children to abuse. While predators may at best be slowed down by this strategy, situational and opportunistic offenders may be fully deterred. Specific tactics for increasing effort include controlling access to facilities, target hardening and controlling tools (Cornish and Clarke, 2003).

Increasing effort may be achieved through excluding potential offenders from places where children are located. Policies instituted by most schools and day-care facilities that regulate casual access to the grounds by visitors (e.g., rules that all visitors must report to the office) are a way to implement this strategy. Increasingly, organizations that deal with children are also screening employees and volunteers to prevent people with previous convictions for sexual offenses from working with children. This strategy is useful for identifying the most obvious predators. However, given that Smallbone and Wortley (2000) found that three-quarters of their sample did not have previous sexual offense convictions, screening alone will not guarantee that these environments are safe. Smallbone and Wortley further found that sexual offenders were three times more likely to have previous convictions for non-sexual offences than for sexual offences, and on this basis it is tempting to suggest that institutions should also screen for general criminality. However, the vast majority of individuals who commit non-sexual offenses do not go on to commit sexual offenses (Hanson and Bussiere, 1998), so such a policy would produce an enormous number of false positives.

Target hardening involves obstructing offenders in their illegal pursuits. Usually this entails employing physical barriers, locks or screens to protect the intended object of their crimes. In the case of the sexual abuse of children, this strategy may be operationalized by the teaching of so-called protective strategies to children (Wyles, 1988). Grooming victims for abuse requires varying degrees of effort for predatory offenders, and in the selection of their victims, they are likely to target vulnerable children who present an easy mark and offer the least resistance. While some commentators have argued that child-focused prevention programs unfairly shift the burden of prevention onto children (Kaufman and Zigler, 1992; Melton, 1992), children's reactions to potential perpetrators can nevertheless have a significant effect on the perpetrator's subsequent behavior. Smallbone and Wortley (2001, 2000) found that the most successful tactic for potential victims when approached by a perpetrator was being assertive and saying "no."[3] Also relatively successful was showing distress, which seems to jog the conscience of the offender. In contrast, struggling and calling for help were not particularly effective. Even well-designed child-focused prevention programs are not, however, without their own risks (Smallbone et al., in preparation). To avoid unintended negative effects for children (e.g., their premature introduction to adult concepts about sexuality; increasing fears about and reducing trust in adults), child-focused prevention programs should arguably concentrate more on general confidence and assertiveness than on specific details about sexual abuse. Since both the risks and consequences of sexual abuse are known to be reduced in secure, protective families (Conte et al., 1989; Kendall-Tackett et al., 1993), perhaps the most effective child-focused approach would be to maximize protection within families.

The facilitators of offending also may be targeted in prevention efforts (i.e., "controlling tools"). The behavioral effects of pornography are controversial, but research suggests it plays a significant role in some sexual offenses. Marshall (1988) found that up to one-third of child molesters said that they viewed pornography immediately prior to offending.[4] Smallbone and Wortley (2000) also found that 19% of offenders said that they showed their victim pornography to incite their curiosity and to help prime them for sexual contact. Such research helps justify censorship laws and law enforcement efforts to restrict the availability of child pornography. Increasingly, pornography, as well as opportunities for networking with other offenders and accessing children for abuse, are provided via the Internet[5] (Tremblay, this volume). Many workplaces have explicit rules prohibiting staff from visiting pornography sites on work computers, a policy which may be backed up by regular audits of Internet use. As Taylor and Quayle (this volume) outline, it is also possible to exercise some control over the operation and content of these sites, for example, by making server managers legally responsible for pornographic sites that they store.

Increasing Risk

The risk of detection is perhaps the most salient variable in the potential offender's decision making. Increasing risks involves making it more likely that the offender's behavior will be observed or detected. Arguably, predatory offenders are most sensitive to risk factors, but they will also have developed the most sophisticated strategies to minimize the dangers of detection. Increasing risk includes extending guardianship, strengthening formal surveillance, increasing natural surveillance, and utilizing place managers (Cornish and Clarke, 2003).

In routine activity theory (Cohen and Felson, 1979), absence of a capable guardian is one of the three preconditions for crime (along with a suitable target and a motivated offender). Extending guardianship seeks to encourage individuals to watch out for crimes that occur within their informal spheres of influence. In the case of sexual abuse of children, the parent/caregiver plays a primary role in safeguarding the child. As Simon and Zgoba (this volume) point out, while most sexual offences against children occur within the home, parents are perpetrators in just 15% of cases. That is, parents may potentially play a preventive role in up to 85% of child sexual abuse cases. Public education programs can be employed to alert parents/caregivers to the need for effective supervision and protection of children in their care (Wyles, 1988). These campaigns need to extend the usual focus on "stranger danger" to include discussion of the risks for children from relatives, neighbors and friends in domestic settings. We are, of course, aware of the inherent social dangers of such campaigns in creating unnecessary suspicion and fuelling a moral panic. Nevertheless, acting with care, perhaps parents/caregivers can be better educated to recognize danger signals such as an offender's repeated or seemingly over enthusiastic attempts to seek opportunities to be alone with a child.

Where there is official guardianship, strategies can be developed to increase the levels of formal surveillance. In institutional settings, those in authority need to take responsibility for supervising the behavior of employees and volunteers. Sensible protocols governing the interaction with children need to be considered. For example, it may be appropriate to have procedures that forbid an employee/volunteer to be alone with a child. Physical modifications to the environment – for example, interviewing rooms with glass panels in the doors – can help increase natural surveillance. Once again, however, there is a clear need to balance the potential benefits of preventive interventions against the potential risks of increasing unwarranted suspicions about physical and emotional contact between adults and children.

Formal surveillance may include tracking the offender's movements via Internet use, credit card transactions and passport control. Awareness of this surveillance may serve as a deterrent, while the records themselves may be used in criminal investigations and prosecutions. Recently in Australia, there were mass arrests of offenders who downloaded child pornography from the Internet and used credit cards to pay for the downloads (Taylor and Quayle, this volume). Similarly, 24 countries currently have legislation that makes it possible to prosecute their citizens who travel overseas to access children on sex-tourism excursions (David, 2000).

In public settings, increasing risk may require greater surveillance of offending hot spots by utilizing place managers. For example, as Table 2 indicates, 12% of extrafamilial offenders said they located children in shopping malls. Those in charge of security at these locations need to be aware of sexual offenders' modus operandi and be on the look out for suspicious behavior. Again, the physical design of facilities may be an issue. For example, 13% of extrafamilial offenders said they had located children at public toilets. The placement and orientation of public toilets need to take maximum advantage of natural surveillance: e.g., they need to be well lit, located in busy locations, and have no concealed entrances (Cockfield and Moss, 2002).

Controlling Prompts

Learning theories emphasize the role of immediate environments in cueing behavior. Situations, then, may contain within them the impetus to offend. Sexual offenses against children may be stimulated by the observation of children in "provocative" (from the perspective of the offender) or vulnerable situations. Controlling prompts involves identifying and removing such situational triggers (Wortley, 2001). This strategy may be particularly important in the offending of situational and opportunistic offenders, but even the behavior of predatory offenders will be mediated by environmental cues.

As shown in Table 5, sexual offending often occurs while the offender is engaged in some intimate activity with the child, such as giving the child a bath. Controlling triggers of this sort is of course very difficult. Where the guardian is not the perpetrator, he/she needs to exercise judgment when delegating these intimate tasks to others. Where the offender is already in therapy, avoiding such high-risk situations will be likely to form part of a relapse prevention program. For other offenders, we may need to rely on them to instigate their own situational prevention strategies. This is perhaps not as unlikely as it may sound. In an early report on Vermont's *Stop It Now!* program, almost one-quarter of all calls to a sexual abuse prevention hotline were from otherwise undetected offenders (Chasan-Taylor and Tabachnick, 1999). Similarly, almost 30% of callers to the *Stop It Now! UK and Ireland* helpline during 2003 were from people expressing concern about their own behavior (Stop It Now! UK and Ireland, 2005). It may be possible to use such opportunities to educate men to recognize and manage situations that they might personally find tempting. If, as we have argued, the potential to be sexually aroused by children is more common than is usually acknowledged, then the current media focus demonizing sexual offenders may be counterproductive because it leaves many men who are struggling with temptations confused about their urges and without guidance.

In some cases, accommodation pressures can create the temptations and opportunities to offend. Sexual offending by adolescents often involves incest among siblings, which may be more common when siblings share beds or bedrooms (Finkelhor, 1984). Similarly, a high prevalence of child sexual abuse has been reported in some semi-remote Australian Aboriginal communities (Aboriginal and Torres Strait Island Task Force on Violence, 1999), and this may be partly facilitated by cramped, open-plan housing where families are forced to share sleeping quarters (Smallbone et al., 1999).

Reducing Permissibility

Offenders may minimize the criminality of their behavior by invoking various excuses to free themselves from the inhibitory effects of self-blame (Sykes and Matza, 1957). Situations can assist in this process by obscuring the offender's contribution to the harm-doing. Sexual offenders are noted for their tendency to justify their behavior with cognitive distortions such as "I was educating the child," "the child enjoyed the relationship," "I could not help myself," and so on. Reducing permissibility involves strategies that help clarify the offender's role in his behavior. This strategy is likely to be most effective with situational and opportunistic offenders who retain an underlying belief that sexual offending against children is morally wrong. Specific techniques include clarifying responsibility, personalizing victims, rule setting and clarifying consequences (Wortley, 2001).

Citing loss of control through alcohol is perhaps the most obvious way that offenders may seek to deny personal responsibility for their offences. Irrespective of debates about whether the effects of alcohol are the result of physiological disinhibition or cognitive expectancies (Marlett et al., 1973), the fact remains that up to two-thirds of sexual offenders against children have serious problems with alcohol (Looman et al., 2004). Excessive alcohol consumption is, of course, a major general public health issue with much broader implications than its contribution to the sexual abuse of children. Nevertheless, the link between alcohol and sexual offending may be particularly strong in some specific settings that are also amenable to situational intervention. We noted earlier the high incidence of child sexual abuse in some Australian Aboriginal communities. The task force investigating this problem identified widespread and chronic alcohol abuse as the single biggest causal factor[6] (Aboriginal and Torres Strait Island Task Force on Violence, 1999). Recently, many of these communities have developed alcohol management plans that involve severe restrictions on the sale of alcohol, and in some case they have established "dry" communities. However, there has at this stage been no formal evaluation of the impact of these measures on sexual offending.

Environmental conditions can also blur for the offender the link between their behavior and the harm done. The tendency for perpetrators to excuse their behavior may be particularly prevalent in residential institutions for children such as orphanages, homes for the intellectually disabled and juvenile correctional facilities. The capacity of "total institutions" to engender abuses of power by staff has been well documented (Goffman, 1959; Haney et al., 1973). Institutional regimes divest residents of human qualities and individuality, facilitating neutralizations by staff that justify abuse ("they're all the same," "they're just a number," etc.). In addition, staff are afforded a degree of anonymity and a cloak of collective responsibility that minimize their sense of personal accountability for their actions ("everyone is doing it," "I am just doing my job"). Abuse may be reduced by empowering and humanizing residents (personalizing victims) and curbing the sense of license that staff may have to act as they please (rule setting, clarifying responsibility). Strategies include: ensuring that residents receive adequate levels of physical care that affords them human dignity; minimizing institutional features of the environment and unnecessary regimentation; introducing explicit codes of conduct and induction procedures for staff that clearly spell out acceptable and unacceptable behavior and leave no room for the exploitation of ambiguity; providing formal opportunities for residents to make complaints if abuse occurs; and opening the institution to outside scrutiny, including instituting a process of regular independent inspections and reviews.

Finally, self-exonerating cognitions may be directly challenged. Again, accessing potential offenders is problematic, and public education campaigns would seem to provide the best forum for getting these messages across. Interestingly, as shown in Table 5, Smallbone and Wortley (2000) found that a common tactic of offenders was to spend time watching TV with their victim prior to the abuse. This would seem to provide an ideal opportunity to reach potential offenders at the very time that offending was being contemplated. These messages might particularly challenge the comforting neutralizations that the offender is performing a service for the child (clarifying consequences) by setting out the harm suffered by children through abuse.

CONCLUSIONS

The application of situational prevention to sexual offenses against children involves two separate questions – is it theoretically plausible, and is there practical utility in doing it? In response to the first question, we argue that situational factors are a crucial and theoretically neglected element of these offenses. Situations are an unavoidable component of all behavior. It is perhaps trite, but nevertheless true, that no behavior can occur without opportunity – an experienced and determined pedophile confined to a deserted island (or prison) will not commit pedophilic acts. But the role of situations is more subtle than this. As research increasingly emphasizes the lack of specialized pedophilic commitment of many sexual offenders, then greater attention needs to be paid to the role that conducive environmental conditions play in facilitating the behavior.

As to the applied implications of a situational perspective, we acknowledge that devising practical interventions for sexual offending is not without its problems. The majority of offenses occur within the home and may be carried out by the very person who is responsible for protecting the child. It is not only difficult to reach such offenders through situational means, but to emphasize the commonplace nature of much sexual abuse runs the risk of encouraging a siege mentality. Care needs to be taken to ensure that sensible protective behaviors do not turn to paranoia. It would be a pity – and ultimately counterproductive from the perspective of encouraging healthy adult-child relationships – if fathers felt they were unable to show affection to their children, if people were reluctant to baby-sit their friends' children, or if teachers felt that they could not comfort a distressed pupil for fear of raising suspicions that they were involved in sexually abusive behaviors.

But equally, the current tendency to demonize sexual offenders and to assume that they form a clearly identifiable group in the community is problematic. As our data show (Smallbone and Wortley, 2000), screening for previous sexual offences will fail to identify most offenders. Moreover, while the focus remains on "stranger danger" people are likely to be less aware of the dangers that exist for their children close to home. The alternative message to stranger danger – that many men experience, if infrequently and fleetingly, a sexual response to a child – is a challenging one. Nevertheless, frank acknowledgement of this may help men deal with these feelings and better prepare parents/caregivers to protect the children under their care.

We have provided some modest suggestions for situational prevention of sexual offenses against children. We do not do not think that our proposals are by any means the last word on the matter. Indeed, we hope that we have stimulated debate and further research on the topic.

Address correspondence to: Richard Wortley, School of Criminology and Criminal Justice, Griffith University, Brisbane 4111, Australia; e-mail: r.wortley@griffith.edu.au.

NOTES

1. These analyses also involved additional cases. The final sample comprised the official records of 362 prisoners and self-report data from 213 prisoners.
2. However, a problem with this term is that it implies the other forms or offending are not situational. As we argue, all crime has a situational element.
3. Smallbone and Wortley (2000) also found that many offenders were seeking an emotional relationship with their victims. Confident and assertive children are less likely to form dependency relationships with offenders and thus will not provide the emotional response many offenders seek. This might also be considered an example of Cornish and Clarke's (2003) reducing rewards.
4. Pornography use may also be conceptualised as a situational prompt. It might also be noted that images of children do not need to be pornographic for them to be stimulating. As Tremblay (this volume) reports, the television program *Malcolm in the Middle* was very popular among the pedophiles in his sample.
5. Arguably there is a case for a fourth setting for offending – a virtual setting.

6. The task force also cited the ready availability of pornography in these communities as a contributing factor to the high levels of sexual abuse.

REFERENCES

Aboriginal and Torres Strait Island Task Force on Violence (1999). *The Aboriginal and Torres Strait Island Task Force on Violence Report.* Brisbane, AUS: Queensland Government.

Barbaree, H.E., and W.L. Marshall (1989). "Erectile Responses Among Heterosexual Child Molesters, Father-Daughter Incest Offenders and Matched Nonoffenders: Five Distinct Age Preference Profiles." *Canadian Journal of Behavioural Science* 21:70–82.

Chasan-Taber, L., and J. Tabachnick (1999). "Evaluation of a Child Sexual Abuse Prevention Program." *Sexual Abuse: A Journal of Research and Treatment* 11:279–292.

Chenery, S., C. Henshaw and K. Pease (1999). "Illegal Parking in Disabled Bays: A Means of Offender Targeting." *Policing and Reducing Crime.* Briefing Note 1/99. London: Home Office Research, Development and Statistics Directorate.

Clarke, R.V. (1997). "Introduction." In: RV. Clarke (ed.), *Situational Crime Prevention: Successful Case Studies* (2nd ed., pp.2–43). Monsey, NY: Criminal Justice Press.

Clarke, R.V. (1995). "Opportunity-Reducing Crime Prevention Strategies and the Role of Motivation." In: P.O. Wikstrom, R.V. Clarke and J. McCord (eds.), *Integrating Crime Prevention Strategies: Propensity and Opportunity* (pp.55–67). Stockholm, National Council for Crime Prevention.

Clarke, R.V. (1992). "Introduction." In: R.V. Clarke (ed.), *Situational Crime Prevention: Successful Case Studies* (pp.3–36). Albany, NY: Harrow and Heston.

Clarke, R.V., and R. Homel (1997). "A Revised Classification of Situational Crime Prevention Techniques." In: S.P. Lab (ed.), *Crime Prevention at the Crossroads* (pp.17–27). Cincinnati, OH: Anderson.

Cockfield, C., and K. Moss (2002). "Sex, Drugs and Broken Bowls: Dealing with Problems of Crime Reduction in Public Conveniences." *Community Safety Journal* 1:37–43.

Cohen, L.E., and M. Felson (1979). "Social Change and Crime Rate Trends: A Routine Activities Approach." *American Sociological Review* 44:588–608.

Conte, J.R., S. Wolf and T. Smith (1989). "What Sexual Offenders Tell Us About Prevention Strategies." *Child Abuse and Neglect* 13:293–301.

Cornish, D.B., and R.V. Clarke (2003). "Opportunities, Precipitators and Criminal Dispositions: A Reply to Wortley's Critique of Situational Crime Prevention." In: M.J. Smith and D.B. Cornish (eds.), *Theory for Practice in Situational Crime Prevention.* (Crime Prevention Studies, vol. 16.) Monsey, NJ: Criminal Justice Press.

Cornish, D.B., and R.V. Clarke (1986). *The Reasoning Criminal*. New York: Springer-Verlag.

David, F. (2000). "Child Sex Tourism." *Trends & Issues in Crime and Criminal Justice* #156. Canberra: Australian Institute of Criminology.

Finkelhor, D. (1984). *Child Sexual Abuse: New Theory and Research*. New York: Free Press.

Goffman, E. (1961). *Asylums: Essays on the Social Situation of Mental Patients and Other Inmates*. Oxford, UK: Aldine.

Gottfredson, M., and T. Hirschi (1990). *A General Theory of Crime*. New York: Macmillan Publishing Co.

Gupta, G.R., and S.M. Cox (1988). "A Typology of Incest and Possible Intervention Strategies." *Journal of Family Violence* 3:299–312.

Haney, C., C. Banks and P. Zimbardo (1973). "Interpersonal Dynamics in a Simulated Prison." *International Journal of Criminology and Penology* 1:69–97.

Hanson, R.K. (2002). "Recidivism and Age: Follow-Up Data from 4673 Sexual Offenders." *Journal of Interpersonal Violence* 17:1046–1062.

Hanson, R.K., and M.T. Bussiere (1998). "Predicting Relapse: A Meta-Analysis of Sexual Offender Recidivism Studies." *Journal of Consulting and Clinical Psychology* 66:348–362.

Hirschi, T. (1988). "On the Compatibility of Rational Choice and Social Control Theories of Crime." In: D.B. Cornish and R.V. Clarke (eds.), *The Reasoning Criminal: Rational Choice Perspectives on Offending*. New York: Springer-Verlag.

Johnston, L., S.M. Hudson and T. Ward (1997). "The Suppression of Sexual Thoughts by Child Molesters: A Preliminary Investigation." *Sexual Abuse: Journal of Research and Treatment* 9:303–319.

Kaufman, K.L. (1989). *Modus Operandi Questionnaire*. Columbus, OH: Children's Hospital.

Kaufman, J., and E. Zigler (1992). "The Prevention of Child Maltreatment: Programming, Research and Policy." In: D.J. Willis, E. W. Holden and M. Rosenberg (eds.), *Prevention of Child Maltreatment: Developmental and Ecological Perspectives* (pp. 269–295). New York: John Wiley.

Kendall-Tackett, K.A., L.M. Williams and D. Finkelhor (1993). "Impact of Sexual Abuse on Children: A Review and Synthesis of Recent Empirical Studies." *Psychological Bulletin* 113:164–180.

Lanyon, R.L. (1986). "Theory and Treatment of Child Molesters." *Journal of Consulting and Clinical Psychology* 53:176–182.

Laws, D.R., and W.L. Marshall (1990). "A Conditioning Theory of the Etiology and Maintenance of Deviant Sexual Preferences and Behavior." In: W.L. Marshall, D.R. Laws and H.E. Barbaree (eds.), *Handbook of Sexual Assault: Issues, Theories, and Treatment of the Offender*. New York: Plenum.

Looman, J., J. Abracen, R. DiFazio, and G. Maillet (2004). "Alcohol and Drug Abuse Among Sexual and Nonsexual Offenders: Relationship to Intimacy Deficits and Coping Strategy." *Sexual Abuse: A Journal of Research and Treatment* 16:117–189.

Malamuth, N.M. (1989). "The Attraction to Sexual Aggression Scale: Part Two." *Journal of Sex Research* 26:324–354.

Marlett, G.A., B. Demming and J.B. Reid (1973). "Loss of Control Drinking in Alcoholics: An Experimental Analogue." *Journal of Abnormal Psychology* 81:233–241.

Marshall, W. L. (1988). "The Use of Explicit Sexual Stimuli by Rapists, Child Molesters and Nonoffender Males." *Journal of Sex Research* 25:267–288.

Marshall, W.L., and H.E. Barbaree (1990). *Handbook of Sexual Assault: Issues, Theories and Treatment of the Offender*. New York: Plenum.

McConaghy, N. (1993). *Sexual Behavior: Problems and Management*. New York: Plenum.

Melton, G.B. (1992). "It's Time for Neighborhood Research and Action." *Child Abuse & Neglect* 16:909–913.

Mischel, W. (1968). *Personality and Assessment*. New York: John Wiley.

Pithers, W.D., J.K. Marques, C.C. Gibat and G.A. Marlatt (1983). "Relapse Prevention with Sexual Aggressives: A Self-Control Model of Treatment and Maintenance of Change." In: J.G. Greer and I.R. Stuart (eds.), *The Sexual Aggressor: Current Perspectives on Treatment* (pp. 214–239). New York: Von Nostrand Reinhold.

Pritchard, C., and C. Bagley (2000). "Multi-Criminal and Violent Groups Amongst Child Sex Offenders: A Heuristic Typology in a 2-Year Cohort of 374 Men in Two English Counties." *Child Abuse and Neglect* 24:579–586.

Simon, L. (2000). "An Examination of the Assumptions of Specialization, Mental Disorder and Dangerousness in Sex Offenders." *Behavioral Sciences and the Law* 18:275–308.

Simon, L. (1997). "Do Criminal Offenders Specialize in Crime Types?" *Applied and Preventive Psychology* 6:35–53.

Smallbone, S.W. (2005). "An Attachment Theoretical Revision of Marshall and Barbaree's (1990) Integrated Theory of the Etiology of Sexual Offending." In: W.L. Marshall, Y.M. Fernandez and L.E. Marshall (eds.), *Sexual Offender Treatment: Issues and Controversies*. Chichester, UK: John Wiley and Sons.

Smallbone, S.W., W.L. Marshall and R.K. Wortley (in preparation). "Evidence-Based Prevention of Sexual Offenses Against Children."

Smallbone, S.W., and R.K. Wortley (2004a). "Criminal Diversity and Paraphilic Interests Among Adult Males Convicted of Sexual Offences Against Children." *International Journal of Offender Therapy and Comparative Criminology* 48:175–188.

Smallbone, S.W., and R.K. Wortley (2004b). "Onset, Persistence and Versatility of Offending Among Adult Males Convicted of Sexual Offenses Against Children." *Sexual Abuse: A Journal of Research and Treatment* 16:285–298.

Smallbone, S.W., and R.K. Wortley (2001). "Child Sexual Abuse: Offender Characteristics and Modus Operandi." *Australian Institute of Criminology Trends and Issues in Crime and Criminal Justice* #193. Canberra: Australian Institute of Criminology.

Smallbone, S.W., and R.K. Wortley (2000). *Child Sexual Abuse in Queensland: Offender Characteristics and Modus Operandi*. Brisbane, AUS: Queensland Crime Commission.

Smallbone, S.W., R.K. Wortley and K. Lancefield (1999). *Sexual Offending by Aboriginal Men in Queensland.* Brisbane, AUS: Queensland Department of Corrective Services.

Soothill, K., B. Francis, S. Sanderson, and E. Ackerley (2000). "Sex Offenders: Specialists, Generalists – or Both?" *British Journal of Criminology* 40:56–67.

Stop It Now! UK & Ireland (2005). *About Stop it Now!* Retrieved February 21, 2005 from http://www.stopitnow.org.uk/about.htm

Sykes, G., and D. Matza (1957). "Techniques of Neutralization: A Theory of Delinquency." *American Journal of Sociology* 22:664–670.

Trasler, G. (1986). "Situational Crime Prevention and Rational Choice: A Critique." In: K. Heal and G. Laycock (eds.), *Situational Crime Prevention: From Theory into Practice* (pp.17–42). London: Her Majesty's Stationery Office.

Tunnell, K.D. (2002). "The Impulsiveness and Routinization of Decision-Making." In: A.R. Piquero and S.G. Tibbetts (eds.), *Rational Choice and Criminal Behavior: Recent Research and Future Challenges.* New York: Routledge.

Weinrott, M.M., and M. Saylor (1991). "Self-Report of Crimes Committed by Sex Offenders." *Journal of Interpersonal Violence* 6:286–300.

Wortley, R.K. (2001). "A Classification of Techniques for Controlling Situational Precipitators of Crime." *Security Journal* 14(4):63–82.

Wortley, R.K. (1998). "A Two-Stage Model of Situational Crime Prevention." *Studies on Crime and Crime Prevention* 7:173–188.

Wortley, R.K. (1997). "Reconsidering the Role of Opportunity in Situational Crime Prevention." In: G. Newman, R. Clarke and S. Shoham (eds.), *Rational Choice and Situational Crime Prevention* (pp. 65–82). Aldershot, Hampshire, UK: Ashgate.

Wortley, R.K. (1996). "Guilt, Shame and Situational Crime Prevention." In: R. Homel (ed.), *The Politics and Practice of Situational Crime Prevention.* (Crime Prevention Studies, vol. 5, pp.115–132.) Monsey, NY: Criminal Justice Press.

Wortley, R.K., and S.W. Smallbone (under review). "Criminal Careers of Child-Sex Offenders."

Wyles, P. (1988). *Missing Children: Advice, Information and Preventative Action for Parents, Teachers and Counsellors.* Canberra: Australian Institute of Criminology.

Situational and Dispositional Factors in Child Sexual Molestation: A Clinical Perspective

by

William L. Marshall

Geris A. Serran

Liam E. Marshall
Rockwood Psychological Services, Kingston, Ontario

Abstract: *Although child molestation, as with other human behavior, is widely recognized as a product of the interaction of individual dispositions and immediate situations, theoretical and empirical research has tended to concentrate more or less exclusively on the dispositional features of child molesters. While research has identified some reasonably stable features of child molesters, it is our lack of knowledge concerning situational and transitory influences that limits our capacity to understand, prevent, and treat child molesters. In this chapter, we present an overview of current clinical evidence for the role of stable and transitory dispositions, and of situational factors, in child molestation.*

The literature on sexual offending includes a wide range of theories, frameworks, and issues. Attempts to understand sexual offending have identified various relevant domains to guide risk assessments and treatment efforts.

Much of our understanding remains in the early stages, with far more research being required, although treatment programs and assessment batteries have become progressively more comprehensive over the past 30 years (Laws and Marshall, 2003; Marshall and Laws, 2003). These developments have been matched by increasingly complex theories about the origins of sexual offending (Finkelhor, 1984; Hall and Hirschman, 1991; Marshall and Barbaree, 1990; Ward and Marshall, 2004). In this paper we will primarily rely on evidence collected on adult males identified by the criminal justice system as child molesters.

Despite the fact that current treatment approaches are quite comprehensive and address a wide range of issues, it is still assumed by many that sexual offending is primarily about sexual deviance. Sexual offenders are viewed as inherently different from the rest of society as well as from other types of criminals. As highlighted by Marshall (1996a), sexual offenders are often viewed as "monsters." Such views consider sexual offenders to be qualitatively different from other people (i.e., "abnormal") leading some to view the aberrant behavior of sexual offenders as genetically or biologically entrenched (Ellis, 1991; Langevin, 1992; Quinsey, 2003). Such theories, however, place little responsibility on the offender for his behavior. Other theories based on the assumption that sexual offenders are qualitatively different from other people, rest on the idea that these men have fixed sexual interests that focus on the types of deviant acts in which they engage. Thus, according to this view, child molesters offend against children because they have an entrenched preference for sex with children. Phallometric assessments are said to reveal these trait-like sexual preferences. Setting aside the various problems with phallometric evaluations (see, e.g., Marshall and Fernandez, 2003a, 2003b, 2000a, 2000b; for a discussion of these problems), the fact is such assessments have not revealed deviant sexual preferences in more than 50% of nonfamilial child molesters nor in more than 20% of incest offenders. In its most absurd form, this theory suggests that simply eliminating these supposed deviant preferences would eliminate the propensity to sexually offend (Bond and Evans, 1967). It seems to us unlikely that child molesters have a trait-like preference for sex with children. It seems more likely to us that while there are some reasonably stable features of these men that contribute to their decision to offend, it is our lack of knowledge concerning situational and transitory influences that limits our capacity to understand, prevent, and treat child molesters. Knowing what sort of circumstances present opportunities to offend is crucial to our understanding of child molestation, but opportunity alone does not produce sexual abuse. The potential child molester's perception of the situation, as an opportunity to be seized or not, is colored by a host of stable and transitory factors. This chapter will explore these influences, as well as the situations that present opportunities and how these situations are created.

Except in rare cases, the decision to sexually offend is clearly made by the perpetrator, often quite far in advance of the crime, and it is associated with carefully planning the offense (Hudson et al., 1999; Polaschek and Hudson, 2004). Part of this planning involves setting up the circumstances in which to offend. As Marshall and Barbaree (1990) note in their early comprehensive theory, an offense cannot take place, no matter what other factors are present, unless an opportunity is either created or occurs by accident.

To date, little research has focused on how such opportunities are created, or how it is that a sexual offender recognizes an unanticipated situation as an opportunity to offend. This latter point might seem to many readers not to be in need of explanation, but many situations described by sexual offenders as opportunities would not be recognized as such by others. For example, a child molester client of ours described an unanticipated situation where he was alone with a 9-year old girl. At one point, the young girl sat back on the chair facing our client and drew up her legs, thereby innocently revealing her underwear. Our client saw this as an unequivocal invitation to sex by the young girl; hopefully the rest of us would either not have noticed or have drawn a more benign interpretation of the child's behavior. From our client's point of view this was a clear situational opportunity to offend; however, his distorted perception of the girl's action might more accurately be described as a "situational precipitator" (see Wortley, 2001 for a discussion of this issue). Thus, we need to examine not only the circumstances under which offending takes place, and how these circumstances might be created by offenders, but also the way in which offenders perceive these circumstances and how these perceptions change as a result of various external and internal influences on the offender. Recent research at our clinic (Webster et al., 2004) is relevant to understanding these influences.

Transcripts of extensive interviews with child molesters are being subjected to grounded theory analyses (see Webster and Marshall [2004] for a discussion of this approach) in order to identify opportunities to offend that have occurred in the past and the factors that influenced whether or not the client took advantage of the opportunity. Although these analyses are in their early stages, it is already clear that child molesters seize far fewer opportunities (i.e., being alone with a potential victim) than are available to them. Some factors that appear to facilitate taking advantage of an opportunity match those that have already been identified in the literature: for example, intoxication, transitory mood fluctuations, boredom, loneliness, sudden increase in relational problems, and interpretation of the child's behavior as indicating a sexual interest. When our analyses are complete we may identify other influential factors.

In this project we are also examining why it is that these child molesters pass on many opportunities to offend. Some hints from our clinical experience suggest that features of the potential victim may be relevant. Some offenders have told us that if a child appears confident, resilient, or defiant, they would not attempt to molest the child. Others have said they simply exercised a determined effort to resist an opportunity, and still others (particularly incest offenders) have said there were occasions when they just did not feel interested in having sex with anyone. These latter remarks seem similar to comments we might expect from adults about their prosocial sexual behavior. Consistent with this idea, we are asking our child molesters similar questions about opportunities (seized or ignored) to engage in sex with a consenting adult partner. We believe this line of research might be a chance to better explore issues to do with *modus operandi*, as well as presenting the chance to strengthen clients' abilities to resist future opportunities to offend.

We suggest that child molestation occurs only when an opportunity to offend (i.e., is either created by the offender or unexpectedly happens) appears in conjunction with the presence of certain stable and transitory dispositional factors in the potential offender. This is a long-standing tradition in the psychological literature. In 1968, Walter Mischel, in his repost to trait theorists of personality, pointed out that behavior is almost always a product of the interaction between dispositional characteristics of the individual and the circumstances in which the person finds him/herself (Mischel, 1968).

This combination of opportunity and dispositional factors produces four sets of possibilities: (1) if an opportunity occurs when the dispositional factors are present, then an offense is very likely to happen; (2) if an opportunity occurs when the dispositional factors are absent, then it is unlikely that an offense will occur; (3) if an opportunity is not available and the dispositional factors are present, then the man may seek to create an opportunity, or he may masturbate to deviant thoughts; and, (4) if an opportunity is not available and the dispositional features are absent, then deviant acts (actually or in fantasy) should not occur. Possibility (2) needs comment. One of our incest offenders told us that he molested his daughter only on Wednesday evenings when his wife was at bingo. He noted that he frequently was not strongly motivated when a Wednesday evening opportunity presented itself, but that he offended anyway. In response to our question about why he would offend when he did not desire to, he said that he routinely took advantage of chances because, he said, "I might feel like it tomorrow (when there would be no chance) and then regret I missed the chance (on Wednesday evening)." We wonder if we might get the same sort of answer from a non-deviant man whose normative sexual activities were similarly routinized to a particular evening of the week.

In this chapter we will describe what is known about the dispositional and situational features that appear to facilitate child sexual abuse. It is important to point out, however, that these features are certain to vary not only across various types of sexual offenders, but also within each subtype. Obviously, the situational features relevant to familial child molesters will be different from those that facilitate nonfamilial offending. Similarly, the pre-offense relationship between the offender and the child will no doubt also influence the types of situations within which offenses occur and will also to some extent determine the dispositional features. For example, Smallbone (2005) has pointed to the influential role in child molestation of the offender's attachment, caregiving, and sexual behavioral systems. He notes that in a situation where an adult male offender and a child are involved in a continuing relationship, the activation of the attachment and caregiving systems are to be expected. Under these conditions, so Smallbone suggests, some men (those whose attachment and caregiving needs are otherwise unfulfilled) will confuse the activation of these two systems with sexual feelings and, as a consequence, they may sexually molest the child. Clearly the joint activation of these three systems will be far more pertinent to our understanding of those acts of child molestation where the offender and the victim have a long-term relationship such as a parent, teacher, religious instructor/caretaker.

DISPOSITIONAL FACTORS

Advocates of relapse prevention approaches to the treatment of child molesters have long argued that offending occurs only when opportunities are created or taken advantage of by the offender, and only when the man is in a particular state (Pithers, 1990; Pithers et al., 1983). However these authors failed to distinguish stable from acute or transitory factors that influenced an offender to abuse, and this failure to distinguish these two types of potential disinhibitors continues. This distinction, however, turns out to be important. For example, Hanson and Harris (2000) found that a stable negative mood state did not predict offending, whereas a transitory negative mood did precipitate an offense.

Stable Dispositions

Stable dispositions function in a trait-like way; that is, they present an enduring state that puts someone at risk. One of the most thoroughly investigated stable dispositions that has been posited as a risk for sexual offending is the person's capacity for intimacy or his attachment style (Bumby and Hansen, 1997; Garlick et al., 1996; Marshall et al., 1997; Smallbone and Dadds, 1998; Ward et al., 1996; Ward et al., 1995). It is quite clear that child molesters do characteristically suffer from a lack of intimacy and, as a result, experience chronic emotional loneliness. It is known that emotional loneliness disinhibits aggression (Check et al., 1985) and that it triggers deviant sexual fantasies in sexual offenders (Looman, 1999; McKibben et al., 1994; Proulx et al., 1996), but the distinction between the effects of chronic and acute emotional loneliness has not yet been made. Given that a sudden breakdown, or problem in a relationship, has been shown to trigger deviant fantasies (Proulx et al., 1996), and that chronic intimacy deficits characterize child molesters, it seems likely that this group of factors (intimacy deficits, loneliness, and insecure attachments) function as both stable and transitory dispositions.

Different attachment styles could be expected to generate different offending patterns. For example, individuals with an anxious/ambivalent (sometimes called "preoccupied") attachment style desperately seek intimacy but see themselves as unlovable to adults. Such individuals may find greater acceptance from children who are not sophisticated enough to judge the true nature of someone who provides them with affection, gifts or other bribes. We (Marshall and Marshall, 2002a; Marshall et al., 2004) have shown that child molesters who groom their victims over a period of time before offending tend to have an anxious/ambivalent attachment style. Interestingly, however, a reasonable number (approximately 35% to 40%) of child molesters have secure attachment styles. These securely attached child molesters also extensively groom their victims and essentially establish, from their point of view, a "romantic" relationship with the child.

Burk and Burkhart (2003) suggest that the severity of an offender's childhood attachment disruption, rather than simply an insecure attachment to his parents, might provide the motivation for sexual offending. They argue that the extreme insecurity associated with a disorganized attachment style creates a vulnerability for more externally based self-regulatory strategies (in this case, sexual offending). Disorganized attachment is most likely to occur in circumstances where the actions of the parent are extremely frightening or threatening (Hesse and Main, 2000): fear is the primary emotion associated with this style of attachment. Burk and Burkhart (2003) claim that, among these men with disorganized attachment, interpersonal control becomes a strong need. As a result, controlling interpersonal behavior emerges, and this can most easily be realized with children, and many of our child molesters also seem to seek vulnerable adults with whom to form a relationship.

As noted earlier, Smallbone (2005) has elaborated a theory of sexual offending within which attachment insecurity plays a pivotal role. He points, however, to the relationship between the attachment system and both the caregiving and sexual systems, in activating behaviors. Attachment is seen, by most researchers, as a complementary system to parenting or caregiver behavior. Both these systems are essential to forming the bonds between adults and children that are necessary for effective functioning, and both involve a close intimate relationship between caregiver and child. Like the attachment and caregiving systems, activation of the sexual system occurs maximally within a close, and continuing, intimate relationship. Under these conditions – which may be apparent in parenting, religious, teaching, or other close continuing professional relationships (e.g., sports coach) – those individuals who have not learned to readily distinguish these three systems, may confuse feelings aroused by activation of the attachment or caregiving systems, with sexual feelings; some of these men may then act on these confused feelings. It is not surprising, then, that most instances of the sexual molestation of children occur within caregiving relationship; most offenders are either related to the victim or are involved in some form of long-term relationship with the child. Special efforts should, therefore, be directed at preventing abuse from occurring within these ostensibly caregiving relationships. This may be difficult where parents are concerned, although education directed at informing parents and relatives of the risks and who the offender might be, as well as teaching children to recognize inappropriate behavior, might serve as preventative strategies. More direct efforts could be made with professionals who come into intimate contact with children, and these potential strategies will be noted in a later section of this paper.

Problems with emotional and sexual self-regulation have been shown to be stable risk factors (Hanson, 2000). Ward and Hudson (2000) have outlined a self-regulation model of the offending process suggesting that sexual offenders either fail to control their behaviour and emotions, or they choose ineffective strategies to achieve their goals, with the result being that they suffer a loss of control. Such losses of self-regulatory control are seen within Ward and Hudson's (2000) model as due to some disruptive life event, such as "a major life transition (e.g., a divorce) or a daily hassle such as an argument" (p. 85). Unfortunately, Ward and Hudson offer little in the way of supporting evidence that these life events do trigger emotional or sexual misregulation exclusively in sexual offenders. If such events trigger misregulation in most people, then Ward and Hudson fail to explain why in sexual offenders it specifically leads to an offense.

If sexual offenders do characteristically have chronic emotional dys-regulation, then no doubt this would place them at risk for numerous problems, but exactly why it should lead to sexual offending is not clear. More to the point, there is as yet little evidence indicating that sexual offenders do, in fact, live life on an emotional roller coaster as this theory suggests. On the other hand, there is gathering evidence suggesting that sexual offenders have problems regulating the expression of their sexuality. Obviously they at least occasionally express their sexual drive in unacceptable ways, but are they typically unrestrained in their sexual expression?

Abel et al. (1988) produced data indicating that sexual offenders (including child molesters) typically displayed multiple paraphilic behaviors. Freund (1990) points to a long history in the literature similarly suggesting that sexual offenders display multiple sexual behaviours, and he described data from his client records that also indicated the occurrence of various sexual outlets among sexual offenders. In our (Marshall and Marshall, 2002b; 2001) work examining the frequency of sexual behaviors in sexual offenders, we have found that almost 50% reach criteria for either sexual addiction (Carnes, 1992) or for hypersexuality (11 or more sexual outlets per week; see Kafka (2003) for a discussion). Consistent with these observations, Cortoni and Marshall (2001) found that sexual offenders were very likely to choose sex (of various kinds and with various types of partners/

victims) as a way of dealing with problems. All these findings suggest that sexual offenders have problems constraining the expression of their sexual feelings and, in this sense, can be construed as having poor self-regulatory control over sex. However, the tendency to be somewhat unconstrained in the expression of sex does not explain why it is that sexual offenders sometimes offend but at other times, even when faced with an opportunity, they resist the chance to offend. Something else must be operating to move this propensity into action.

Recent research in our clinic (Marshall et al., 2000; Serran, 2004) has shown that child molesters have dysfunctional coping styles (a stable disposition). A person's characteristic coping style will lead to the display of either effective coping strategies or ineffective ones. The general psychological literature identifies three types of coping styles: (1) Task-focused; (2) Avoidance-focused; and (3) Emotion-focused (Endler and Parker, 1994). A task-focused style refers to the ideal problem-solving approach (see D'Zurilla [1998] for details), whereas the latter two styles are dysfunctional when they are maintained beyond an initial immediate response. In avoidance-focused coping the person successfully ignores dealing with the problem by engaging in a distracting activity such as having sex, becoming intoxicated, or working long hours. Emotion-focused coping involves centering all attention on the emotional responses to the problem, such as being angry or sad, or, for many child molesters, engaging in self-pity. Both of these coping responses are dysfunctional when they persist as the person's only response, although they occur as transitory states in most people's immediate reactions to distressing events. Our research (Marshall et al., 2000) has demonstrated that child molesters tend to remain fixated on an emotion-focused approach. This emotion-focused response not only fails to solve the problem, it also leaves the child molester in a distressed state that is likely to trigger offending. This is consistent with Hanson and Harris's (2000) observation that an acute negative mood state is an immediate precursor of sexual offending, and appears to add the link necessary to Ward and Hudson's (2000) model.

A variety of cognitive processes and products have been identified as contributing to, or facilitating, sexual offending (Abel et al., 1989; Langton and Marshall, 2001, 2000; Marshall and Langton, 2004; Ward et al., 1997). Attitudes, beliefs and perceptions have been reported that support sexual offending, all of which appear to result from deeply held schemas about women, children, sex, and the world, as well as about issues of the self and a sense of entitlement (Mann, 2004; Serran et al., 2004). Schemas help us make sense of our world in a way that is consistent with past experiences and with current goals. Some schemas are only activated under certain conditions, so that the pro-offending perceptions of child molesters may only be apparent when the desire to molest a child occurs or when an opportunity presents itself. However, these distorted schemas are permanently present in child molesters even though they may not be readily triggered under the circumstances of an evaluation of the client. Once again, we see that stable features related to child sexual abuse may only be triggered by particular experiences and circumstances that more immediately predict offending.

A similar case can be made for substance abuse. Some child molesters use intoxicants to disinhibit their constraints against offending, in which case intoxication is a transitory or acute factor. For others, the chronic use of alcohol or some other drug so depletes the person's capacity for rational decision making that all sorts of dysfunctional behavior (including sexual offending) emerges (Abracen et al., 2000; Langevin et al., 1990; Lightfoot and Barbaree, 1993; Travin and Protter, 1993). Thus, chronic alcohol and drug abuse can cause some men to suspend what might otherwise be their concerns about the immediate and long-term consequences, for themselves and others, of their behavior (Steele and Josephs, 1990). In this respect substance abuse may function as a stable dispositional factor in child molestation. Using an intoxicant to deliberately facilitate offending (i.e., remove perceived barriers), on the other hand, is clearly a transitory or acute factor.

Over the past several years, we have made a case for the role of low self-esteem in sexual offending (Marshall et al., 1999; Marshall et al., 1996). The general literature indicates that low self-esteem as a chronic state undermines the person's belief that s/he can meet her/his needs prosocially and causes her/him to seek comfort and self-affirmation in inappropriate ways (Baumeister, 1993). We (Marshall et al., 1996) have suggested that among child molesters their low self-esteem leads them to seek comfort in sex with children, who are seen by these men as non-threatening and non-demanding (Howells, 1979). There is now evidence that child molesters are, indeed, low in self-esteem (Marshall, 1997; Marshall et al., 1997; Marshall et al., 1996; Marshall and Mazzucco, 1995). However, recent research by Hanson (2000) indicates that low self-esteem does not predict sexual offending, which suggests it is neither a stable nor a transitory dispositional factor. But in our recent attempts (Marshall et al., 2001) to examine the influence of an induced negative mood on the responses of child molesters to various tests (e.g., phallometry, self-esteem, attachments), we have made an observation that may point to a role for self-esteem as a dispositional factor. In one of our studies we assessed the self-esteem of child molesters prior to and after exposing them to a mood-induction procedure that has been shown to be effective in the general psychological literature (Velten, 1968). Our goal was to appraise the effects on self-esteem of the negative mood induced by the procedure. Instead what we found was that the only subjects who were responsive to the mood-induction procedure were those who were already low in self-esteem. These observations suggest that low self-esteem may be a stable dispositional (and risk) factor, but only through its indirect effect on making the person responsive to mood-altering experiences. Thus, low self-esteem may make a person more vulnerable to respond to various upsetting, transitory, events (e.g., problems in relationships, loss of a job) by experiencing a negative mood. Since child molesters characteristically respond to these distressing experiences by engaging in emotional coping (e.g., focussing only on angry feelings or experiencing self-pity), it will be their negative mood that will be the best proximal predictor of offending, rather than their chronic low self-esteem which initiated the chain of events leading to the negative mood.

No doubt there are other stable dispositional factors, some of which have been identified and some yet to be discovered. However, the ones we have discussed should serve to illustrate the issues. We now turn to transitory features.

Transitory Dispositions

Transitory dispositions are those states that act proximally to facilitate offending. We have already seen that a number of dispositional factors can be both stable influences on offending as well as transitory facilitators. This is true concerning the use of intoxicants, in the activation of dominant schemas, and in the momentary experience of loneliness. There are, however, other specific transitory experiences that appear to precipitate offending.

Relapse prevention theory and treatment have contributed to our understanding of sexual offenses. Essentially, proponents of the relapse prevention approach suggest that offending is likely to occur when sexual offenders encounter high-risk situations which threaten their control over deviant tendencies (Laws, 1989). These high-risk situations are said to involve either exposure to a possible victim (what we are calling "situational factors"), or the experience of some event or internal state (what we are calling "dispositional factors") that might cause them to seek a victim. The most frequent types of events or states described in the literature concern interpersonal conflicts and negative mood states, which are said to potentiate the offender's recognition of, and propensity to seize, opportunities where victims are present. If child molesters fail to cope appropriately in response to interpersonal conflict, they may experience a transitory negative mood or they may turn to alcohol or drugs to escape dwelling on their problem. Both these responses to inadequate coping have been identified as acute risk factors for sexual offending (Hanson and Harris, 2000).

Research suggests that negative emotional states are often present prior to sexually aggressive behavior. Pithers et al. (1989) reported that negative situational factors (e.g., job loss, conflict with a spouse) or negative emotions (e.g., anger, anxiety, depression) were present prior to a sexual offense. Since recidivism studies have shown that an acute change in mood is predictive of recidivism, emotional states can be considered important factors in offending. Even more relevant is that stable mood states are not as problematic as an acute change. Thus, events that trigger a particular shift in mood state could serve as triggers to subsequent offending behavior.

When in a negative mood state, child molesters are more likely to resort to deviant fantasies (Looman, 1995; McKibben et al., 1994; Proulx et al., 1996). Looman (1995) found that child molesters reported they were more likely to sexually fantasize about a child rather than an adult when experiencing conflict in relationships, or when feeling depressed or angry. Proulx and colleagues found that when sexual offenders experienced conflict, anger, loneliness, or humiliation, their frequency of deviant fantasies and masturbation to these fantasies increased. Pithers et al. (1989) demonstrated that negative mood states frequently precede an offense, and may serve as a situational trigger. When experiencing a negative mood state, a child molester might seize or create an opportunity to offend. Specifically, anger, loneliness, humiliation, depression, feelings of inadequacy and conflict in a relationship have produced a disinhibition of deviant fantasies (Looman, 1995; McKibben et al., 1994; Proulx et al., 1996). Once in a negative mood state, a child molester may seek an opportunity to offend or seize the chance to offend when an opportunity arises.

Although the early version of relapse prevention applied to sexual offenders has recently been criticized (Laws et al., 2000; Ward and Hudson, 1996; Ward et al., 1995), the essence of predisposing factors and situational risks, remains part of the revised model. Ward and his colleagues (Ward and Hudson, 1998; Ward et al., 1995) have revised the model and identified several different pathways to offending. In their research Ward and his colleagues found that some offenders followed a positive-affective pathway to offending (i.e., they offended when they were feeling good), and one-fourth of the sample were described as having a covert negative-affect pathway, while the remainder pursued a negative-affect approach associated with implicit planning. Offenders were identified as possessing either approach or avoidance goals where sexual offending was concerned. Thus, some clearly wished to continue to offend, while others attempted, unsuccessfully, to desist. This understanding has important consequences for a situational understanding of offending. Approach goal abusers do not see sexual contact between adults and children as a problem even though they realize that this view is not shared by society. For these offenders, positive-affective states, explicit planning, and cognitive distortions are the central features of their offense process. The goal of avoidant child molesters is to refrain from offending, but their self-regulation deficits (e.g., inadequate coping skills [underregulation] or inappropriate strategies [misregulation]) result in offending. Although Ward and his colleagues do not suggest this, it seems likely that their different pathways may also describe the same offender at different stages in his offending career. These distinctions among different pathways to offending are important, as different dispositional and situational variables will differentially affect the offense patterns of these groups of offenders.

SITUATIONAL FACTORS

Having access to victims is essential for an opportunity to offend to occur. It is often assumed (particularly by adherents of the early version of the relapse prevention approach) that most instances of sexual offending involve the offender creating opportunities to offend. While this may be true for some child molesters (e.g., repeat offenders), we can also expect that sexual offenders are likely to display the same flexibility in seeking to satisfy their deviant desires that the rest of us show in seeking to meet our more prosocial goals. Thus, child molesters are likely to seize an unexpected opportunity, and they are also likely to display different pathways, or modus operandi variability, on different occasions. This is a point that is missing from the otherwise exemplary pathways model described by Hudson and his colleagues (Hudson et al., 1999; Polaschek and Hudson, 2004).

Flexibility in modus operandi presents limitations on our ability to develop specific prevention strategies for individual clients to manage their post-treatment lives, but it does not stand in the way of generating overall preventative strategies to reduce the incidence of sexual offending. This variability in strategies is revealed by the numerous ways in which a specific child molester manages to get access to his victims and secure their cooperation. In some cases, a child molester may develop detailed plans to gain access to victims, including manipulating situations and other people so he can be alone with a child. On other occasions he may groom or coerce his victim into complying with sexual activities. On still other occasions he may engage in covert planning, where he allows events to unfold in a way that permits him access to a victim. It is not always clear, however, when planning is covert nor what exactly is meant by "covert."

In some of the early expositions of the relapse prevention model, descriptions of covert planning came close to implying unconscious processes. The following example from one of our clients would likely be described as "covert planning," but it is clearly not below the client's awareness. Our client had been experiencing repeated sexual arousal toward the 10-year old daughter of his wife's best friend. One Saturday his wife was speaking at some length on the phone to her friend. After some time our client interrupted his wife's conversation, suggesting she should invite her friend to visit, knowing at some low level of awareness that the friend would likely bring her daughter. Once the friend and her daughter arrived, he suggested they stay for supper knowing that this would require his wife to go shopping for food. Not surprisingly, his wife suggested her friend accompany her shopping while our client stayed home to look after the children. Once the women were gone, our client molested the young girl. At interviews, and early in treatment, he claimed he had not planned to offend; the opportunity, he said, just happened. Perhaps this man's "plans" are best understood in terms of "cognitive deconstruction" (see Ward et al., [1995] for the application of this construct to sexual offending), where the offender suspends concerns for anything but the explicit small steps he must take to achieve his goal; in doing so the offender blinds himself to his real intentions.

Child molesters gain access to victims through a variety of means. Choosing relationships with women who have children is one means by which child molesters seek opportunities to offend. Similarly, engaging in activities where they have unsupervised contact with children provides an opportunity to offend. Child molesters typically create such opportunities.

As Polaschek and Hudson (2004) note, a series of factors increases the propensity of sexual offenders to offend, but once these factors are established the offender then engages in "distal" planning to set up the opportunity to offend.

A recent study of child molesters by Sullivan and Beech (2004) offers an interesting perspective on this long-term planning. They examined the detailed reports extracted from child molesters attending a residential clinic. Information from these offenders came from structured interviews, case file data, and details revealed throughout a comprehensive treatment program. In particular, Sullivan and Beech examined reports from 41 child molesters who offended against children in their professional care. These subjects included religious professionals (n = 27), teachers (n = 10), and childcare workers (n = 4). Of these men, 15% said they chose their profession for the sole reason to get access to victims. A further 42% said having the opportunity to access victims was part of their motivation in seeking the job, and 20% were not sure how important getting an opportunity to offend was in choosing their career; only 25% declared that having a chance to offend was not part of their job choice. Thus, 75% of these offenders were aware at some level that choosing their career was influenced by the potential it offered to molest a child. Since 90% of them admitted to being aware of their sexual attraction to children before entering their professional careers, it is tempting to think that they chose their jobs at least in part because it provided a chance to sexually abuse children. However, since this information comes from identified offenders, it may be that their explanations for their career choice are simply reflections of their broader need to see themselves as suffering from a disposition over which they have little control. In this respect they may be attempting to reduce their responsibility for their crimes. In addition, a significant number of priests and members of Catholic orders whom we have seen in treatment have told us they entered seminaries because they thought such a career would "cure" their sexual problem. Nevertheless, it is clear that appropriate and detailed screening of men entering professions or volunteer organizations where access to children is part of the job, is essential to any adequate program aimed at preventing child sexual abuse.

In terms of the actual tactics employed by child molesting professionals (teachers, priests, etc.) to gain the compliance of their child victims, again Sullivan and Beech (2004) have relevant information. Almost 80% of their professional subjects said they took the child away from the scrutiny of the normal work environment as part of their offense planning. Of these offenders, 85% said that taking the child away overnight, or having the child stay overnight at the offender's home, was their preferred tactic. Taking the child away was seen by these offenders as not only maximizing an opportunity to molest the child, but also as a ploy that would be likely to receive parental support since these trips typically involved activities, or visits to places, that parents approved of.

Once these professionals (i.e., those child molesters who were engaged in a professional role with their victim) had the child alone, 67% of Sullivan and Beech's subjects said they used emotionally coercive tactics to gain the child's compliance. In an earlier study of clerics who molested children, Langevin et al. (2000) reported that far more of the clerics used physical force to gain their victims' cooperation than did a comparison group of non-professional child molesters. Another tactic employed by these professional offenders was to show the children pornography (usually adult heterosexual pornography), and this has been observed in studies on non-professional child molesters. Lang and Frenzel (1988), for example, found that 15% of incest offenders and 10% of nonfamilial child molesters showed their victims pornography as part of their attempts to gain victim compliance. Similarly, Langevin and Curnoe (2004) observed that 17% of child molesters exposed their victims to pornography to facilitate cooperation; those who molested nonfamilial boys showed the greatest use of this tactic (32% showed victims adult heterosexual pornography). Having pornography readily available in the household appears to be a clear risk factor for incest offenders: similarly to Lang and Frenzel's (1988) findings, Langevin and Curnoe (2004) reported that 16% of their incest offenders used this tactic to encourage their victim's participation. This remarkable variation in tactics (i.e., grooming, use of force, pornography exposure) appears likely to be related to features of the pre-offense relationship between the offender and his victim, to features of the victim (e.g., degree of submissiveness, degree of personal resilience), and to features of the setting where the offense occurs (e.g., child is isolated from others, or adults are in near proximity).

One of the primary questions about child molestation that is involved in attempts to plan prevention strategies concerns the consistency these offenders display in their offending. If child molesters consistently do the same things from offense to offense, then this consistency could provide the basis for identifying features that could become part of prevention plans. As we have seen, those who offend through their professional contacts with children demonstrate long-term planning that includes entering their profession as well as adopting specific tactics to be alone with a child. We now know some of the features that predict reoffending (see Hanson, [2000], Hanson and Bussière [1998], Hanson and Harris [2000] for a discussion of these issues), and it seems reasonable to suppose that these same features might predict the likelihood that someone who has not yet offended, will offend in the future. While factors that initiate a behavior are not always the same as those that maintain an ongoing behavior, until we learn otherwise these known predictors of relapse could serve as an initial basis for screening applicants for professions that involve potential contact with children. Those same features, plus what we know about the modus operandi of child molesters, could serve as the basis for monitoring such professionals during their employment. Marshall (in press) has outlined a prevention program along these lines for men entering Catholic seminaries and for graduates of the seminaries.

When attempting to identify the modus operandi of those child molesters whose employment does not provide them with opportunities to offend, it is well to keep in mind our previous note that child molesters are likely to be flexible in their strategies. Indeed the evidence supports versatility in offending. The modus operandi of sexual offenders is defined by Warren et al. (1999) as involving the offender's way of planning, how he gets access to and controls his victims, as well as his methods to avoid detection. To this list Kaufman, Hilliker and Daleinden (1996) add consistency in victim choice and characteristic offense features. Several researchers (Guay et al., 2001; Hanson et al., 1995; Soothill et al., 2000) have reported that when sexual offenders reoffend they tend to repeat previous behaviors and select the same type of victim. On the other hand, other researchers have found considerable variability across offenses in terms of behaviors, victim choice, and offense type (Abel et al., 1988; Grubin and Kennedy, 1991; Simon, 1997, 2000). Similarly, Studer et al. (2000) noted that more than half of their incest offenders reported prior nonfamilial victims and 13% of the nonfamilial child molesters said they had molested children within their family. There is no doubt that some child molesters are specialists, in the sense that they consistently choose similar victims (same age and gender) and engage in the same behaviors over repeated offenses (use of force, same type of sexual acts), while others are generalists.

This does not, however, reduce the importance of attempting to discern a consistency in modus operandi within individual offenders. In fact, in a recent large-scale study (n = 1,400), Sjöstedt et al. (2004) found considerable stability over time in offenders' victim preference, sexual acts during the offense, threats to victim, and type of victim injury.

We (Marshall and Marshall, 2001a, 2001b) have identified a significant proportion of child molesters who are sexually preoccupied and who, as a consequence, show little constraint in the expression of their sexual behaviors. These men appear to be a subgroup that match those described by Abel et al. (1998) as multiply paraphilic. We would not expect these offenders to show stability in the features examined in the above-mentioned studies of modus operandi, but perhaps other child molesters would show consistency. Thus, the apparent contradictions in the reports of modus operandi in these studies may be the result of differing samples of offenders.

However, the issue of individual consistency, as studied in the modus operandi research, has limited relevance for prevention planning, since most child molesters offend in circumstances (e.g., in the home) over which society's agents have little control. Clearly the main feature that can be prevented is the circumstance of the offender being alone with a child. However, even if we could identify a clear set of consistent features of the environment that is likely to trigger an offense in a man so disposed, it is hard to see how we could implement strategies to deter offending. The fact that most sexual offences against children occur within the home immediately poses limits on preventive strategies. While we could make guardians (i.e., parents, siblings, other relatives) more aware of the risks within the home setting, this is more easily implemented with known offenders. With known offenders, restrictions can be placed on whom they live with, and their support-group members (including members of their own household) can be alerted to the risks specific to the individual offender. In attempts to prevent offending from occurring in the first place, it is primarily among those men who are employed or volunteer for a job that puts them in a position where they can offend against a child, that we can articulate a clear set of steps (i.e., selection for the positions, and monitoring once in the job) to reduce the likelihood of offending. Careful and thorough interviews and assessments focusing on known features of child molesters, could serve as an effective screening process that would eliminate some who might offend. Similarly careful monitoring of such professionals and volunteers would seem essential. Such monitoring should watch for indications that the man is spending excessive time with a child, and other similar indications of a "special" relationship between the man and a child. In addition, persistent expressions by a child of discomfort about being with the man should be seen as indicating possible problems. As noted, these strategies have been enunciated in detail by Marshall (in press) concerning those entering and graduating from Catholic seminaries.

IMPLICATIONS FOR TREATMENT

When assessing and treating sexual offenders, we are often quick to dismiss the explanations they provide as excuses. However, within their explanations there often lies a kernel of truth. For example, when a man who has sexually assaulted his stepdaughter claims that if he had not been drinking he would not have offended, this might be partially true. Alcohol could serve to allow him to engage in a behavior that, sober, he would not consider doing. Similarly, stressful situations, relationship difficulties, and negative emotions (boredom, rejection, and anger) can all serve as triggers to offend. Rather than assume the offender is attempting to excuse his behavior, it is worthwhile to explore these issues because a thorough understanding of the circumstances under which he is more likely to offend can result in a more comprehensive treatment and release/discharge set of plans. What are seen as excuses by the offender should be seen by therapists as potential explanatory factors to be incorporated as targets of treatment and as features of future self-management plans.

Just as the factors we have considered can increase the likelihood of offending, similar factors can serve to decrease offending behavior. In treatment, Ward (2002) suggests that the goal should incorporate the "good lives" model; that is, the development of a way of living that is beneficial and fulfilling for the individual. Effective rehabilitation, Ward (2002; Eccleston and Ward, this volume; Marshall and Ward et al., in press) says, ensures that offenders possess the skills, knowledge, and resources to live more satisfying lives. According to this view, if offenders are meeting their needs appropriately their motivation to offend will be reduced. Within the "good lives" approach, then, the goal of treatment is to determine what prevents these men from living a positive, healthy lifestyle and to provide them with the attitudes, beliefs and skills to succeed. Within this approach, therapists are encouraged to challenge child molesters to adopt goals that lead to a healthier approach to life. Following from this model, primary prevention programs could target young males with the goal of enhancing their capacity to lead a fulfilled and healthy life. Since the good lives model, and the basic goals of a good life, have been clearly articulated and empirically supported in the general psychological literature (Deci and Ryan, 2000; Emmons, 1999; Schmauk and Sheldon, 2001), such a primary prevention program would simply implement training procedures meant to enhance the skills necessary for each individual to meet the goals of his own good lives model.

While the good lives model offers an alternative set of treatment goals that are no doubt very valuable, it remains essential to include in treatment the design of strategies that will reduce the likely occurrence of opportunities to offend. However, since approach goals are more easily achieved than avoidance goals (Mann et al., 2004), helping sexual offenders choose goals that are incompatible with offending (e.g., choosing adult partners and activities that are satisfying and do not involve children) is the best approach.

CONCLUSIONS

Research presently available provides some, albeit limited, guidance in formulating plans to prevent sexual abuse of children. However, more detailed, and specifically-targeted research is needed before truly effective plans can be developed. Once such plans are developed, their implementation will no doubt be resisted by those concerned about privacy and individual rights. Even if, and when, such plans are implemented, the bulk of sexual abusers of children can be expected to escape the net of prevention. Since most victims are molested by family members or trusted friends, it is unlikely that general prevention plans will intrude sufficiently on the lives of these offenders to prevent abuse from occurring. Indeed, the major obstacle to any program aimed at prevention of child sexual abuse is the trust these offenders are typically able to generate in those who might otherwise protect a child. Any program that attempts to reduce this trust runs the risk of seriously damaging the trust societies depend on for their healthful functioning. Nevertheless, the obstacles notwithstanding, we must press ahead with attempts to reduce the incidence of the sexual victimization of innocent children, not just for their sake, although that should be reason enough, but also for the future health of our societies.

Address correspondence to: W.L. Marshall, Rockwood Psychological Services, Suite 403, 303 Bagot Street, Kingston, Ontario, K7K 5W7, Canada; e-mail: bill@rockwoodpsyc.com.

REFERENCES

Abel, G.G., D.K. Gore, C.L. Holland, N. Camp, J.V. Becker and J. Rathner (1989). "The Measurement of the Cognitive Distortions of Child Molesters." *Annals of Sex Research* 2:135–152.

Abel, G.G., J.V. Becker, J. Cunningham-Rathner, M. Mittelman and J.L.Rouleau (1988). "Multiple Paraphilic Diagnoses Among Sex Offenders." *Bulletin of the American Academy of Psychiatry and the Law* 16:153–168.

Abracen, J., J. Looman, J. and D. Anderson (2000). "Alcohol and Drug Abuse in Sexual and Nonsexual Violent Offenders." *Sexual Abuse: A Journal of Research and Treatment* 12:263–274.

Baumeister, R.F. (1993). *Self-Esteem: The Puzzle of Low Self-Regard.* New York: Plenum Press.

Bond, I.K. and D.R. Evans (1967). "Avoidance Therapy: Its Use in Two Cases of Underwear Fetishism." *Canadian Medical Association Journal* 96:1160–1162.

Bumby, K.M. and D.J. Hansen (1997). "Intimacy Deficits, Fear of Intimacy and Loneliness Among Sex Offenders." *Criminal Justice and Behavior* 24:315–331.

Burk, L.R. and B.R. Burkhart (2003). "Disorganized Attachment as a Diathesis for Sexual Deviance: Developmental Experience and the Motivation for Sexual Offending." *Aggression and Violent Behavior* 8:487–512.

Bushman, B.J., R.F. Baumeister and C.M. Philips (2001). "Do People Aggress to Improve Their Mood? Catharsis, Beliefs, Affect Regulation Opportunity and Aggressive Responding." *Journal of Personality and Social Psychology* 81:17–31.

Carnes, P. (1992). *Out of the Shadows: Understanding Sexual Addiction* (2nd ed.). Minneapolis, MN: CompCare Publishers.

Check, J.V.P., D. Perlman and N.M. Malamuth (1985). "Loneliness and Aggressive Behavior." *Journal of Social and Personal Relations* 2:243–252.

Cortoni, F.A. and W.L. Marshall (2001). "Sex as a Coping Strategy and its Relationship to Juvenile Sexual History and Intimacy in Sexual Offenders." *Sexual Abuse: A Journal of Research and Treatment* 13:27–43.

Deci, E.L. and R.M. Ryan (2000). "The 'What' and 'Why' of Goal Pursuits: Human Needs and the Self-Determination of Behavior." *Psychological Inquiry* 11:227–268.

D'Zurilla, T.J. (1988). "Problem-Solving Therapies." In: K.S. Dobson (ed.), *Handbook of Cognitive-Behavioral Therapies* (pp. 85–135). New York: Pergamon Press.

Ellis, L. (1991). "A Synthesized (Biosocial) Theory of Rape." *Journal of Consulting and Clinical Psychology* 59:631–642.

Emmons, R.A. (1999). *The Psychology of Ultimate Concerns.* New York: Guilford Press.

Endler, N.S. and J.D.A. Parker (1994). "Assessment of Multidimensional Coping: Task, Emotion, and Avoidance Strategies." *Psychological Assessment* 6:50–60.

Finkelhor, D. (1984). *Child Sexual Abuse: New Theory and Research*. New York: Free Press.

Freund, K. (1990). "Courtship Disorder." In: W.L. Marshall, D.R. Laws and H.E. Barbaree (eds.), *Handbook of Sexual Assault: Issues, Theories and Treatment of the Offender* (pp. 195–207). New York: Plenum Press.

Garlick, Y., W.L. Marshall and D. Thornton (1996). "Intimacy Deficits and Attribution of Blame Among Sexual Offenders." *Legal and Criminological Psychology* 1:251–258.

Grubin, D.H. and H.G. Kennedy (1991). "The Classification of Sexual Offenders." *Criminal Behaviour and Mental Health* 1:123–129.

Guay, J-P., J. Proulx, M. Cusson and M. Ouiment (2001). "Victim-Choice Polymorphia Among Serious Sex Offenders." *Archives of Sexual Behavior* 30:521–533.

Hall, G.C.N. and R. Hirschman, R. (1991). "Toward a Theory of Sexual Aggression: A Quadripartite Model." *Journal of Consulting and Clinical Psychology* 59:662–669.

Hanson, R.K. (2000). "What Is So Special About Relapse Prevention?" In: D.R. Laws, S.M. Hudson and T. Ward (eds.), *Remaking Relapse Prevention with Sex Offenders* (pp. 27–38). Thousand Oaks, CA: Sage Publications.

Hanson, R.K. and M.T. Bussière (1998). "Predicting Relapse: A Meta-Analysis of Sexual Offender Recidivism Studies." *Journal of Consulting and Clinical Psychology* 66:348–362.

Hanson, R.K., R. Gizzarelli and H. Scott (1994). "The Attitudes of Incest Offenders: Sexual Entitlement and Acceptance of Sex with Children." *Criminal Justice and Behavior* 21:187–202.

Hanson, R.K. and A.J.R. Harris (2000). "Where Should We Intervene? Dynamic Predictors of Sexual Offense Recidivism." *Criminal Justice and Behavior* 27:6–35.

Hanson, R.K., H. Scott and R.A. Steffy (1995). "A Comparison of Child Molesters and Nonsexual Criminals: Risk Predictors and Long-Term Recidivism." *Journal of Research in Crime and Delinquency* 32:325–337.

Hesse, E. and M. Main (2000). "Disorganized Infant, Child and Adult Attachment: Collapse in Behavioral and Attentional Strategies." *Journal of the American Psychoanalytic Association* 48:1097–1127.

Howells, K. (1979). "Some Meanings of Children for Pedophiles." In: M. Cook and G.D. Wilson (eds.), *Love and Attraction: An International Conference* (pp. 519–526). Oxford: Pergamon Press.

Hudson, S.M., T. Ward and J.C. McCormack (1999). "Offense Pathways in Sexual Offenders." *Journal of International Violence* 8:779–798.

Kafka, M.P. (2003). "The Rationale for the Role of Medications in the Treatment of Catholic Clergy Who Sexually Molest Children and Adolescents." In: R.K. Hanson, F. Pfäfflin and M. Lütz (eds.), *Sexual Abuse in the Catholic Church: Scientific and Legal Perspectives*. Vatican City: Libreria Editrice Vaticana.

Kaufman, K.L., D.R. Hilliker and E.L. Daleinden (1996). "Subgroup Differences in the Modus Operandi of Adolescent Sexual Offenders." *Child Maltreatment: A Journal of the American Professional Society on the Abuse of Children* 1:17–24.

Lang, R.A. and R.R. Frenzel (1988). "How Sex Offenders Lure Children." *Annals of Sex Research* 1:303–318.

Langevin, R. (1992). "Biological Factors Contributing to Paraphilic Behavior." *Psychiatric Annals* 22:307–314.

Langevin, R. and S. Curnoe (2004). "The Use of Pornography During the Commission of Sexual Offenses." *International Journal of Offender Therapy and Comparative Criminology* 48:572–586.

Langevin, R., R. Lang and P. Wright (1990). "Substance Abuse Among Sex Offenders." *Annals of Sex Research* 3:397–424.

Langton, C. and W.L. Marshall (2001). "Cognition in Rapists: Theoretical Patterns by Typological Breakdown." *Aggression and Violent Behavior: A Review Journal* 6:499–518.

Langton, C. and W.L. Marshall (2000). "The Role of Cognitive Distortions in Relapse Prevention Programs." In: D.R. Laws, S.M. Hudson and T. Ward (eds.), *Remaking Relapse Prevention With Sex Offenders: A Sourcebook* (pp. 167–186). Newbury Park, CA: Sage Publications.

Laws, D.R. (1989). *Relapse Prevention with Sex Offenders.* New York: Guilford Press.

Laws, D.R., S.M. Hudson and T. Ward (2000). "The Original Model of Relapse Prevention with Sex Offenders: Promises Unfulfilled." In: D.R. Laws, S.M. Hudson and T. Ward (eds.), *Remaking Relapse Prevention with Sex Offenders: A Sourcebook* (pp. 3–24). Thousand Oaks, CA: Sage Publication.

Laws, D.R. and W.L. Marshall (2003). "A Brief History of Behavioral and Cognitive-Behavioral Approaches to Sexual Offender Treatment. Part 1. Early Developments." *Sexual Abuse: A Journal of Research and Treatment* 15:75–92.

Lightfoot, L.O. and H.W. Barbaree (1993). "The Relationship between Substance Use and Abuse and Sexual Offending in Adolescents." In: H.E. Barbaree, W.L., Marshall and S.M. Hudson (eds.), *The Juvenile Sex Offender* (pp. 203–224). New York: Guilford Press.

Looman, J. (1999). "Mood, Conflict and Deviant Sexual Fantasies." In: B. Schwartz (ed.), *The Sex Offender: Theoretical Advances, Treating Special Populations and Legal Developments* (vol. 3, pp. 3.1–3.11). Kingston, NJ: Civic Research Institute.

Mann, R.E. (2004). "Innovations in Sex Offender Treatment." *Journal of Sexual Aggression* 10:141–152.

Mann, R.E., S.D. Webster, C. Schofield and W.L. Marshall (2004). "Approach Versus Avoidance Goals in Relapse Prevention with Sexual Offenders." *Sexual Abuse: A Journal of Research and Treatment* 16:65–75.

Marshall, W.L. (in press). "Preventing Sexual Crimes against Children: Integrating Clinical and Criminological Perspectives." Forthcoming in *Seminary.*

Marshall, W.L. (1997). "The Relationship between Self-Esteem and Deviant Sexual Arousal in Nonfamilial Child Molesters." *Behavior Modification* 21:86–96.

Marshall, W.L. (1996a). "The Sexual Offender: Monster, Victim or Everyman?" *Sexual Abuse: A Journal of Research and Treatment* 8:317–335.

Marshall, W.L. (1996b). "Assessment, Treatment and Theorizing About Sex Offenders: Developments Over the Past 20 Years and Future Directions." *Criminal Justice and Behavior* 23:162–199.

Marshall, W.L. (1993). "The Role of Attachment, Intimacy and Loneliness in the Etiology and Maintenance of Sexual Offending." *Sexual and Marital Therapy* 8:109–121.

Marshall, W.L. (1989). "Intimacy, Loneliness and Sexual Offenders." *Behaviour Research and Therapy* 27:491–503.

Marshall, W.L., D. Anderson and Y.M. Fernandez (1999). *Cognitive Behavioural Treatment of Sexual Offenders.* Chichester, UK: John Wiley & Sons.

Marshall, W.L., D. Anderson and F. Champagne (1996). "Self-Esteem and its Relationship to Sexual Offending." *Psychology, Crime & Law* 3:81–106.

Marshall, W.L. and H.E. Barbaree (1990). "An Integrated Theory of Sexual Offending." In: W.L. Marshall, D.R. Laws and H.E. Barbaree (eds.), *Handbook of Sexual Assault: Issues, Theories, and Treatment of the Offender* (pp. 257–275). New York: Plenum Press.

Marshall, W.L., F. Champagne, C. Brown and S. Miller (1997). "Empathy, Intimacy, Loneliness, and Self-Esteem in Nonfamilial Child Molesters." *Journal of Child Sexual Abuse* 6:87–97.

Marshall, W.L. and Y.M. Fernandez (2003a). "Sexual Preferences: Are They Useful in the Assessment and Treatment of Sexual Offenders." *Aggression and Violent Behavior: A Review Journal* 8:131–143.

Marshall, W.L. and Y.M. Fernandez (2003b). *Phallometric Testing with Sexual Offenders: Theory, Research and Practice.* Brandon, VT: Safer Society Press.

Marshall, W.L. and Y.M. Fernandez (2000c). "Phallometric Testing with Sexual Offenders: Limits to its Value." *Clinical Psychology Review* 20:807–822.

Marshall, W.L. and Y.M. Fernandez (2000b). "Phallometry in Forensic Practice." *Journal of Forensic Psychology Practice* 1:77–87.

Marshall, W.L. and C. Langton (2004). "Unwanted Thoughts and Fantasies Experienced by Sexual Offenders: Their Nature, Persistence and Treatment." In: D. Clark (ed.), *Intrusive Thoughts in Clinical Disorders: Theory, Research and Treatment* (pp. 199–225). New York: Guilford Press.

Marshall, W.L. and D.R. Laws (2003). "A Brief History of Behavioral and Cognitive Behavioral Approaches to Sexual Offender Treatment. Part 2. The Modern Era." *Sexual Abuse: A Journal of Research and Treatment* 15:93–120.

Marshall, L.E. and W.L. Marshall (2002). "The Role of Attachment in Sexual Offending: An Examination of Preoccupied-Attachment-Style Offending Behavior." In: B. Schwartz (ed.), *The Sex Offender: Current Treatment Modalities and Systems Issues* (vol. 4, pp. 3.1–3.8). Kingston, NJ: Civic Research Institute.

Marshall, W.L. and L.E. Marshall (2002). "Cómo Ilega Alguien A Convertirse En Un Delincuente Sexual." In: S. Redondo (ed.), *Delincuencia Sexualy Sociedad* (pp. 235–250). Valencia: Ariel Publishing.

Marshall, L.E. and W.L. Marshall (2001a, May). "Sexual Compulsivity as Part of Sexual Offending Behavior." Workshop presented at the National Conference of the National Council on Sexual Addiction and Compulsivity, San Diego.

Marshall, L.E. and W.L. Marshall (2001b). "Excessive Sexual Desire Disorder Among Sexual Offenders: The Development of a Research Project." *Sexual Addiction and Compulsivity: The Journal of Treatment and Prevention* 8:301–307.

Marshall, W.L. and A. Mazzucco (1995). "Self-Esteem and Parental Attachments in Child Molesters." *Sexual Abuse: A Journal of Research and Treatment* 7:279–285.

Marshall, L.E., H. Moulden and W.L. Marshall (2004, October). "An Examination of the Relationship between Preoccupied Attachment and Offence Behavior in

Incarcerated Sexual Offenders." Paper presented at the 23rd Annual Research and Treatment Conference of the Association for the Treatment of Sexual Abusers, Albuquerque, New Mexico.

Marshall, L.E., H. Moulden and W.L. Marshall (2001, November). "Mood Induction with Sexual Offenders." Paper presented at the 20th Annual Research and Treatment Conference of the Association for the Treatment of Sexual Abusers, San Antonio, Texas.

Marshall, W.L., G.A. Serran and F.A. Cortoni (2000). "Childhood Attachments, Sexual Abuse and Their Relationship to Adult Coping in Child Molesters." *Sexual Abuse: A Journal of Research and Treatment* 12:17–26.

Marshall, W.L., T. Ward, R.E. Mann, H. Moulden, Y.M. Fernandez, G.A. Serran and L.E. Marshall (in press). "Working Positively with Sexual Offenders: Maximizing the Effectiveness of Treatment." *Journal of Interpersonal Violence*.

McKibben, A., J. Proulx and R. Lusignan (1994). "Relationship between Conflict, Affect and Deviant Sexual Behavior in Rapists and Pedophiles." *Behaviour Research and Therapy* 32:571–575.

Mischel, W. (1968). *Personality and Assessment*. New York: John Wiley & Sons.

Pithers, W.D. (1990). "Relapse Prevention with Sexual Aggressors: A Method for Maintaining Therapeutic Gain and Enhancing External Supervision." In: W.L. Marshall, D.R. Laws and H.E. Barbaree (eds.), *Handbook of Sexual Assault: Issues, Theories and Treatment of the Offender* (pp. 343–361). New York: Plenum Press.

Pithers, W.D., L.S. Beal, J. Armstrong and J. Petty (1989). "Identification of Risk Factors Through Clinical Interviews and Analysis of Records." In: D.R. Laws (ed.), *Relapse Prevention with Sex Offenders* (pp. 77–87). New York: Guilford Press.

Pithers, W.D., J.K. Marques, C.C. Gibat and G.A. Marlatt (1983). "Relapse Prevention with Sexual Aggressors: A Self-Control Model of Treatment and Maintenance of Change." In: J.G. Greer and I.R. Stuart (eds.), *The Sexual Aggressor: Current Perspectives on Treatment* (pp. 214–239). New York: Van Nostrand Reinhold.

Polaschek, D.L.L. and S.M. Hudson (2004). "Pathways to Rape: Preliminary Examination of Patterns in the Offense Process of Rapists and their Rehabilitation Implications." *Journal of Sexual Aggression* 10:7–20.

Proulx, J., A. McKibben and R. Lusignan (1996). "Relationships between Affective Components and Sexual Behaviors in Sexual Aggressors." *Sexual Abuse: A Journal of Research and Treatment* 8:279–289.

Quinsey, V.L. (2003). "The Etiology of Anomalous Sexual Preferences in Men." *Annals of the New York Academy of Sciences* 989:105–117.

Schmauk, P. and K.M. Sheldon (2001). *Life Goals and Well-Being*. Toronto: Hogrefe & Huber Publishers.

Serran, G.A. (2004). "Changes in the Coping Strategies of Extrafamilial Child Molesters Following Cognitive Behaviour Relapse Prevention Treatment." Unpublished doctoral thesis, University of Ottawa, Canada.

Serran, G.A., J. Looman and I. Dickie (2004, October). "The Role of Schemas in Sexual Offending." Paper presented at the 23rd Annual Research and Treatment Conference of the Association for the Treatment of Sexual Abusers, Albuquerque, New Mexico.

Simon, L. (2000). "An Examination of the Assumptions of Specialization, Mental Disorder and Dangerousness in Sex Offenders." *Behavioral Sciences and the Law* 18:275–308.

Simon, L. (1997). "Do Criminal Offenders Specialize in Crime Types?" *Applied and Preventive Psychology* 6:35–53.

Sjöstedt. G., N. Långström, K. Sturidsson and M. Grann (2004). "Stability of Modus Operandi in Sexual Offending." *Criminal Justice and Behavior* 31:609–623.

Smallbone, S.W. (2005). "An Attachment Theoretical Revision of Marshall and Barbaree's (1990) Integrated Theory of Sexual Offending." In: W.L. Marshall, Y.M. Fernandez, L.E. Marshall, and G.A. Serran (eds.), *Sexual Offender Treatment: Issues and Controversies*. London: John Wiley and Sons.

Smallbone, S.W. and M.R. Dadds (1998). "Childhood Attachment and Adult Attachment in Incarcerated Adult Male Sex Offenders." *Journal of Interpersonal Violence* 13:555–573.

Smallbone, S.W. and R. Wortley (2004). "Criminal Diversity and Paraphilic Interests among Adult Males Convicted of Sexual Offences against Children." *International Journal of Offender Therapy and Comparative Criminology* 48:175–188.

Soothill, K., B. Francis, B. Sanderson and E. Ackerley (2000). "Sex Offenders: Specialists, Generalists – Or Both? A 32-year Criminological Study." *British Journal of Criminology* 40:56–67.

Steele, C.M. and R.A. Josephs (1990). "Alcohol Myopia: Its Prized and Dangerous Effects." *American Psychologist* 45:921–933.

Studer, L.H., S.R. Clelland, A.S. Aylwin, J.R. Reddon and A. Monro (2000). "Rethinking Risk Assessment for Incest Offenders." *International Journal of Law and Psychiatry* 23:15–22.

Sullivan, J. and A. Beech (2004). "A Comparative Study of Demographic Data Relating to Intra- and Extra-Familial Child Sexual Abusers and Professional Perpetrators." *Journal of Sexual Aggression* 10:39–50.

Travin, S. and B. Protter (1993). *Sexual Perversion: Integrative Treatment Approaches for the Clinician*. New York: Plenum Press.

Velten, E.A. (1968). "A Laboratory Task for the Induction of Mood States." *Behaviour Research and Therapy* 6:473–482.

Ward, T. (2002). "Good Lives and the Rehabilitation of Offenders: Promises and Problems." *Aggression and Violent Behavior: A Review Journal* 7:513–528.

Ward, T. and S.M. Hudson (2000). "A Self-Regulation Model of Relapse Prevention." In: D.R. Laws, S.M. Hudson and T. Ward (eds.), *Remaking Relapse Prevention with Sex Offenders: A Sourcebook* (pp. 79–101). Thousand Oaks, CA: Sage Publications.

Ward, T. and S.M. Hudson (1998). "A Model of the Relapse Process in Sexual Offenders." *Journal of Interpersonal Violence* 13:400–425.

Ward, T. and S.M. Hudson (1996). "Relapse Prevention: A Critical Analysis." *Sexual Abuse: A Journal of Research and Treatment* 8:177–200.

Ward, T., S.M. Hudson, L. Johnston and W.L. Marshall (1997). "Cognitive Distortions in Sex Offenders: An Integrative Review." *Clinical Psychology Review* 17:479–507.

Ward, T., S.M. Hudson and W.L. Marshall (1996). "Attachment Style in Sex Offenders: A Preliminary Study." *Journal of Sex Research* 33:17–26.

Ward, T., S.M. Hudson and W.L. Marshall (1995). "Cognitive Distortions and Affective Deficits in Sex Offenders: A Cognitive Deconstructionist Interpretation." *Sexual Abuse: A Journal of Research and Treatment* 7:67–83.

Ward, T., S.M. Hudson, W.L. Marshall and R. Siegert (1995). "Attachment Style and Intimacy Deficits in Sex Offenders: A Theoretical Framework." *Sexual Abuse: A Journal of Research and Treatment* 7:317–335.

Ward, T., S.M. Hudson and R.J. Siegert (1995). "A Critical Comment on Pithers' Relapse Prevention Model." *Sexual Abuse: A Journal of Research and Treatment* 7:167–175.

Ward, T., K. Louden, S.M. Hudson and W.L. Marshall (1995). "A Descriptive Model of the Offense Chain for Child Molesters." *Journal of Interpersonal Violence* 10:452–472.

Ward, T. and W.L. Marshall (2004). "Good Lives, Aetiology and the Rehabilitation of Sex Offenders: A Bridging Theory." *Journal of Sexual Aggression* 10:153–169.

Warren, J., R. Reboussin, R.R. Hazelwood, N.A. Gibbs, S.L. Trumbetta and A. Cummings (1999). "Crime Scene Analysis and the Escalation of Violence in Serial Rape." *Forensic Science International* 100:37–56.

Webster, S.D. and W.L. Marshall (2004). "Generating Data with Sexual Offenders Using Qualitative Material: A Paradigm to Complement Not Compete with Quantitative Methodology." *Journal of Sexual Aggression* 10:117–122.

Webster, S., H. Moulden and W.L. Marshall (2004). "A Grounded Theory Analysis of Opportunities to Offend among Child Molesters." Unpublished manuscript. Rockwood Psychological Services, Suite 403, 303 Bagot Street, Kingston, Ontario, Canada K7K 5W7.

Wortley, R. (2001). "A Classification of Techniques for Controlling Situational Precipitators of Crime." *Security Journal* 14:63–82.

Sex Crimes against Children: Legislation, Prevention and Investigation

by

Leonore M. J. Simon

Department of Criminal Justice and Criminology, East Tennessee State University

and

Kristen Zgoba

New Jersey Department of Corrections

Abstract: *Legislation targeting sex offenders was enacted in the U.S. during 1980s and 1990s with the goal of preventing child molestations. These sex offender policies generally aim to prevent sex crimes by focusing on some aspect of the offender, and they range from offender registration with the police to participation in sex offender treatment. In contrast, situational crime prevention (SCP) methods bypass offender-focused approaches, emphasizing modification of situational factors that initiate or facilitate the commission of crimes. This chapter makes suggestions for legislation, prevention, and investigation of child molestation based on empirical data that compare sex crimes with three other violent felonies. Findings indicate that: most sex crimes involve child victims; sex crime rates are comparable to rates of other violent crimes; sex crimes are rarely perpetrated by strangers; most male sex crime victims are victimized under the age of 12; most female sex crime victims are victimized during and after puberty; sex crimes have a decreased* *probability of arrest compared to other violent crimes; and sex crimes committed by family members and acquaintances have a decreased probability of arrest compared to sex crimes committed by strangers. Implications of the findings for legislation, prevention, and investigation are explored.*

INTRODUCTION

Cases of child molestation have all but eclipsed similarly heinous crimes in the media and in society (Scott, 2001). In the U.S., this moral panic (Jenkins, 1998) over child molestation began in the early 1980s,[1] when states rediscovered child sexual abuse and began to arrest, prosecute, and incarcerate child molesters in large numbers. For example, between 1980 and 1994, while the overall prison population increased 206%, the number of imprisoned sex offenders grew by 330% (Greenfeld, 1997). In 1998, the number of adult sex offenders in state prisons numbered 94,000 (Beck and Mumola, 1999), increasing to 118,500 in 2002 (Harrison and Beck, 2003), a 26% increase.[2]

The increase in incarceration of child molesters after 1980 was followed in the 1990s by a series of legal policies intended to increase the social control of sex offenders (Simon, 2003), at a time when the number of actual child molestation cases was declining (Jones and Finkelhor, 2001), as were the general crime rates. Policies directed toward sex offenders include Megan's Law[3] or community notification statutes, mandatory sex offender registration statutes, mandatory sex offender treatment, and involuntary commitment to mental hospitals for offenders assessed as sexually violent predators. The policies were developed in response to highly publicized and particularly heinous cases of child molestation by strangers (Simon, 2003). Washington State, for instance, enacted its community notification legislation after a seven-year-old boy was raped and mutilated by a convicted sex offender (Simon, 2003). New Jersey enacted the same type of legislation after a seven-year-old girl was raped and murdered by another convicted sex offender who lived across the street from her (Simon, 2003). A major goal of the resulting 1990s' policies is to prevent child molestation by strangers (Simon and Black, 2004).

The sex offender policies are designed to prevent child molestation by focusing on some aspect of the offender. For instance, sex offender registration requires convicted sex offenders to register with the local police each time they move. If a new sex crime occurs, and no suspect is immediately evident, police often round up the usual suspects – convicted, registered sex offenders. Sexually violent predator statutes involuntarily commit convicted sex offenders (after they have served their prison terms) to indefinite terms when they are deemed dangerous. These involuntary committed sex offenders are rarely released after their commitments. Sex offender treatment programs, operating in and outside of prison in the majority of states (West et al., 2000; Freeman-Longo et al., 1994; Zgoba, 2004; Zgoba et al., 2003), emphasize changing the offender's sexually deviant fantasies, sexual urges, and behavior.[4] Unfortunately, the effects of treatment do not consistently translate into lower recidivism rates (Simon, 1998). Sex offenders who receive specialized sex offender treatment are encouraged to identify and eliminate deviant sexual fantasies. However, many studies show that sex offenders can eliminate the sexual fantasies but go on to sexually offend again. In some cases, sex offenders participating in treatment have recidivism rates comparable to offenders who do not receive the treatment (Zgoba, 2004; Zgoba and Simon, 2006).

Child Molestation, Criminology, and the Versatility of Sex Criminals

Although legal scholars are critically examining the legality of policies singling out sex offenders (e.g., Winick, 2003), and clinical treatment providers are actively researching the efficacy of sex offender treatment (e.g., Rice and Harris, 2003) or assessment of dangerousness (e.g., Hanson, 2003), until recently criminologists have ignored this area of research and policy (e.g., Kruttschnitt et al., 2000; Presser and Gunnison, 1999). The neglect by criminology and criminal justice may explain why nationally collected and published criminal justice statistics generally still do not disaggregate sex offenders and their victims to distinguish child molestation cases from forcible rapes of adults. For instance, published statistics on state and federal inmates disaggregate sex offenses in only one table by enumerating the number of prisoners incarcerated for "rape and other sexual assault" (Harrison and Beck, 2003, Table 15, p. 10). The fact that the other sexual assault category is almost three times the size of the rape category can be seen in the table, but this comparison is otherwise neither emphasized nor explained in the text. Similarly, a statistical report on felony sentences in state courts (Durose and Langan, 2003) includes the categories of rape and sexual assault under violent crimes, but does not disaggregate the sex crimes by age of the victim. The report includes a table that indicates that in the year 2000 there were almost twice as many state felony convictions for sexual assault (20,900) than there were for rape (10,600), but it contains no information on what percentage of these convictions involved victims who were children (Durose and Langan, 2003, Table 1, p. 2). The disjuncture between enactment of sex offender policies in the 1980s and 1990s, and the absence as of 2003 of national data on child molestation cases, thwarts efforts by researchers and policymakers to assess the proportion of sex crimes that involve child victims. Moreover, the absence of the relevant data prevents the sex offender policies from being evaluated for their effectiveness in preventing sex crimes against children.

The neglect of sex offender research and policy by criminologists results in misconceptions that child molestations are committed by individuals afflicted with a sexual deviance or mental disorder (Simon, 2000, 1997). Such misconceptions are rooted in the research of clinical treatment providers, who assess and treat select samples of child molesters after they enter the criminal justice system (e.g., Rice and Harris, 2003). Most of the research on child molesters ignores the molesters' criminal records before and after their incarceration for child molestation, resulting in the myth that sex offenders do not commit non-sex crimes.

In contrast to clinicians, criminologists acknowledge that, although there may be a few specialist offenders, the overwhelming weight of the empirical evidence supports the idea of versatility of offending (e.g., Britt, 1994; Gottfredson and Hirschi, 1990; Hindelang et al., 1981; Hindelang, 1971; Hirschi, 1969; Klein, 1984; Simon, 1996, 1995, 1994; Smallbone and Wortley, 2004a; Wolfgang et al., 1972). Studies finding versatility in offending generally conclude that offenders commit a wide variety of crime types. The proportion of offenders who could be regarded as specialists – that is, offenders who commit only one crime at a high rate – ranges from 1% (Simon, 1994) to 10% (Peterson and Braiker, 1981).

Similarly to the findings of general offender versatility, research on the offending histories of sex offenders has found that sex offenders do not specialize in sex crimes. For instance, in a study of 136 consecutive, convicted child molesters, Simon et al. (1992) found that 50% of the offenders had a prior non-sex crime record. In a subsequent study comparing 142 child molestation cases, 51 rape cases, and 290 violent offense cases, more than 70% of the rapists and violent offenders and 54% of the molesters possessed prior criminal records containing non-sex crimes (Simon, 2000). Similarly, Smallbone and Wortley (2004b), in their study of 362 convicted child molesters, found that 52% of their sample had previous convictions for non-sex offenses. Moreover, in a study of 207 incarcerated child molesters, Smallbone and Wortley (2004a) found that 69% of the molesters had previous convictions for non-sex offenses. As is the case with other crimes, there may be a few specialists who commit only sex crimes at a high rate. However, the majority of child molesters are versatile in their offending patterns, possessing criminal records that contain more arrests and convictions for myriad non-molestation offenses and few, if any, child molestations or other sex crimes.

Although empirical observations of criminal versatility have existed for years, versatility is directly incorporated into control theory (Gottfredson and Hirschi, 1990). Control theory suggests that crime provides immediate pleasure or benefit to the offender. The specific form of the pleasure can range from mood enhancement to monetary gain (Britt, 1994). The crime itself is seen as opportunistic and requiring little skill or planning. Offenders seek immediate gratification, do not consider the long-term consequences of their behavior, display egocentricity, have low self-control, and act impulsively. Because offenders are not governed by the long-term consequences of their acts, they are "likely to engage in a host of immediately pleasurable activities – from sex to drugs to assault – without pattern, rhyme, or reason" (T. Hirschi, personal communication, March 25, 1996). Instead of specializing in crime types, control theory suggests that criminal offenders are versatile in crimes and other antisocial or self-destructive, risky behaviors such as alcohol abuse, smoking, sexual promiscuity, reckless driving, and accidents. According to control theory, sex crimes, like other criminal acts, have a hedonistic component (Simon, 2000, 1998, 1997). Offenders molest children and rape women because they derive immediate sexual gratification from the acts, failing to consider the long-term consequences of their acts such as legal sanctions and disruptions in relationships.

Situational Crime Prevention as an Alternative to Offender-focused Policies

Because child molesters have a generalized problem with self-control, rather than a specific sexual deviance or mental disorder (Simon, 2000), offense-focused prevention strategies may be more effective than current offender-focused policies. Although predominantly a theory about the role of self-control in offending, control theory emphasizes the importance of situational crime prevention (SCP)-related factors in defining the necessary conditions for the occurrence of specific crimes and in suggesting how specific crimes can be prevented (Gottfredson and Hirschi, 1990).

Consequently, preventing child molestation by increasing controls through SCP methods is consistent with control theory, offering an attractive alternative to crime reduction efforts targeting offender behavior, such as by improving parental child rearing practices or rehabilitating the offender, both of which may take years to effect changes (Australian Institute of Criminology (AIC), 2003; Clarke and Eck, 2003; Clarke and Mayhew, 1980; Clarke, 1997; Clarke, 1995; Gottfredson and Hirschi, 1990; Simon, 1998). For instance, incarcerated sex criminals who receive sex offender treatment in prison have comparable recidivism rates to sex offenders not receiving the treatment (Zgoba, 2004; Zgoba and Simon, 2006). Thus, the goal of reducing or preventing future sex crimes may be more effectively accomplished by SCP approaches than through current sex offender policies like treating the offender.

SCP is a unique criminological approach which suggests that offender behavior interacts with circumstances in the environment to produce criminal acts (Clarke and Eck, 2003; Clarke, 1997; Clarke, 1995 Clarke and Mayhew, 1980; Wortley, 2002, 2001). According to SCP, prevention of crime can occur by modifying aspects of the environment that initiate or facilitate the commission of crimes (Wortley and Smallbone, this volume, chapter 2). Devising effective SCP programs depends on analyses of specific types of crimes in specific situations. According to Clarke (1997, p. 2), situational crime prevention " . . . [p]roceeds from an analysis of the circumstances giving rise to specific kinds of crime, it introduces discrete managerial and environmental change to reduce the opportunity for those crimes to occur. Thus it is focused on the settings for crime, rather than upon those committing criminal acts. It seeks to forestall the occurrence of crime, rather than to detect and sanction offenders." In summary, situational crime prevention comprises opportunity-reducing measures that are directed at specific types of crime, tailor the design of the environment, and make crime more risky and difficult for offenders (Clarke, 1997).

Wortley (2002, 2001) notes that opportunity reduction represents only half of the equation, and that the motivation to commit a crime may itself be situationally-dependent. Wortley distinguishes between the relationship of "precipitators" and "opportunities" in a two-stage model.

He suggests that in the first stage criminal behavior may be entirely pre-vented if situational precipitators or instigators are controlled. When crimi-nal behavior is not prevented in the first stage, the second stage involves the individual's weighing of the costs and benefits that are expected to follow. The second stage of the model corresponds to Clarke's initial four types of opportunity-reduction techniques (Clarke, 1997; Wortley, 2002, 2001). Wortley's insights have resulted in a revised model of SCP that incorporates some of the precipitating factors under the heading of reduc-ing provocations (Cornish and Clarke, 2003). The addition of precipitators has had both a theoretical and a practical influence on the original tech-niques suggested by Clarke (1997).

SCP's intellectual foundation includes theories of environmental criminology (Brantingham and Brantingham, 1984, 1981), rational choice (Cornish and Clarke, 1986) and routine activities (Cohen and Felson, 1979). Environmental criminology examines the manner by which the physical environment facilitates the perpetration of a crime (Brantingham and Brantingham, 1984, 1981), whereas rational choice theory suggests that offenders weigh the risks and the benefits of committing a crime (Cornish and Clarke, 1986). Routine activity theory examines the intersec-tion of environment and offender, and suggests that the necessary elements for a crime to occur consist of a motivated offender, an attractive target, and an absence of capable guardianship of the target (Cohen and Felson, 1979).

SCP and Preventing Child Molestation

SCP has focused largely on the prevention of instrumental crimes that benefit the offender tangibly, as opposed to more personally expressive crimes (e.g., Clarke and Eck, 2003; Gill, 2000). For example, SCP has been applied to residential and business burglaries, credit card theft, em-ployee theft, shoplifting, vandalism to elevators and bus stops, theft from cars, purse snatchings, obscene phone calls, pay phone toll fraud, and check forgeries (e.g., Clarke and Eck, 2003; Clarke, 1997).

In contrast, child molestation prevention tactics primarily rely upon secondary and tertiary prevention techniques. For example, children are taught to report whether they have been touched inappropriately or told to keep a secret, whereas adults are trained to identify and report children who are molested. However, such strategies fail to prevent the sexual victimization of children.

This chapter adds to the body of SCP research by presenting data on sex crime incidents that challenge common misconceptions of sex offenders and their victims. Taking account of the empirical realities of sex crime incidents can facilitate the development of successful prevention strategies targeting child molestation. Moreover, this chapter demonstrates how sex crime incidents differ from other violent felony incidents in regard to incidence rates, victim and offender characteristics, the victim-offender relationship, and arrest rates. These differences suggest that approaches to preventing child molestation may differ substantially from approaches used to prevent some types of violent felonies and be similar to those used in other types of felonies. The implications of the findings for legislation, prevention, and investigation are explored.

DATA SOURCES AND ELEMENTS

The data are from the National Incident-Based Reporting System (NIBRS) for the year 2000, which is distributed by the Federal Bureau of Investigation (FBI)[5] and maintained by the National Archive of Criminal Justice Data (NACJD) at the Inter-University Consortium for Political and Social Research (ICPSR). Until the recent availability of the National Incident-Based Reporting System (NIBRS), designed to eventually replace the Uniform Crime Reports (UCR), national data sources were not able to provide specific information on sex crimes, such the age of the victim and other characteristics of sex crime incidents. Prior to NIBRS, researchers of sex crimes have long struggled with the shortcomings of police report and victimization data in addressing sex crimes against children (Snyder, 2000). For police (UCR) data, these shortcomings include: the limitation of police data to one narrow category; the forcible rape of females; the absence of information on the age of the victim; the absence of information of the offender's relationship to the victim; and the fact that only one crime is counted in incidents involving multiple offenses (U.S. Bureau of Justice Statistics, 1997b; Rantala and Edwards, 2000). Victimization data from the National Crime Victimization Survey (NCVS) contain survey data on individuals 12 years of age and older (e.g., Hart, 2003; Rennison, 2003, 2002), omitting victimization data on sex crimes experienced by individuals younger than age 12.

NIBRS reports on 46 types of crime incidents and arrests within 22 categories (U.S. Bureau of Justice Statistics, 1997b).[6] Like the UCR, participation in NIBRS is voluntary, and anecdotal accounts suggest that law enforcement agencies may not be sufficiently funded for the time and personnel it takes to compile and report all the data. For those reasons, the year 2000 data supplied by NIBRS-certified states cover only 17% of the United States' population and represent 15% of the nation's crime volume (U.S. FBI, 2002). Other limitations of the data include the tendency of police reports to often underestimate the number of sex crimes and other violent felonies committed by offenders known to the victim.

Although there is no way to ascertain the representativeness of the sample, the 2000 NIBRS data indicate that the number of sex crimes reported to the police (42,610) was almost as large as the number of robberies (45,010), a common stranger crime. Therefore, accepting the inherent limitations of the data, the sheer number of reports and detailed information available on each incident provides researchers and policymakers with a unique opportunity to analyze the characteristics of sex crimes.

NIBRS is used in this chapter to examine the characteristics of four forcible sexual crimes (forcible rape, forcible sodomy, sexual assault with an object, and forcible fondling); the characteristics of two non-forcible sexual crimes (incest and statutory rape); and the characteristics of three non-sex violent crimes (kidnapping, aggravated assault, and robbery) reported to NIBRS. The FBI definitions and instructions for coding of the sex crimes are presented in the appendix. In particular, this chapter examines the rate of sex crimes, the percentage of victims of sex crimes who are children, the ages and genders of the victims, the victim-offender relationships, and the predictors of arrest for sex crimes compared to other violent crimes.

The original data structure allowed multiple records for most of the record types in the data set (victim, offender, arrestee, offense, and property). The raw relational NIBRS data were converted from an incident-based data set to a victim-based set. Incident data were written to each victim record, as was other detailed information (age, race, sex, offender-victim relationship, victim injury). A series of other variables reflecting incident characteristics was added to each victim record (use of force or weapon, number of offenders, number of victims, number of crimes, offender age, offender sex, offender race, and the reporting state). Thus, even though the data structure was victim-based, each record contained incident-based information. The result was a moderately sized record, which could be processed by standard statistical analysis software.

Distribution and Rates of Sex and Comparison Violent Crimes

The NIBRS data include smaller jurisdictions. The cities range in size from 191 to 936,498, with an average population of 128,734. The population size for the 25th percentile is 20,297; for the 50th percentile, 58,721; and for the 75th percentile, 532,680. The distribution of offenses includes 14,740 forcible rapes, 3,816 forcible sodomy cases, 2,362 sexual assaults with an object, 18,801 forcible fondlings, 471 incest cases, 2,420 statutory rapes, 7,647 kidnappings, 122,380 aggravated assaults, and 45,010 robberies. The largest categories of sex crimes are forcible fondling (18,801) and forcible rape (14,446).[7] The smallest category is incest, with just 471 cases. The 0.95 rate of sex crimes per 1,000 people is almost as high as the rate of robberies (1.01); the rates for kidnapping and aggravated assault are 0.17 and 2.75, respectively.

Age and Gender of the Victim

Compared with other violent crimes, sex crimes reported to the police are more likely to be committed against children. Seventy-two percent (72%) of sex crime victims are under the age of 18, compared to 35% in kidnappings, 17% in aggravated assault, and 12% in robbery. The percentage of sex crime victims under age six is 12%, compared to 9% in kidnapping, 2% in aggravated assault, and 0% in robbery. The percentage of sex crime victims between the ages of 6 and 11 is 19%, compared to 10% in kidnapping, 2% in robbery victims, and 3% in aggravated assault. The percentage of sex crime victims between the ages of 12 and 17 is 40%, compared to 15% in kidnapping, 10% in robbery, and 12% in aggravated assault. However, in adulthood, sex crime victimization is less common than is victimization in other violent felonies. For instance, 13% of sex crime victims are between the ages of 19 and 24, compared to 24% in kidnapping, 27% in robbery, and 25% in aggravated assault. Moreover, 8% of sex crime victims are between the ages of 25 and 34, compared to 22% in kidnapping, 22% in robbery, and 26% in aggravated assault. Throughout the remaining lifespan, sex crimes continue to decrease relative to other violent felonies. Thus, 8% of sex crime victims are 34 and older, compared to 20% in kidnapping, 39% in robbery, and 32% in aggravated assault.

The majority of victims of sex crimes (86%) and kidnappings (71%) are female, whereas most victims of aggravated assaults (59%) and robberies

(67%) are male. Although females constitute the majority of sex crime victims over all, the majority of males who are sexually victimized are victimized under the age of 12, whereas the majority of females who are victimized are victimized from age 12 into adulthood. Thus, although only 14% of all sex crime victims are male, of all males who are sexually victimized, 27% are victimized while they are under the age of 5, compared to 10% of all females who are sexually victimized at that age. Of all males who are sexually victimized, another 35.5% are victimized between the ages of 6 to 11, compared to 16% of all females who are sexually victimized at that age. Forty-three percent of all females who are sexually victimized are victimized between the ages of 12 and 17, compared to 26% of all sexually victimized males who are victimized at that age. The trend for higher female sexual victimization continues from age 12 throughout adulthood.

Similarly to the sex crimes, males constitute a minority of kidnapping victims. Among all male kidnapping victims, 20% are victimized under the age of 5 compared to 8% of all females who are kidnapped at that age. In addition, among all males who are kidnapped, 20% are kidnapped between the ages of 6 and 11 compared to 9% of all females who are kidnapped in that age group. However, during puberty kidnapping victimization of females begins to exceed that of males. Of all females who are kidnapped, 17% are between the ages of 12 and 17, compared to 15% of all males who are kidnapped in that age group. Of all females who are kidnapped, 28% are between the ages of 18 and 25, compared to 17% of all males who are kidnapped. Thus, female kidnapping continues to exceed that of males throughout the remaining lifespan (and appears to be a form of domestic violence). No substantial differences exist between male and female victimization in aggravated assault and robbery.

Other Descriptive Characteristics of Victims and Incidents

Forcible sodomy (19%) is the sex crime most likely, and statutory rape (5%) the sex crime least likely, to involve multiple victims. Practically all statutory rape cases (99.9%) involve juvenile victims, whereas only slightly more than half of the forcible rape cases (52%) do. The sex crime with the largest percentage of juvenile offenders is forcible sodomy (41%), whereas only 15% of statutory rape cases involve juvenile offenders. Considering that both statutory rape and incest are classified by the FBI as non-forcible sex crimes, it is surprising that both these crimes have a high percentage of offenses involving the use of force or a weapon, with 74% for statutory rape and 69% for incest. Moreover, the highest percentage of victim injuries among the sex crimes is found in statutory rape (39%) and incest (33%) cases, whereas the lowest percentage of victim injury is found in the forcible fondling cases (10%).

Kidnappings are the most likely of the comparison crimes to involve juvenile victims (35%), compared to aggravated assaults (17%) and robberies (12%). The sex crimes that tend to be perpetrated by white offenders range from 68% of forcible rapes to 80% forcible fondlings; the majority of kidnapping (60%) and aggravated assaults (60%) are also perpetrated by white offenders, whereas only 27% of robberies are committed by white offenders.

Victim-Offender Relationships

Table 1 presents the victim-offender relationships in sexual crimes. Contrary to the assumptions of sex offender legislation, only 16% of juvenile victims are victimized by strangers. Almost half of sexual victimizations occur at the hands of acquaintances, a category of individuals who do not fit neatly into one of the other four categories: intimate, parents, other family, or strangers.

Table 1: Victim-Offender Relationships in Sex Crimes

Victim Age	Offenders					
	Parent	Intimate	Family	Acquaintance	Stranger	Total
All Victims	11.2	7.7	11.9	48.3	21.0	100.0
Juveniles	14.8	5.4	15.4	48.7	15.7	100.0
0 to 5	25.9	0.1	25.8	35.1	13.1	100.0
6 to 11	19.5	0.3	24.5	43.0	12.7	100.0
12 to 17	9.2	9.3	8.1	55.5	17.9	100.0
Adults	1.9	15.0	3.0	46.5	33.6	100.0
18 to 24	3.2	9.6	3.0	53.5	30.7	100.0
25 to 34	1.8	18.0	2.5	43.8	33.9	100.0
35+	0.8	17.1	3.8	41.9	36.4	100.0

Table 2 presents the victim-offender relationships in kidnapping cases. Two-thirds of kidnappings of juvenile victims are perpetrated by family members, intimates and acquaintances, with only a third perpetrated by strangers. In fact, the largest percentages of juvenile victims are kidnapped by their parents (37%).

Table 3 shows the victim-offender relationship and age of victims in aggravated assault cases. The table shows that the majority of assaulted juveniles are victimized by family members and acquaintances, with only one-quarter being assaulted by strangers. The younger the child is, the more likely she is to be assaulted by a parent, with almost half of children who are assaulted under the age of 6 being assaulted by their parents.

Table 4 shows the victim-offender relationship in robbery cases. The majority of juvenile robbery victims (77%) are victimized by strangers. Almost twice as many juvenile (22%) as adult (12%) robberies are perpetrated by acquaintances.

The Probability of Arrest

An arrest is made in 28% of the sex crimes, ranging from a low of 24% in forcible rape to a high of 37% in statutory rape cases. Fewer than half of the other violent crimes result in an arrest, with 21% of robberies, 39% of kidnappings, and 46% of assaults resulting in arrest. Tables 5 and 6

Table 2: Victim-Offender Relationships in Kidnapping

| | Offenders | | | | | |
Victim Age	Parent	Intimate	Family	Acquaintance	Stranger	Total
All Victims	13.0	29.0	3.3	19.5	35.1	100.0
Juveniles	36.7	4.3	4.8	20.4	33.8	100.0
0 to 5	64.6	0.3	7.9	11.9	15.3	100.0
6 to 11	46.1	0.2	4.8	13.6	35.3	100.0
12 to 17	13.5	9.5	2.7	30.0	44.3	100.0
Adults	0.6	42.3	2.6	19.3	35.3	100.0
18 to 24	1.1	41.1	1.7	22.0	34.1	100.0
25 to 34	0.5	47.5	1.4	17.0	33.6	100.0
35+	0.1	37.9	4.9	18.5	38.5	100.0

Table 3: Victim-Offender Relationships in Aggravated Assault Crimes

| | Offenders | | | | | |
Victim Age	Parent	Intimate	Family	Acquaintance	Stranger	Total
All Victims	3.4	20.9	7.7	37.8	30.1	100.0
Juveniles	14.9	2.6	8.4	48.6	25.4	100.0
0 to 5	47.6	0.1	7.9	22.4	22.0	100.0
6 to 11	20.8	0.1	9.8	49.5	19.8	100.0
12 to 17	9.2	3.6	8.1	51.8	27.4	100.0
Adults	1.0	25.2	7.7	36.1	29.9	100.0
18 to 24	1.9	20.1	4.6	39.7	33.7	100.0
25 to 34	0.9	23.3	5.5	34.4	31.0	100.0
35+	0.5	26.7	12.0	34.6	26.2	100.0

Table 4: Victim-Offender Relationships in Robbery Crimes

| | Offenders | | | | | |
Victim Age	Parent	Intimate	Family	Acquaintance	Stranger	Total
All Victims	0.0	1.2	0.4	12.9	85.4	100.0
Juveniles	0.1	0.5	0.2	22.1	77.2	100.0
0 to 5	0.0	0.0	0.0	10.8	89.2	100.0
6 to 11	0.2	0.0	0.5	20.7	78.6	100.0
12 to 17	0.1	0.6	0.2	22.5	76.7	100.0
Adults	0.0	1.3	0.5	11.9	86.4	100.0
18 to 24	0.0	1.4	0.4	13.6	84.6	100.0
25 to 34	0.0	1.9	0.3	11.1	86.7	100.0
35+	0.0	0.8	0.6	11.1	87.5	100.0

show the results of logistic regression analyses examining correlates associated with the probability of arrest. For purposes of the first analysis, crime types were dummy-coded with robbery as the reference category. For purposes of the second analysis, crime types were dummy-coded with sex crimes as the reference category. For both analyses, the victim-offender relationships were dummy-coded with stranger as the comparison group.

Table 5: Logistic Regression Predicting the Arrest of Sex and Comparison Offenders (using robbery as the reference category)

Offense	UC (S.E.)	Odds Ratio
Murder	1.14 (.25)	3.12***
Burglary	0.24 (.05)	1.23***
Assault	0.74 (.02)	2.10***
Kidnapping	0.46 (.04)	1.58***
Rape	0.42 (.05)	1.52***
Fondling	0.33 (.03)	1.34***
Sodomy	0.74 (.08)	2.10***
Object	0.08 (.06)	1.08
Incest	0.19 (.64)	1.21
Statutory	0.42 (.50)	1.52
Acquaintance	0.18 (.01)	1.20***
Child	−0.21 (.05)	0.82***
Intimate	0.53 (.06)	1.71***
Family	0.69 (.03)	1.99***
One victim	−0.45 (.01)	0.64***
Victim injury	0.29 (.01)	1.34***
Victim age	0.01 (.00)	1.01***
Victim male	−0.01 (.01)	1.02
Victim white	0.18 (.02)	1.20***
Weapon	0.18 (.02)	1.20***
One crime	−0.09 (.03)	0.92**
One offender	−0.06 (.01)	0.95***
Offender age	0.01 (.00)	1.00***
Offender male	0.01 (.02)	1.01
Offender white	0.27 (.02)	1.31***
Rape / intimate	−0.31 (.09)	0.74***
Rape / child	0.62 (.10)	1.85***
Rape / victim age	−0.02 (.00)	0.98***
Rape / burglary	0.67 (.15)	1.96***
Sodomy / family	−0.63 (.10)	0.53***
Sodomy / victim age	−0.02 (.00)	0.98***
Fond / victim male	−0.26 (.05)	0.77***
Fond / family	−0.51 (.06)	0.60***
Assault / intimate	0.24 (.07)	1.27***

(continued)

Table 5: *(continued)*

Offense	UC (S.E.)	Odds Ratio
Assault / child	0.71 (.06)	2.03***
Kidnap / intimate	0.66 (.08)	1.93***
Kidnap / child	−0.34 (.11)	0.71***
Nagelkerke (pseudo)	$R^2 = .12$	
Chi-square (df)	14729.77	
p-value	.0001	

UC = unstandardised coefficient; SE = standard error
* $p < .05$; ** $p < .01$; *** $p < .001$

Interactions were tested to determine whether the probability of arrest varied by type of crime, relationship, or victim age.

Main Effects: Offense Type and Victim-Offender Relationship

For the analysis with robbery as the reference category, sex crimes (except sexual assault with an object, incest, and statutory rape), kidnapping, and aggravated assault are more likely to result in arrest than are robberies. Acquaintances, intimates, and other family members are more likely than strangers to be arrested. Parents are significantly less likely than strangers to be arrested.

For the analysis with sex crimes as the reference category, robberies are more likely to result in arrest than are sex crimes. Other family members are significantly more likely to be arrested than are strangers. Parents are significantly less likely than strangers to be arrested.

Main Effects: Victim and Offender Characteristics

For the analysis with robbery as the reference category, victim and incident characteristics influence the probability of arrest. Victim injury, victim age (older), victim race (white), and multiple victims increase the probability of arrest. Offender characteristics also influence the probability of arrest. Offender age (older), offender race (white), the involvement of multiple offenders, and the commission of multiple offenses, all increase the probability of arrest.

Table 6: Logistic Regression Predicting the Arrest of Sex and Comparison Offenders

Offense	UC (S.E.)	Odds Ratio
Assault	0.13 (.09)	1.14
Kidnapping	−0.45 (.13)	1.58
Robbery	0.10 (14)	2.63***
Acquaintance	0.02 (.01)	1.02
Child	−0.25 (.04)	0.78***
Intimate	−0.77 (.05)	0.93
Family	0.10 (.04)	1.12**
Victim injury	0.20 (.02)	1.22***
Victim age	−0.01 (.00)	0.99***
Victim male	−0.05 (.02)	0.96
Victim white	0.03 (.03)	1.03
Weapon	0.21 (.02)	1.24***
One crime	−0.69 (.05)	0.50***
Offender age	0.04 (.00)	1.00***
Offender male	0.49 (.59)	1.63***
Offender white	0.24 (.02)	1.27***
Assault / intimate	0.55 (.05)	1.73***
Assault / child	0.54 (.05)	1.72***
Assault / victim white	0.18 (.03)	1.20***
Assault / offender male	−0.47 (.06)	0.63***
Assault / one crime	0.52 (.06)	1.69***
Assault / family	0.38 (.05)	1.46***
Assault / victim age	0.02 (.00)	1.02***
Assault / victim male	0.07 (.03)	1.07*
Assault / victim injury	0.07 (.03)	1.07*
Kidnap / intimate	0.63 (.09)	1.88***
Kidnap / victim age	0.02 (.00)	1.02***
Kidnap / weapon	0.54 (.08)	1.71***
Kidnap / offender age	−0.01 (.00)	0.99*
Robbery / intimate	0.52 (.06)	1.68***
Robbery / victim age	0.01 (.00)	1.01***
Robbery / weapon	−0.52 (.06)	0.59***
Robbery / offender male	−0.88 (.09)	0.41***

(continued)

Table 6: *(continued)*

Offense	UC (S.E.)	Odds Ratio
Robbery / one crime	0.44 (.08)	1.55***
Robbery / victim white	0.27 (.05)	1.30***
Robbery / one victim	−0.43 (.03)	0.65***

Nagelkerke (pseudo)	$R^2 = .10$	
Chi-square (df)	11688.65 (36)	
p – value	.0001	

UC = unstandardised coefficient; SE = standard error
*$p < .05$; **$p < .01$; ***$p < .001$

For the analysis with sex crimes as the reference category, victim and incident characteristics influence the probability of arrest. Victim injury, offender weapon, offender age, offender gender (male), offender race (white), and the offender's commission of multiple offenses, all increase the probability of arrest, whereas younger victims decrease the probability of arrest.

Interaction Effects

For the analysis with robbery as the reference category, over and above the main effects of the offense, victim, relationship, and offender variables, certain interactions influence the probability of arrest. Aggravated assault by parents and intimates, kidnappings by intimates, forcible rapes by parents, and forcible rapes occurring during a burglary, all increase the probability of arrest. Kidnapping by parents, forcible rapes by intimates, forcible rapes of younger victims, forcible sodomy of younger victims by family members, and forcible fondling of female victims by family members, all decrease the probability of arrest.

For the analysis with sex crimes as the reference category, over and above the main effects of the offense, victim, relationship, and offender variables, certain interactions influence the probability of arrest. Aggravated assaults by intimates, parents, other family members, against white victims, older victims, male victims, by offenders who commit one offense, and offenders who injure the victim, all increase the probability of arrest, whereas aggravated assaults by male offenders decrease the probability of arrest. Kidnappings by intimates, of older victims, by younger offenders, and by offenders using a weapon increase the probability of arrest. Robberies by intimates, of older victims, of multiple victims, by female offenders, by offenders who do not use a weapon, by white offenders, and by offenders who commit one offense, all increase the probability of arrest.

SUMMARY AND IMPLICATIONS OF FINDINGS

Prevention

Although policies targeting sex crimes and offenders have been in existence since the early 1980s, until the recent creation of the NIBRS, national statistics on sex crimes lacked essential specifics, such as the age of the victims and other characteristics of the offenses. The findings of these unique NIBRS data indicate that the rate of sex crimes, a predominantly non-stranger offense, is almost as high as the rate of robberies, a common stranger crime. Unlike robbery, kidnapping, and aggravated assault, in which only a fraction of offenses involve juvenile victims, almost three-quarters of sex crime victims are children under age 18. Moreover, unlike other violent felonies, almost 80% of all sex crimes are committed by family members and acquaintances.

SCP methods in the past have focused mostly on property crimes committed by strangers. The existence of a trusted relationship with the victim poses the greatest challenge to SCP methods in targeting child molestation and other sex crimes. Although prevention efforts aimed at parents may be the most difficult to devise and implement, parents constitute only 14.8% of perpetrators of sex crimes of juveniles. Family members constitute another 16% of perpetrators, and prevention efforts targeting them might prove similarly difficult. In contrast, acquaintances commit almost half (49%) of all sex crimes against juveniles, and these offenses may be more amenable to SCP methods because they occur outside of the largely private arena of the familial relationship. Unfortunately, the current data do not provide sufficient detail on the specific relationships within the category of acquaintances to guide specific prevention efforts. We can only assume that acquaintances are individuals outside the family who have varying relationships with the family and/or the child. At a minimum, the SCP strategy of increasing effort by controlling access suggests that limiting access to children by individuals outside the immediate family could prevent potential acquaintance offenders from molesting children. Limiting access does not necessarily entail barring all contact with acquaintances. Instead, the SCP strategy of increasing risks by extending guardianship suggests that increasing parental or family supervision of acquaintance contact with children, to ensure that children are not left alone with acquaintances, may prevent many acquaintance molestations. Focusing SCP efforts on the largest category of offenders, acquaintances, could conceivably prevent almost half of all child molestations.

Because children often come into contact with acquaintances outside the home in places like school, church, and day care, the SCP strategy of increasing efforts by controlling access to facilities could reduce or prevent child molestations. One way to control access to facilities like school, day care, and churches that serve children would be to screen people who work there or who work with children in the facilities. Both control theory and findings on the versatility of offenders suggest that individuals who have criminal records containing any type of crime would be more likely than individuals without such records to molest children. Control theory also suggests that people with low self-control are not only more likely to commit crimes, but may also engage in analogous, risky behaviors such as substance abuse, reckless driving (and resulting automobile accidents), and other behaviors that provide immediate pleasure at the expense of negative long-term costs. Therefore, screening prospective employees for drug and alcohol abuse and poor driving records could reduce the number of employees with low self-control, who are more likely than employees with higher self-control to molest children. And screening prospective employees on the above grounds may be justified by non-control theory interests. (Non-control theory interests refer to unique aspects of the NIBRS data that are not reflected in the theory, such as young boys being at higher risk of sexual victimization than young girls. Non-control theory interests also refer to SCP strategies not associated with low self-control.) To ensure the safety of children, one may not want to entrust the care of young children to individuals with a history of substance abuse or poor driving records.

The data indicate that although males constitute only 14% of sex crime victims, among all males who are sexually victimized, the majority are sexually victimized under the age of 12. This may be compared to females, whose risk of sexual victimization begins to exceed that of males at older ages, beginning at age 12 and continuing throughout the lifespan. The data do not explain why males under the age of 12 and females after the age of 11 are at higher risk for sexual victimization. However, sexual victimization of young boys and teenage girls is inconsistent with responsible parental supervision. In routine activity theory (Cohen and Felson, 1979), the absence of a capable guardian is one of the necessary conditions for crime. SCP methods aimed at increasing risks through extending guardianship suggest that increasing responsible adult supervision of males under 12 years and females after the age of 11 may reduce victimization in these age groups (unless the parents are the perpetrators). In addition, parents may not understand the risks of permitting their children to have unsupervised contact with acquaintances because the media often focus on the danger of stranger molestation. At the same time, sensational media coverage of acquaintance molestation obscures the risk to children from family members. For example, as the media covered the recent child molestation trial of entertainer Michael Jackson in an almost circus-like atmosphere, no media attention was given to the hundreds of children in the child welfare system in Santa Barbara, California who are molested by family members and non-celebrity acquaintances. The SCP strategy of increasing effort by target hardening could make use of the media in high-profile cases, like the one involving Michael Jackson, to highlight statistics about the risk of child molestation by family members and acquaintances. This form of target hardening would focus on parents and family members who may be unaware that their own children are at less risk for child molestation from strangers than from the people they know and trust.

Only 16% of juvenile sex crime victims, 34% of juvenile kidnapping victims, and 25% of juvenile aggravated assault victims are victimized by strangers, compared to 77% of juvenile robbery victims. Consequently, robbery is the only crime against juveniles where the majority of perpetrators are strangers. A large percentage of sex crimes, kidnappings, and aggravated assaults against juveniles are perpetrated by parents and other family members. For example, 42% of the kidnappings, 30% of the sex crimes, and 23% of the aggravated assaults of juveniles are committed by parents and other family members. The SCP strategy of reducing permissibility may be relevant to all three non-robbery crimes. In non-robbery crimes against children, parents and family members may share rationalizations or cognitive distortions about their offenses. For example, child molesters frequently rationalize their behavior by blaming the victim as the one who seduced the offender, or by insisting that they (the molesters) were educating the victim about sex. Kidnappings of children are often instigated by the non-custodial parent, who probably engages in cognitive distortions about the unfairness of the legal custody proceedings that awarded custody to the custodial parent. Aggravated assaults of children by parents and family members also may involve cognitive distortions about the victim provoking the violence by conduct such as soiling her pants and crying. Using public education and media campaigns to challenge and correct the distorted thinking in these three crimes could make use of the SCP strategy of removing permissibility and clarifying the offender's role in his/her behavior as well as preventing potential offenders from neutralizing thoughts of violence towards their children.

Sex crimes are less likely to result in arrest than other violent crimes, except for robbery. The two types of sex crimes that are most likely to result in arrest are forcible rape of a child by a parent and forcible rape during a burglary. Other sex crimes, such as those against younger children by family members, are unlikely to result in arrest. The data do not explain why the forcible rape of a child by a parent increases the probability of arrest. SCP strategies could target situations involving younger children and family members, which often do not result in arrest, by using the strategy of increasing effort and target hardening in order to educate parents about the risks of molestation of their children by other family members. Also, the SCP strategy of increasing effort by controlling access to young children could involve parental supervision of contact between family members and young children. Supervising contact between children and family members with a criminal record also can control access. Thus, responsible parental supervision can serve as both a means to control access and extend guardianship of children.

Because 12% of sex crime victims are under the age of 6, and because these victims include neonates, infants, toddlers, and very young children, prevention and arrest in these cases may be more problematic. Moreover, the data do not indicate how cases involving such young victims come to the attention of police. Information on how these cases come to the attention of police is important for SCP strategies aimed at such cases.

Legislation

The findings that sex crimes may be as numerous as robberies, and that the majority of sex crime victims are children, suggest a need for special sex crime policies. However, current policies like sex offender registration and community notification aim to protect children from stranger child molesters, which constitute the minority of cases. The legislation does not protect the majority of children from family members and acquaintances. With the data indicating that only 16% of juveniles are molested by strangers, targeting stranger molestation through legislation is misdirected and unwittingly places children in greater danger by lulling parents into a false sense of security (Palermo and Farkas, 2001; Simon, 1997; John Jay Study, 2004). The purpose of new legislation would be to protect children from sex crimes at the hands of family members and acquaintances.

After two decades of legislation targeting the arrest and prosecution of sex offenders, it is disturbing that the arrest rates for all sex crimes are lower than for other violent crimes except for robbery, which is predominantly a stranger crime. Moreover, the only non-stranger relationship that is most likely to result in arrest for a sex crime is a parent who commits a forcible rape. Other sex crimes committed by family members have a decreased probability of arrest. New legislation might consider creating mandatory arrest policies, similar to the ones developed in domestic violence cases, in cases where a family member or acquaintance is suspected. Domestic violence mandatory arrest legislation and law enforcement policies were developed to resolve the problem of police reluctance to arrest an offender simply because the situation involved domestic matters (e.g., Hirschel and Hutchinson, 2003). A similar reluctance to arrest family members in sex crimes could be addressed by the implementation of such policies.

Investigation

Several of the findings have implications for investigation of sex crimes. For those 12% of victims who are under the age of six, investigation practices and legal rules may need to be modified where a family member or acquaintance was the sole caretaker at the time of the offense and the child is too young to testify or the child is unable to talk when infants and toddlers are the victims.

The finding of the greater risk of sexual victimization for young boys than for young girls under the age of 12 suggests that increased intensity of investigations of sex offenses against boys should be undertaken by law enforcement in cases of molestation by acquaintances. Most available statistics suggest that boys are rarely molested compared to girls. The statistics on male victimization may reflect greater denial on the part of parents and law enforcement in cases where the perpetrator is male because of the stigma of sexual relations between males.

The offense versatility found in sex offenders should alert law enforcement to the fact that sex offenders are not specialists in sex crimes. Consequently, in investigating new sex crimes, the common practice of rounding up all the usual suspects (i.e., convicted, registered sex offenders) should be abandoned in favor of widening the net to all criminal offenders. The finding that almost 80% of all sex offenders are family members and acquaintances should guide law enforcement to apply the same zeal in investigating sex crimes by known offenders as they do to stranger offenders. Such zeal could also be applied to the decision to arrest sex offenders where a family member or acquaintance is suspected.

CONCLUSIONS

This chapter compares sex crimes with other violent felonies. Findings indicate that, compared to other violent felonies, almost three-quarters of sex crime victims are children. In addition, compared to other violent felonies, the majority of sex crime victims are children molested by family members and acquaintances, not strangers. Moreover, after decades of policies targeting sex offenders, sex crimes have a decreased probability of arrest compared to other violent felonies.

The finding that sex crimes are almost as numerous as robberies, the prototypical stranger violent crime, suggests a need to replace current sex offender policies that target stranger molesters. Instead, new sex offender policies are needed to address the fact that the majority of molesters are family members and acquaintances.

Moreover, current sex offender policies are designed to prevent child molestation by focusing on some aspect of the offender, such as compelling him to register as a sex offender or treating him with therapy. Because sex offenders have a generalized problem with self-control rather than a specific deviance or mental disorder, offense-focused prevention strategies may be more effective in preventing child molestation.

Based on the findings, this chapter makes suggestions for how SCP methods can be applied in the largest category of child molestations, those committed by acquaintances. SCP methods in the past have been applied mainly to instrumental crimes by strangers. Application of prevention efforts to interpersonal crimes by non-strangers could prevent the majority of non-robbery violent crimes, particularly child molestation and other sex crimes, where the majority of the offenders are known to the victims.

The established research on the versatility of offending has not reached most police departments that still round up the usual suspects – convicted, registered sex criminals – after a new sex crime occurs. Broadening the suspect pool to all convicted offenders is more likely to contain the sought-out offender than are suspect pools containing only registered sex offenders. This and other suggestions for investigation of sex crimes are made.

Sex offender legislation, prevention, and investigation policies and procedures are most effective when based on the empirical realities of sex crimes instead of media myths based on stranger danger. Because most sex crimes are not committed by random strangers, they are more easily prevented by an informed public and more easily solved by police officers. Unfortunately, the vast majority of people in society are not informed or educated on situational prevention methods that could prevent many crimes in general, and sex crimes in particular, that are committed by family members and acquaintances. In addition, most police officers in this country are not educated about sex crimes, which are often referred to specialized sex crimes units.

Just over one-quarter of sex crimes are perpetrated against adults. Police data are particularly susceptible to underestimates of sex crimes, particularly sex crimes against adults. For example, a police officer/student recently bragged in class that the majority of rapes never happen, and that out of 20 rape accusations his department received, only one had been confirmed. Most police officers are not trained to accept the fact that most rapes, like child molestations, involve offenders who are known to the victim, and police often become immediately suspicious of the victim who reports such a rape. The same problem may result in child molestation cases involving offenders known to the victim – the hesitancy of police to arrest sex crime offenders compared to other violent felonies may be due to the likely existence of a relationship between the victim and the offender in sex crimes cases. If true, the poor treatment of sex crime cases in the legal system may be the strongest argument for utilizing situational crime prevention methods to prevent sex crimes altogether.

Future research is needed to examine the effectiveness of situational crime prevention efforts in reducing sex crimes. As the data indicate, the facts that sex crimes are as numerous as robberies and that the victims are mostly children suggest that preventing sex crimes should be a criminal justice policy priority. Given the failure of offender-focused efforts that include registration, incarceration, and treatment, policymakers might consider a national focus on situational prevention strategies that are designed to prevent crimes (and victimization) from occurring in the first place.

Address correspondence to: Prof. Leonore Simon, Department of Criminal Justice and Criminology, Box 70555, 201 Rogers-Stout Hall, East Tennessee State University, Johnson City, TN 37614; e-mail: simonlmj@gmail.com.

NOTES

1. The rediscovery of child sexual abuse in the 1980s can be traced back to the 1962 publication on the Battered Child Syndrome by Dr. Henry Kempe (Kempe, 1962) and subsequent national legislation in the 1970s that created financial incentives for states to create child protection agencies, enact mandatory reporting statutes, investigate child abuse, and create record-keeping systems (Mangold, 2003). Since 1980, child protection agencies, working with law enforcement and prosecutors, have treated sexual abuse cases with the zeal of a "moral panic" (Jenkins, 1998). Although current national statistics give us a general idea of the numbers of sexual offenders in the criminal justice system today, comparable statistics for sexual offenders in the 1970s are hard to come by for many reasons. First, the term sexual assault came into being in the 1970s as a result of the rape law reform movement, suggesting that the greatest number of sexual offenses in the 1970s probably consisted of forcible rapes of adult women. Second, in the 1970s national criminal justice statistics on sex crimes against children were either completely unavailable or they lacked key details about the offenders and offenses.

2. The current national data are not broken down by age of the victim.

3. Megan's Law is named after seven-year-old Megan Kanka, a New Jersey girl who was raped and killed by a known child molester who had moved across the street from the family without their knowledge. The law provides the public with certain information on the whereabouts of sex offenders so that members of local communities may protect themselves and their children. Megan's Law statutes are often referred to as community notification statutes because they require police to notify community members of a dangerous sex offender residing in or moving into the community.

4. Note that, for a clinical diagnosis of paraphilia or pedophilia, an individual does not need to engage in sexual activity with a child (or other inappropriate individual or nonhuman object, for paraphilia). To be diagnosed with pedophilia, for example, an individual needs to have fantasized about sexual activity with a prepubescent child for at least six months, so long as the fantasies or sexual urges cause clinically significant distress or impairment in social, occupational, or other important areas of functioning (Simon, 2000). Consequently, a major component of some sex offender treatment programs is eliminating the deviant sexual fantasies or preference alone, although recidivism is best predicted from prior criminal history and not sexual preference for children (Simon, 2000).

5. The law enforcement agency's data are certified once they have met the FBI's strict reporting standards.

6. A crime incident is defined as one or more offenses committed by the same offender or group of offenders acting in concert at the same time and place. An incident may or may not result in an arrest. NIBRS reports on 22 categories of crime types, such as arson, weapon law violations, gambling offenses and so on. One crime incident can contain multiple crimes, and therefore multiple categories of crimes per incident. For example, a person who kills someone at a bar could also be committing some type of weapons violation as well as other crimes in addition to murder as part of the same incident.

7. The FBI definitions and instructions on coding are included in the Appendix. The reader might want to examine the definitions and coding instructions for forcible rape and statutory rape because the instructions are confusing when it comes to coding the offenses that involve young victims. The contradictory and confusing instructions provided by the FBI may explain why the two non-forcible crimes, incest and statutory rape, appear more violent than the so-called forcible sexual crimes.

REFERENCES

American Psychiatric Association. (1999). *Dangerous Sexual Offenders: A Task Force Report of the American Psychiatric Association*. Washington, DC: American Psychiatric Association.

Australian Institute of Criminology (June 17, 2003). *Understanding Situational Crime Prevention*. (AIC Crime Reduction Matters #3; http://aic.gov.au/publications/crm/crm003.pdf.) Canberra, AUS: Author. (ISSN 1448-1383.)

Beck, A. and C. Mumola (1999). *Prisoners in 1998*. Washington, DC: Bureau of Justice Statistics.

Brantingham, P.J. and P.L. Brantingham (1984). *Patterns in Crime*. New York: Macmillan.

Brantingham, P.L. and P.J. Brantingham (1981). *Environmental Criminology*. Beverly Hills, CA: Sage Publications.

Britt, C.L. (1994). "Versatility." In: T. Hirschi and M.R. Gottfredson (eds.), *The Generality of Deviance* (pp. 173–192). New Brunswick, NJ: Transaction Press.

Clarke, R.V. (1997). *Situational Crime Prevention: Successful Case Studies, vol.2*. New York: Harrow and Heston.

Clarke, R. (1995). "Situational Crime Prevention." In: M. Tonry and D. Farrington (eds.), *Building a Safer Society: Strategic Approaches to Crime Prevention*. Chicago: The University of Chicago Press.

Clarke, R.V. and J. Eck (2003). *Become a Problem-Solving Crime Analyst*. London: Jill Dando Institute of Crime Science, University College London.

Clarke, R.V. and P. Mayhew (1980). *Designing Out Crime*. London: HMSO.

Cohen, L. and M. Felson (1979). "Social Change and Crime Rate Trends: A Routine Activity Approach." *American Sociological Review* 44:588–608.

Cornish, D.B. and R.V. Clarke (1986). *The Reasoning Criminal: Rational Choice Perspectives on Offending*. New York: Springer-Verlag.

Cornwell, J., J. Jacobi and P. Witt (1999). "The New Jersey Sexually Violent Predator Act: Analysis and Recommendations for the Treatment of Sexual Offenders in New Jersey." *Seton Hall Legislative Journal* 24:1–42.

Durose, M. and P. Langan (2003). *Felony Sentences in State Courts*. Washington, DC: Bureau of Justice Statistics.

Freeman, R. and G. Blanchard (1998). *Sexual Abuse in America: Epidemic of the 21st Century*. Brandon, VT: Safer Society Press.

Freeman-Longo, R.E. and L. Berliner (1996). "Public Notification and Sexual Offender Release." *Sexual Abuse: A Journal of Research and Treatment*, 8(2):89–104.

Freeman-Longo, R., S. Bird, W.F. Stevenson and J.A. Fiske (1995). *1994 Nationwide Survey of Treatment Programs & Models: Serving Abuse Reactive Children and Adolescent & Adult Sexual Offenders*. Brandon, VT: Safer Society Press.

Gill, M. (2000). *Commercial Robbery: Offenders' Perspectives on Security and Crime Prevention*. London: Blackstone Press.

Gottfredson, M. and T. Hirschi (1990). *A General Theory of Crime*. Stanford: Stanford University Press.

Greenfeld, L. (1997). *Sex Offenses and Offenders: An Analysis of Data on Rape and Sexual Assault.* (U.S. Department of Justice Special Report – NCJ 163392.) Washington, DC: US Department of Justice, Bureau of Justice Statistics.

Hanson, R.K. (2003). "Who is Dangerous and when are they Safe? Assessment with Sexual Offenders." In: B.J. Winick and J.Q. LaFond (eds.), *Protecting Society from Sexually Dangerous Offenders: Law, Justice, and Therapy.* Washington, DC: American Psychological Association, Law and Public Policy Series.

Hanson, K. and M. Bussiere (1998). "Predicting Relapse: A Meta-Analysis of Sexual Offender Recidivism Studies." *Journal of Consulting and Clinical Psychology,* 66(2):348–362.

Hanson, K., A. Gordon and A. Harris (2002). "First Report on a Collaborative Outcome Data Project on the Effectiveness of Psychological Treatment for Sexual Offenders." *Sexual Abuse: A Journal of Research and Treatment* 14(2):169–194.

Harrison, P.M. and A.J. Beck (2003). *Prisoners in 2002.* Washington, DC: Bureau of Justice Statistics.

Hart, T.C. (2003). *Reporting Crime to the Police, 1992–2000.* Washington, DC: U.S. Bureau of Justice Statistics.

Henry, F. and K. Kaufman (1999). "The Prevention of Sexual Abuse." *Sexual Abuse: A Journal of Research and Treatment* 11(4):255–325.

Hindelang, M.J. (1971). "Age, Sex, and the Versatility of Delinquent Involvements." *Social Problems* 18:522–535.

Hindelang, M.J., T. Hirschi and J.G. Weis (1981). *Measuring Delinquency.* Beverly Hills, CA: Sage.

Hirschel, D. and I. Hutchinson (2003). "The Voices of Domestic Violence Victims: Predictors of Victim Reference for Arrest and the Relationship between Preference for Arrest and Revictimization." *Crime and Delinquency* 49:313–336.

Hirschi, T. (1969). *Causes of Delinquency.* Berkeley, CA: University of California Press.

Jenkins, P. (1998). *Moral Panic: Changing Concepts of the Child Molester in Modern America.* New Haven, CT: Yale University Press.

John Jay College of Criminal Justice (2004). *The Nature and Scope of Sexual Abuse of Minors by Catholic Priests and Deacons in the United States, 1950–2002.* Washington, DC: United States Conference of Catholic Bishops.

Jones, L. and D. Finkelhor (2001). *The Decline in Child Sexual Abuse Cases.* Washington, DC: Office of Juvenile Justice and Delinquency.

Kempe, C.H., F.N. Silverman, B.F. Steele, W. Droegmuller and H.K. Silver (1962). "The Battered Child Syndrome." *Journal of the American Medical Association* 181:17–24.

Klein, M. (1995). *The American Street Gang.* New York: Oxford University Press.

Klein, M.W. (1984). "Offense Specialization and Versatility among Juveniles." *British Journal of Criminology* 24:185–1994.

Kruttschnitt, C., C. Uggen and K. Shelton (2000). "Predictors of Desistance among Sex Offenders." *Justice Quarterly* 17:61–88.

Langan, P. and D. Levin (2002). *Recidivism of Prisoners Released in 1994 (NCJ 193427)*. Washington, DC: United States Department of Justice, Bureau of Justice Statistics.

Laws, R. (2000). "Sexual Offending as a Public Health Problem: A North American Perspective." *Journal of Sexual Aggression* 5(1):30–44.

Marshall, W. (1996). "The Sexual Offender: Monster, Victim, or Everyman?" *Sexual Abuse: A Journal of Research and Treatment* 8(4):317–335.

Palermo, G.B. and M.A. Farkas (2001). *The Dilemma of the Sexual Offender.* Springfield, IL: Charles C. Thomas Publishing, Ltd.

Peterson, M. and H.B. Braiker (1981). *Who Commits Crime: A Survey of Prison Inmates.* Cambridge, MA: Oelgessschlager, Gunn, and Hain.

Prentky, R.A., R.A. Knight and A.F. Lee (1997). *Child Sexual Molestation: Research Issues.* Washington, DC: National Institute of Justice.

Prentky, R., A. Lee, R. Knight and D. Cerco (1997). "Recidivism Rates of Child Molesters and Rapists: A Methodological Analysis." *Law and Human Behavior* 21:635–659.

Presser, L. and E. Gunnison (1999). "Strange Bedfellows: Is Sex Offender Notification a Form of Community Justice?" *Crime & Delinquency* 45:299–315.

Rantala, R. and T.J. Edwards (2000). *Effects of NIBRS on Crime Statistics.* Washington, DC: U.S. Bureau of Justice Statistics.

Rennison, C. (2003). *Criminal Victimization, 2002.* Washington, DC: U.S. Bureau of Justice Statistics.

Rennison, C. (2002). *Criminal Victimization 2001: Changes 2000–01 with Trends 1993–2001.* (U.S. Department of Justice Special Report – NCJ 194610). Washington, DC: U.S Department of Justice, Bureau of Justice Statistics.

Rice, M.E. and G.T. Harris (2003). "What We Know and Don't Know about Treating Adult Sex Offenders." In: B.J. Winick and J.Q. LaFond (eds.), *Protecting Society from Sexually Dangerous Offenders: Law, Justice, and Therapy.* Washington, DC: American Psychological Association Law and Public Policy Series.

Scott, S. (2001). *The Politics and Experience of Ritual Abuse: Beyond Belief.* Buckingham, UK: Open University Press.

Simon, L.M. (2003). "Matching Legal Policies with Known Offenders." In: B.J. Winick and J.Q. LaFond (eds.), *Protecting Society from Sexually Dangerous Offenders: Law, Justice, and Therapy.* Washington, DC: American Psychological Association Law and Public Policy Series.

Simon, L.M (2000). "An Examination of the Assumptions of Specialization, Mental Disorder, and Dangerousness of Sex Offenders." *Behavioral Sciences and the Law* 18:275–308.

Simon, L.M. (1999). "Sex Offender Legislation and the Antitherapeutic Effects on Victims." *Arizona Law Review Symposium on Therapeutic Jurisprudence* 41:485–533.

Simon, L.M. (1998). "Does Criminal Offender Treatment Work?" *Applied and Preventive Psychology* 7:137–159.

Simon, L.M. (1997). "Do Criminal Offenders Specialize in Crime Types?" *Applied and Preventive Psychology* 6:35–53.

Simon, L.M. (1996). "The Legal Processing of Domestic Violence Cases." In: D. Shuman and B. Sales (eds.), *Law, Mental Health, and Mental Disorder*. Pacific Grove, CA: Brooks/Cole.

Simon, L.M. (1995). "A Therapeutic Jurisprudence Approach to Domestic Violence Cases." *Psychology, Public Policy, and Law* 1:43–79.

Simon, L.M. (1994). "The Victim-Offender Relationship." In: T. Hirschi and M. Gottfredson (eds.), *The Generality of Deviance*. New Brunswick, NJ: Transaction Press.

Simon, L.M. and J.A. Black (2004). "Assessment of Sex Offender Policies Using Police Data: A Therapeutic Jurisprudence Analysis." Paper presented at the annual meeting of the Western Society of Criminology, Long Beach, CA.

Simon, L.M, B.D. Sales, A. Kaszniak and K. Marvin (1992). "Characteristics of Child Molesters: Implications for the Fixated-Regressed Dichotomy." *Journal of Interpersonal Violence* 7:211–225.

Smallbone, S. and R.Wortley (2004a). "Onset, Persistence and Versatility of Offending among Adult Males Convicted of Sexual Offenses against Children." *Sexual Abuse: A Journal of Research and Treatment* 16:285–298.

Smallbone, S. and R. Wortley (2004b). "Criminal Diversity and Paraphilic Interests among Adult Males Convicted of Sexual Offenses against Children." *International Journal of Offender Therapy and Comparative Criminology* 48:175–188.

Smallbone, S., J. Wheaton and D. Hourigan (2003). "Trait Empathy and Criminal Versatility in Sexual Offenders." *Sexual Abuse: A Journal of Research and Treatment* 15(1):49–60.

Snyder, H. (2002). *Sexual Assault of Young Children as Reported to Law Enforcement: Victim, Incident, and Offender Characteristics*. Washington, DC: Bureau of Justice Statistics.

U.S. Bureau of Justice Statistics (1997b). *Implementing the National Incident-Based Reporting System: A Project Status Report*. Washington, DC: U.S. Department of Justice. (Publication NCJ-165581.)

U.S. Federal Bureau of Investigation (2002). "NIBRS Status Report 2002." (The first author has a copy of this report in her files and will send it to anyone interested. A more recent version of the report may be found at: http://www.jrsa.org/ibrrc/background-status/nibrs_states.shtml.)

Van Dam, C. (2001). *Identifying Child Molesters: Preventing Child Sexual Abuse by Recognizing the Patterns of the Offenders*. New York: Haworth Press.

West, M., C. Hromans and P. Wenger (2000). "Survey of State Sex Offender Treatment Programs." Denver: Colorado Department of Corrections. (August, 2000; 435 p.)

Winick, B.J. (2003). "A Therapeutic Jurisprudence Analysis of Sex Offender Registration and Community Notification Laws." In: B.J. Winick and J.Q. LaFond (eds.), *Protecting Society from Sexually Dangerous Offenders: Law, Justice, and Ther-*

apy. Washington, DC: American Psychological Association, Law and Public Policy Series.

Wolfgang, M.E., R.M. Figlio and T. Sellin (1972). *Delinquency in a Birth Cohort.* Chicago, IL: University of Chicago Press.

Wortley, R. (2002). *Situational Prison Control: Crime Prevention in Correctional Institutions.* Cambridge, UK: Cambridge University Press.

Wortley, R. (2001). "A Classification of Techniques for Controlling Situational Precipitators of Crime." *Security Journal* 14:63–82.

Zgoba, K. (2004). *Variations in the Recidivism of Treated and Non-treated Sexual Offenders in New Jersey: An Examination of Three Time Frames.* Ph.D dissertation, Rutgers University.

Zgoba, K., W. Sager and P. Witt (2003). "Evaluation of New Jersey's Sexual Offender Treatment Program at the Adult Diagnostic Treatment Center: Preliminary Results." *The Journal of Psychiatry and Law* 31:133–165.

Zgoba, K. and L.M. Simon (2006, in press). "Recidivism Rates of Sex Offenders Up to Seven Years Later: Does Treatment Matter?" Forthcoming in *Criminal Justice Review.*

APPENDIX

FBI Definitions and Instructions

Forcible Rape

Definition – The carnal knowledge of a person, forcibly and/or against that person's will; or not forcibly or against the person's will where the victim in incapable or giving consent because of his/her temporary or permanent mental or physical incapacity (or because of his/her youth).

This offense includes the forcible rape of both males and females. In cases where several offenders rape one person, report one Forcible Rape. Do not count the number of offenders. If force was used or threatened, the crime should be classified as Forcible Rape regardless of the age of the victim. If no force or threat of force was used and the victim was under the statutory age of consent, the crime should be classified as Statutory Rape. The ability of the victim to give consent must be a professional determination by the law enforcement agency. The age of the victim, of course, plays a critical role in this determination. Individuals do not mature mentally at the same rate. Certainly, no 4-year-old is capable of consenting, whereas victims aged 10 or 12 may need to be assessed within the specific circumstances.

Forcible Fondling

Definition – The touching of the private body parts of another person for the purpose of sexual gratification, forcibly and/or against that person's will; or, not forcibly or against the person's will where the victim is incapable of giving consent because of his/her youth or because of his/her temporary or permanent mental incapacity. Forcible fondling includes "indecent liberties" and "child molesting." Because Forcible Fondling is an element of Forcible Rape, Forcible Sodomy, and Sexual Assault With An Object, it should be reported only if it is the sole forcible sex offense committed against a victim.

Forcible Sodomy

Definition – Oral or anal sexual intercourse with another person, forcibly and/or against that person's will; or not forcibly or against the person's will where the victim is incapable of giving consent because of his/her youth or because of his/her temporary or permanent mental or physical incapacity. If a victim is both raped and sodomized in one incident, then both offenses should be reported.

Sexual Assault with an Object

Definition – To use an object or instrument to unlawfully penetrate, however slightly, the genital or anal opening of the body of another person, forcibly and/or against that person's will; or not forcibly or against the person's will where the victim is incapable of giving consent because of his/her youth or because of his/her temporary or permanent mental or physical incapacity. An "object" or "instrument" is anything used by the offender other than the offender's genitalia. Examples are a finger, bottle, handgun, stick, etc.

Definitions of Non-Forcible Sex Crimes

Statutory Rape

Definition – Nonforcible sexual intercourse with a person who is under the statutory age of consent.

If force was used or threatened or the victim was incapable of giving consent because of his/her youth or mental impairment, either temporary or permanent, the offense should be classified as Forcible Rape, not Statutory Rape.

Incest

Definition – Nonforcible sexual intercourse between persons who are related to each other within the degrees wherein marriage is prohibited by law.

Kidnapping

Definition – The unlawful seizure, transportation, and/or detention of a person against his/her will, or of a minor without the consent of his/her custodian parent(s) or legal guardian. This offense includes not only kidnapping and abduction, but hostage situations as well. Although the object of a kidnapping may be to obtain money or property, this category is intended to capture information only on the persons actually kidnapped or abducted, not those persons or organizations paying ransoms. Therefore, for each kidnapping incident, report as victims only those persons taken or detained against their will.

Robbery

Definition – The taking, or attempting to take, anything of value under confrontational circumstances from the control, custody, or care of another person by force or threat of force or violence and/or by putting the victim in fear of immediate harm. Robbery involves the offender taking or attempting to take something of value from a victim, aggravated by the element of force or threat of force. The victim, who usually is the owner or person having custody of the property, is directly confronted by the perpetrator and is threatened with force or is put in fear that force will be used. If there is no direct confrontation and the victim is not in fear of immediate harm, an extortion should be reported. In pocket-pickings or purse-snatchings, direct confrontation does occur, but force or threat of force is absent. However, if during a purse-snatching or other such crime, force or threat of force is used to overcome the active resistance of the victim, the offense is to be classified as robbery. Cases involving pretended weapons or where the weapon is not seen by the victim but the robber claims to possess one are also classified by Robbery and the alleged weapon reported. If an immediate "on-view" arrest proves that there was no weapon, the offense is classified as Robbery, but the weapon is reported as "None." In any instance of robbery, report one offense for each distinct operation. As in the case of other crimes against property, only one offense is reported regardless of the number of victims involved. The victims of a robbery include not only those persons and other entities (businesses, financial institutions, etc.) from whom property was taken, but also those persons toward whom the robber(s) directed force or threat of force in perpetrating the offense. Therefore, although the primary victim in a bank robbery would be the bank, the teller toward whom the robber pointed a gun and made a demand should also be reported as a victim, as well as any other person upon whom an assault was committed during the course of the robbery.

Aggravated Assault

Definition – An unlawful attack by one person upon another wherein the offender uses a weapon or displays it in a threatening manner, or the victim suffers obvious severe or aggravated bodily injury involving apparent broken bones, loss of teeth, possible internal injury, severe laceration, or loss of consciousness. For purposes of Aggravated Assault reporting, a "weapon" is a commonly known weapon (a gun, knife, club, etc.) or any other item which, although not usually thought of as a weapon, becomes one when used in a manner that could cause the types of severe bodily injury described in the above definition. A "severe laceration" is one which should receive medical attention. A "loss of consciousness" must be the direct result of force inflicted on the victim by the offender. Aggravated Assault includes: assaults or attempts to kill or murder; poisoning; assault with a dangerous or deadly weapon; maiming, mayhem, assault with explosives; and assault with disease (as in cases when the offender is aware that he/she is infected with a deadly disease by biting, spitting, etc.) All assaults by one person upon another with the intent to kill, maim, or inflict severe bodily injury with the use of any dangerous weapon are classified as Aggravated Assault. It is not necessary that injury result from an aggravated assault when a gun, knife, or other weapon is used which could cause serious personal injury. By definition, there can be no attempted assaults. On occasion, it is the practice to charge assailants in assault cases with assault and battery or simple assault even though a knife, gun, or other weapon was used in the incident. For UCR purposes, this type of assault is to be classified as aggravated.

An Empirically Based Situational Prevention Model for Child Sexual Abuse

by

Keith L. Kaufman

Heather Mosher

Megan Carter

and

Laura Estes
Department of Psychology, Portland State University

Abstract: *Situational crime prevention focuses on the reduction of opportunities to engage in criminal behavior, and has been successfully applied to prevent general crimes (Clarke, 1995). While this model seems to offer promise, an attempt has not yet been undertaken to apply the model to preventing child sexual abuse. The purpose of this chapter is to outline the development of a situational prevention model to enhance our understanding of child sexual abuse risks and potential prevention approaches. The chapter begins with a discussion of the historical context underlying the child sexual abuse prevention movement, and then summarizes the empirical literature on sexual offenders'* modus operandi *(i.e., patterns of perpetration) as a foundation for model development. Details are provided to describe the proposed model and its components. Prevention strategies are presented*

Crime Prevention Studies, volume 19 (2006), pp. 101–144.

to address the various risks related to model components, and directions for future research and programming are discussed.

CHILD SEXUAL ABUSE PREVENTION: BACKGROUND AND HISTORICAL CONTEXT

Child sexual abuse (CSA) has been defined as sexual contact with a child or adolescent that occurs due to coercion, force or within the context of a relationship that is exploitative as a result of caregiving responsibility or an age difference (Centers for Disease Control and Prevention [CDC], 1985; Finkelhor, 1992), or as "maltreatment that involves the child in sexual activity to provide sexual gratification or financial benefit to the perpetrator" (*Child Maltreatment Report*, 2001). A broad range of sexual acts may constitute abuse, from non-contact offenses (e.g., voyeurism) to acts of varying physical intrusiveness (e.g., fondling, intercourse; Walker et al., 1988). CSA is considered a national public health concern with serious consequences for victims, offenders, and the larger community (Mercy, 1999). Despite some evidence that rates have been on the decline in the U.S. (Jones and Finkelhor, 2004), the number of children, teens, and their families impacted by CSA remains a significant national concern. According to the *Child Maltreatment* (2002) report, which summarized statistics from the National Child Abuse and Neglect Data System, 896,000 children were confirmed victims of child abuse/neglect, with 10% of them experiencing child sexual abuse. While not all victims exhibit severe or long-term consequences of their abuse (National Clearinghouse on Child Abuse and Neglect Information, 2004; Rind and Tromovich, 1997), evidence suggests that many victims and their families are adversely affected over a sustained period of time (Browne and Finkelhor, 1986; Budin and Johnson, 1989; National Clearinghouse on Child Abuse and Neglect Information, 2004). For many victims, the effects of sexual abuse can be numerous and often severe, and the effects frequently continue into adulthood (Cohen and Roth, 1987; Collings, 1995; Finkelhor et al., 1989; Hunter, 1990a, 1990b; Roth and Lebowitz, 1988). Some initial and long-term effects include fear, anxiety, depression, anger, hostility, aggression, shame, guilt, loneliness, and inappropriate sexual behaviors (Anderson et al., 1981; Browne and Finkelhor, 1986; DeFrancis, 1969; Hunter, 1990a), as well as difficulties in sexual adjustment (Briere, 1984; Langmade, 1983; Meiselman, 1978).

Recognition of the prevalence and consequences of CSA, in combination with increased media attention in the early to mid-1980s, spurred the development of child-focused, school-based prevention programs nationwide (Reppucci and Haugaard, 1989; Wurtele, 2002, 1987). Estimates suggest that 88% of elementary school districts in the U.S. have offered prevention programs, with about 66% of children exposed to such programs (Breen et al., 1991; Finkelhor and Dziuba-Leatherman, 1995). For more than 25 years, these programs have sought to keep children safe by attempting to make them less vulnerable to the advances of adult and adolescent sexual offenders. A broad range of children and young teens have been participants in such programs, which have included children as young as preschoolers (Finkelhor and Dziuba-Leatherman, 1995; Tutty, 2002) and as old as teens in high school (Conte, 1986; Wurtele, 2002). These programs have typically involved both skills training and abuse disclosure components. The primary intent of the skills training has been to strengthen children's abilities to recognize potentially abusive situations and teach them strategies to resist sexual assault (Wurtele and Miller-Perrin, 1992). Initiatives have varied from a single class lasting no more than two hours to multiple sessions held over days or weeks (Tutty, 1994, 1992). Content has most often been based on a standardized curriculum, which has been taught by community prevention program staff, trained volunteers, school personnel or teachers. Programs have strived to teach a variety of skills according to children's developmental capabilities (see Rispens et al., 1997) including body ownership, threat recognition, abuse refusal skills, and in some cases, self-defense (Conte et al., 1985; Ray-Keil, 1988). The disclosure component of school-based prevention programs has typically involved clarifying that: CSA is wrong; it is not the victim's fault; and that disclosing abuse can lead to getting help to both the victim and the offender. The programs offer a safe and private context for children to talk to the teacher or trainer about incidents of abuse.

Despite indications that child-focused, school-based CSA prevention programs have been successful in fostering abuse disclosures (Beland, 1986; Kolko et al., 1989; Kolko et al., 1987), there is minimal evidence to support the efficacy of their prevention components (see Kaufman et al., [2002] for a detailed critique and review). In fact, programs of this nature have been sharply criticized since the late 1980s for a lack of empirical foundation (Kolko, 1988; Reppucci and Haugaard, 1989). In particular, Reppucci and Haugaard (1989) note a lack of knowledge regarding the types of skills that will reduce children's vulnerability to sexual abuse. Moreover, these programs have neglected to incorporate empirical findings indicating that: offenders use a complex grooming process (i.e., behaviors leading up to and intended to foster compliance in sexually abusive acts) to commit CSA; the vast majority of victims either know or are related to their offender (perhaps in excess of 90%; Greenfeld, 1997); and offenders can be quite sophisticated in the manner in which they approach their victims (Kaufman et al., 1998; Kaufman et al., 1996). Instead they have often adopted a "one size fits all" perspective, choosing to ignore important nuances associated with the victim-offender relationship. Further, children's physical (i.e., smaller size) and developmental limitations (e.g., deference to adult authority, cognitive immaturity, lack of sexual knowledge) place them at a significant disadvantage in negotiating with older teens and adults regarding their safety (Reppucci et al., 1999). Clearly, these differences cannot be overcome by simply providing children classroom-based information and skills training. Finally, the research findings indicate that offenders have continued to perpetrate CSA despite children's participation in school-based CSA prevention programs (Berliner and Conte, 1988; Conte et al., 1985; Kaufman et al., 2002) and children's attempts to stop offenders from abusing them (Barber and Kaufman, in preparation).

Taken together, the literature suggests that children are not in an optimal position to be responsible for their own well-being with regard to CSA. Rather, it is more appropriate to shift the burden to adults who are better able to ensure children's safety. At the same time, it is important to recognize that only a small proportion of school-based prevention programs (11%) have included parents in any manner (e.g., receiving handouts or direct training; Finkelhor and Dziuba-Leatherman, 1995). Over the past five to seven years the public health approach has been suggested as a general framework for thinking about how to integrate a broad array of adults into the process of protecting children and adolescents from CSA (Mercy, 1999). The public health approach emphasizes primary prevention, which identifies behavioral and situational risk factors associated with a problem and takes steps to educate the community and protect them from these risks (Hamburg, 1998). This approach also encourages the development of skills and strengths that would mitigate against certain risks associated with CSA (Hamburg, 1998). Through the public health approach, community members, professionals, parents, caregivers, and other family members can be mobilized as agents of change. At the same time, children can continue to be given explicit permission to disclose abuse, no matter what their relationship is to the perpetrator. This shift in responsibility for children's safety will require more thoughtful use of existing prevention models as well as the development of empirical research to guide the application of these frameworks to the problem of child sexual abuse.

Research as a Foundation for Tailoring CSA Prevention: Offenders' Modus Operandi

Developing a comprehensive understanding of risk factors that underlie the perpetration of sexual violence with child and adolescent populations is critical to the tailoring of prevention models to CSA. The development of an empirical foundation in this area has included CDC-funded research designed to enhance our understanding of offenders' patterns of perpetration. This study also investigated risk factors related to caregivers' supervision of children and teens who may be at risk (i.e., for victimization or perpetration; Kaufman et al., 2004). Research on modus operandi has been described as providing a mechanism to fulfill a longstanding mandate to better educate the public regarding CSA situations (Cohn, 1986; Reppucci and Haugaard, 1989).

Prior to obtaining CDC support, Kaufman and his colleagues undertook a systematic investigation to empirically examine the process of sexual offending (Kaufman et al., 1996; Kaufman et al., 1994). They proposed a temporal framework intended to describe offenders' behavior prior to, during, and following sexual abuse. Referred to as "modus operandi," this framework places behaviors along a temporal continuum, beginning with offenders' efforts to access victims and including strategies intended to: 1) lure the victim, 2) gain the potential victim's and their family members' trust, 3) obtain the victim's compliance in sexually abusive behaviors, and 4) maintain the victim's silence following the onset of the abuse. The notion of modus operandi has also provided the field with instruments to empirically examine offenders' behavior patterns across the offender-victim relationship. Modus operandi strategies (also referred to, in part, as "grooming") can be directed at either a child/teen and/or his/her parent, and are intended to "set-up" an individual to be sexually abused. Of particular relevance to the field of prevention is the observable nature of many of these modus operandi behaviors. Behaviors that are observable and can be identified as common patterns in sexual offending represent excellent targets for the development of prevention efforts involving parents, family members, professionals and community members. Descriptions of these patterns can be used to alert the public to common strategies that offenders use to sexually abuse children as well as to debunk many of the myths associated with sexual offending (e.g., that many offenders are strangers). Research of this nature may also assist in the development of models that may foster CSA prevention.

Adopting the Situational Prevention Model to Guide CSA Prevention

Situational factors have been utilized in crime prevention (Clarke, 1995), and they represent a category of risk factors that may strengthen a public health approach to the prevention of CSA. Situational factors represent "precipitators" within the crime setting itself that may prompt, provoke, pressure or permit an individual to offend (Wortley, 2001). According to Wortley (2001), "environmental cues tempt us, jog our memory, create expectations, evoke moods, stimulate us, warn us, and set examples for us to follow" (p. 65). Situational crime prevention is based on the premise that much of crime is contextual and opportunistic, and that altering the context will diminish opportunities for crime (*Design against Crime Report*, 2000). Changing the crime situation involves focusing on the reduction of opportunities for criminal behavior, increasing the risk of detection and minimizing the rewards for probable offenders (Clarke and Homel, 1997). The emphasis in situational crime prevention is on modifying environmental factors that provoke offenders' attitudes and motives as well as create opportunities for the commission of crimes. Clarke and Homel (1997) suggested strategies that: (1) increased offenders' perceived effort to perpetrate a crime; (2) increased the risks associated with the crime; (3) reduced anticipated rewards; and (4) removed excuses that made offending more acceptable. Examples of situational prevention approaches include increasing lighting and video surveillance in parking structures, increasing the use of signs to clarify consequences for shoplifting, and designing housing projects to decrease anonymity, increase interactions, and reduce opportunities for crime (Wortley, 2001).

Typically, situational approaches have tended to focus on environmental factors in public spaces, crimes against property, and the behavior of individuals perpetrating crimes against strangers (Clarke, 1995; Clarke and Homel, 1997). As such, it is not surprising that efforts have not been undertaken to apply this approach to the problem of child sexual abuse, a problem that typically occurs in private spaces (e.g., the victim or offender's home). While specific estimates are unavailable, it seems that the majority of sexual offenders targeting non-stranger victims utilize a broad array of approaches to foster the success of their abusive advances. Despite this, a situational perspective may offer some insights into CSA perpetrated by offenders known and unknown to the victim.

The Situational Model in Perspective: Etiological Factors in CSA

While situational factors may contribute significantly to a proportion of cases, it is important to recognize the breadth of factors that contribute to the etiology of CSA. The ecological model has been offered as an organizing framework (Tan et al., 1991), and it suggests that factors may include dimensions related to the offender, the victim and their family, community and institutional contexts, and societal influences (see Table 1). Situational conceptualizations have sought to account for offender motivations (Cornish and Clarke, 2003; Wortley, 2001); however, research findings suggest that individuals' offending behaviors may be the result of a broader constellation of precipitating factors including those related to psychological (e.g., poor self-esteem, difficulties regulating anger; Gray and Pithers, 1993; Wurtele and Miller-Perrin, 1992; Yates, 2003), interpersonal (e.g., limited social and dating skills, a lack of empathy, objectification of children; Gray and Pithers, 1993; Wurtele and Miller-Perrin, 1992; Yates, 2003), psychosexual (e.g., history of sexual abuse, sexual arousal toward children; Wurtele and Miller-Perrin, 1992; Yates, 2003) and psycho-educational (e.g., sexual knowledge deficits) dimensions.

Victim-related etiological factors may include developmental influences, cognitive deficits, and family-related concerns. Children and younger adolescents' developmental immaturity make them particularly vulnerable to perpetrators' (i.e., adult and older adolescents') advances. While normative in nature, developmental differences between victims and their offenders are manifested in areas of cognitive processing, social functioning, moral reasoning, and in relating to authority figures. These differences allow offenders to use misinformation, manipulation, subtle coercion, and direct threats both to obtain compliance in abusive sexual acts and to ensure victim silence following the onset of the abuse (Kaufman et al., 1998). Cognitively-impaired children and teens (e.g., mentally retarded, developmentally delayed) also represent attractive targets for CSA

Table 1: Etiological Dimensions Related to Child Sexual Abuse

Etiological Dimensions	Factors Within Etiological Dimensions		Situational Role
	Factor	Illustrative Risk	
Victim Specific	Developmental	Children's compliance with	Situational considerations play
	Social	adult authority	a minimal role for intra-indi-
	Moral		vidual victim factors
	Authority		
	Psychological	Poor self-esteem	
	Cognitive	Mental retardation	
	Interpersonal Skills	Socially isolated	
Offender Specific	Psychological	Lack of empathy	Minimal role for intra-
	Psychosexual	Arousal to children	individual offender
	Cognitive Distortions	Children as objects	factors
	Interpersonal Skills	Poor dating skills	

Table 1: *(continued)*

Etiological Dimensions	Factors Within Etiological Dimensions		Situational Role
	Factor	Illustrative Risk	
Family/Relationships	Violence	Domestic violence	Minimal role for family factors, more related to relationships
	Dysfunction	Marital conflict	
	Configuration	Single-parent family	
	Dating	Dating older peers	
	Friendships	Frequent visits by acquaintances	
Institutional & Community Context	Life Style	Uses bus/subway	Situational considerations play a significant role for institutional and community factors
	Routine Activities	Parent works two jobs	
	Physical Environment	Lives in public housing	
	Violence Facilitators	Pornography involved	
	Victim Context	Lack of supervision	
	Offender Context	Inadequate community management	
Societal Influences	Media	Portrays sexual violence as acceptable	Situational considerations play a significant role
	Criminal Justice System	Lack of investment in treatment & supervision	

offenders. Psychological (e.g., poor self-esteem, depression) and interpersonal difficulties (e.g., social isolation) experienced by children and teens have also been associated with an increased risk for sexual assault.

The literature has also focused attention on family-level (Blaske et al., 1989; Hazelwood and Warren, 1989; Lisak, 1994; Lisak and Roth, 1990; McCormack et al., 2002) and societal (Ellis, 1993; Finkelhor, 1982) risk factors in sexual offenders' backgrounds. Many social learning and family theories adopt a holistic approach to understanding the etiology of CSA, viewing problems as existing in the dynamics of the family network and society at large rather than in the pathology of the individual (Haley, 1980; Minuchen, 1974; Satir, 1983). Some examples of possible family-level risk factors include inefficient or sporadic supervision (Kaufman et al., 2002), lack of privacy (Wurtele, 2002; Wurtele and Miller-Perrin, 1992), poor or negative communication (Blaske et al., 1989), and a negative parent-child bond (Hazelwood and Warren, 1989; Lisak, 1994; Lisak and Roth, 1990). Possible risk factors at the societal-level include portrayal of children as sexual objects or property in the media (e.g., pornography; Russell, 1995; Wurtele and Miller-Perrin, 1992), male socialization of patriarchal authority (Finkelhor, 1982), and lack of sexuality education (Wurtele and Miller-Perrin, 1992). These theories are important in developing a broader understanding of the complexities of CSA. However, due to the heterogeneity of perpetrators and the complex nature of CSA, no one theory adequately explains the factors that lead an adult to sexually abuse a child (Bickley and Beech, 2001) or the contextual factors that promote its occurrence.

Using Modus Operandi Research to Tailor the Situational Prevention Model to CSA

Clearly, the Situational Prevention Model may only account for a portion of the etiological factors associated with CSA. This model does, however, offer a unique means of addressing particular types of offenders and CSA crimes. In particular, the model seems to fit best for perpetration involving non-familial cases of abuse (i.e., neighbors, family friends, strangers). This model also offers a number of distinct advantages. For example, applying situational prevention to the area of CSA can be useful in emphasizing public responsibility for making communities safer for children, rather than simply focusing on individual and family risk factors or asking children to protect themselves. Further, situational crime prevention emphasizes offenders' and potential offenders' individual accountability and responsibility. A public response is required to reduce the incidence of CSA. Prevention relies on detection and improvements in society and its institutions. Situational prevention may offer a way to expand prevention initiatives that typically focus on potential offender or victim characteristics, by shifting the focus from dispositional characteristics to situational explanations of crime with respect to offenders' motives.

Despite its usefulness in general crime prevention, it is important to recognize the true scope of situational crime prevention for CSA. As previously noted, situational conceptualizations tend to focus on the environment, on public spaces, and on crimes against property. This may limit the model's relevance to the area of CSA, where secrecy, intra-familial abuse, and perpetration in private spaces often predominate. Given the multiple pathways associated with other forms of crime, it is not surprising to find that sexual offending against children and teens is associated with a variety of etiological dimensions. There is broad consensus among researchers that sexual offenders are heterogeneous and that sexual offending against children is a multi-dimensional, multi-determined phenomenon. Studies show considerable variation in patterns of offending against children and in the characteristics and motives of offenders themselves (Kaufman et al., 1998, 1994). To be effective, CSA prevention initiatives should utilize an integrated strategy that considers different contexts (e.g., home, community, organizations, and Internet) that may motivate and permit an individual to sexually offend. It is necessary to identify the different risk factors in each context and to devise prevention strategies which address these contexts.

In response to this need, the goal of this chapter is to develop a situational crime prevention model to guide the prevention of CSA and to examine this model in the context of research on offenders' patterns of perpetration or modus operandi. Although large-scale studies of offenders' modus operandi have revealed general patterns of grooming, findings have also demonstrated that a particular offender's modus operandi can differ based upon a variety of factors including: offender age (juvenile vs. adult); victim gender; offender-victim relatedness (i.e., intra-familial vs. extra-familial); and culture. However, a detailed discussion of subgroup differences in modus operandi is beyond the scope of this chapter, given its conceptual nature. Rather, modus operandi findings will be used to illustrate discussion of various aspects of a situational model for CSA. For a more in-depth discussion of modus operandi sub-group differences, see the following literature on juvenile sexual offenders (Barbaree et al., 1998; Fehrenbach et al., 1986; Kaufman et al., 1996), victim characteristics (Conte et al., 1989; Finkelhor, 1986; Veneziano et al., 2000), offender-victim relatedness (Kaufman et al., 1998), and culture (Kaufman et al., 2004).

A CSA SITUATIONAL PREVENTION MODEL

In situational crime prevention, opportunities that facilitate crime are identified and prevention measures are sought to reduce crime opportunities and to deflect offenders. Adapted from the work of Clarke (1995), the model presented in Figure 1 maintains a similar overall structure, but provides factors in each category specific to CSA and integrates research on offenders' "modus operandi." The purpose of the model is to describe the situational factors that influence opportunities for CSA and the interplay between these opportunities and offender factors. As such, the "Crime Opportunity Structure" is at the heart of this model. Opportunities are most directly influenced by the victim's situation (e.g., walking alone to school), target locations (e.g., parks), and the involvement of facilitators (e.g., alcohol use by the victim and/or the offender). These direct influences (i.e., victims, target locations, facilitators) are more generally shaped by lifestyle and routine activities (e.g., parents' work demands, time with babysitters) as well as the characteristics of the physical environment (e.g., lack of privacy in the home, or abandoned buildings in the neighborhood) in which they live. There is also a critical interplay between the crime opportunity structure and offender-specific factors (e.g., number of offenders in the area, quality of offenders' supervision). This interplay involves both offenders' perceptions of the risks associated with and the opportunities to commit CSA as well as their motivation to commit CSA. Model components are all impacted by the prevailing socio-economic structure (e.g., particular demographics, geography, economics, legal institutions) and associated sub-cultural influences (e.g., local judicial practices, use of traditional criminological rationales by justice system and treatment professionals, and local systems' control over offenders). Taken together, this model offers a framework for exploring dimensions that contribute to CSA opportunities, the role of modus operandi in shaping these factors, and prevention strategies that may be employed to address these factors.

The remainder of this chapter explores research support for the various components of a situational model of CSA (i.e., Lifestyle and Routine

Figure 1: Situational Prevention Model of Child Sexual Abuse

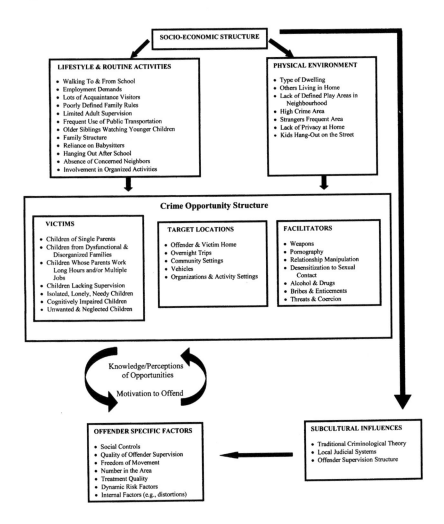

Activity; Physical Environment; Crime Opportunity Structure; Offender Specific Factors; Socio-Economic Structure; Sub-Cultural Factors; see Figure 1). Particular attention is paid to the role of offenders' modus operandi and the utility of such findings in describing the model's application to CSA. Prevention strategies which address key situational risks are proposed and suggestions are offered for future directions in research and prevention.

Lifestyle and Routine Activity Risk Factors

Clarke (1995) has suggested that individuals' lifestyles, as well as their routine activities, represent areas that may have significance for situational prevention. While heavily influenced by socio-economic realities (e.g., a family's need to use public transportation because they cannot afford a car), these factors may significantly influence aspects of the Crime Opportunity Structure (see Table 1). For example, a lifestyle that requires the use of public transportation for young teens may frequently place them in higher risk "target locations" (e.g., side streets, bus stop), which, in turn, invokes "victim factors" (e.g., out of the view of potential supervisors), making it easier for offenders to use crime "facilitators" (e.g., being offered a beer) to decrease victims' inhibitions and increases the likelihood of a CSA crime to occur.

Pertinent lifestyle and routine activities include factors specific to CSA (e.g., high-frequency use of babysitters, many acquaintance visitors to the home) and dynamics that promote crime in general (e.g., parents working multiple jobs, poor supervision). With regard to CSA-specific factors, research has suggested that both intra and extra-familial adult and juvenile offenders use babysitting assignments as a primary means of accessing and isolating children for the purpose of sexual abuse (Kaufman et al., 1998). Kaufman and his colleagues (Kaufman et al., 1998) found that babysitting was used by more adolescent offenders than any other strategy to gain victim access (i.e., about 50% of both intra and extra-familial offenders reported use of this strategy). Frequent visits from family acquaintances, neighbors, and boyfriends may also reflect a lifestyle factor that increases children's risk for CSA. This is especially possible in light of literature that suggests offenders' propensity to establish friendships or dating relationships with parents to facilitate access to their children for the purpose of CSA (Lang and Frenzel, 1988; Smallbone and Wortley, 2001), and extra-familial offenders' reliance on playing with and providing attention to potential victims to gain their trust (Kaufman et al., 1994). The risk for CSA may be heightened in families where rules are poorly defined and parental supervision is unavailable, resulting in more opportunities for acquaintances to enter the home and interact with children. More general lifestyle and routine activity factors (e.g., working two jobs, single-parent family) may also increase opportunities for CSA by: reducing parents' availability for supervision; increasing the need for babysitters (i.e., siblings, family members or individuals outside of the family); or increasing the amount of time that potential victims are allowed to spend in high risk "target locations" unsupervised (e.g., hanging out on the street, at the mall).

Physical Environment

In many cases, the physical environment in which a family resides is determined by socio-economic influences. Poorly lit streets, apartment "security doors" that don't lock, overcrowded housing, and high rates of crime are endemic in poorer areas of cities and towns. In contrast to situational factors that may be largely under the control of individuals, many characteristics of the physical environment are beyond their ability to influence. Rather, they are within the purview of landlords, local decision makers (e.g., planning boards, city council members), and state legislators.

Adverse physical environments (e.g., high-density, low-cost dwellings referred to in many cities as "the projects") tend to create risks for crime in general. A few exceptions may be differentially related to increased crime opportunities for CSA in particular. For example, home environments that involve multiple families, extended families, and/or unrelated adults sharing the same domicile may lead to greater opportunity for CSA to occur (Wurtele and Miller-Perrin, 1992). A family's dire financial circumstances may also increase the probability that less-desirable individuals may be present in their household (i.e., primarily based upon their ability to contribute to the rent). Living arrangements of this nature may result in the presence of multiple adults with "pseudo parental authority," frequent babysitting by non-family or extended family adult and adolescent members of the household, and the presence of individuals who otherwise would not be considered appropriate for sharing a home with children. Homes that lack privacy may also create environments that increase opportunities for CSA (e.g., sharing a bedroom; Kaufman et al., 1994). While often a concern in overcrowded and poorly maintained households (e.g., broken bathroom locks), this issue need not be restricted to low income neighborhoods. Families lacking appropriate sexual boundaries, rules about personal privacy, and containing family members with mental health problems or cognitive impairment may be especially at risk for CSA (Finkelhor and Hotaling, 1984; Herman and Hirschman, 1981). Finally, community environments that do not offer safe play areas for children increase opportunities for offenders to access potential victims (Kaufman et al., 1994). The absence of community centers, parks, and playgrounds will not keep children and teens from playing outside, it will, however, decrease potential community supervision and increase offenders' access to children and teens.

Crime Opportunity Structure

The crime opportunity structure is a conceptual framework illustrating the myriad of pathways and situational factors that allow opportunities for CSA crimes to occur. This structure consists of three main components: (1) target locations; (2) victims; and (3) crime facilitators (Clarke, 1995). The scale and nature of CSA crime opportunities are based upon both the dynamic interactions among its three main components and the influence of other factors in the model (e.g., lifestyle, offender-specific factors, and socio-economic structure). To illustrate this dynamic process, consider the following scenario: Sarah, a nine year old girl, is left unsupervised every day from the time that she gets home from school until just before bed time when her single mother, Janice, returns home from her second job. Her mother cannot afford to pay for babysitting, but someone that she's dating, Bob, offers to watch her daughter. Janice is relieved because she worries about her daughter being home alone, particularly given the neighborhood in which they live. Sarah is an only child and doesn't have many friends. Bob showers Sarah with love and attention, and forms a special relationship with her. Secrets develop between them as Bob allows Sarah to break rules that her mother has established. He gives her money, and sometimes some of his beer while they watch TV together. Bob has also become more and more physically affectionate with Sarah. Over time, Bob lets Sarah watch movies containing increasing amounts of sexuality. It is not unusual for Bob to use the remote to replay movie scenes, sometimes encouraging Sarah to do the same. Each time, Bob comments on the actors' sexual behavior and encourages Sarah to talk about the scenes as well. One day, Bob puts on a porno tape and suggests to Sarah that he can teach her how to do some of the things that the grown-ups are doing on the tape. Sarah is somewhat reluctant, but Bob reminds her that her mom would be upset if he told her about the rules that she's been breaking over the past few months. Sarah doesn't really like what Bob tells her to do, but she's afraid that her mom will be mad at her and maybe even have Bob go away. Bob is her best friend and really good to her . . . most of the time, so she does what he says and keeps it to herself. This hypothetical scenario illustrates how certain lifestyles and routine activities can play a central role in facilitating opportunities for the development of an abusive relationship. It also suggests ways in which children's vulnerabilities (e.g., needy, lacking parental attention) may be capitalized upon by offenders, and how crime facilitators (i.e., pornography, desensitization to physical touch) are used in "setting-up" and maintaining the abusive scenario.

By understanding the dynamic interplay among these components (i.e., victims, targets, and facilitators) within the crime opportunity structure, we can better design prevention strategies that reduce the potential for abuse to occur. The situational prevention model provides a framework for developing CSA-related situational crime prevention strategies that incorporate information gained from research on CSA risk factors and offenders' modus operandi. The following section describes the major parameters of the crime opportunity structure: target location; victims; and facilitators. This includes a brief description of each parameter as well as a more detailed articulation of its application to CSA.

Target Locations

Features of the physical environment, lifestyle patterns, and routine activities of the population determine the level of crime opportunity in a particular setting or "target location." For example, target locations for burglary crimes include cars, convenience stores, and automated teller machines lacking security protections or guardianship (Clarke, 1995). The various features and patterns at a target location can either hinder or facilitate the interplay among the three crime elements (i.e., targets, victims, facilitators), and thus affect how easily a crime might occur in a specific location. One strategy to reduce crime opportunities is to "harden targets" by increasing the effort required to perpetrate the crime and the associated risk of detection (Clarke, 1995).

In contrast to the public nature of most crimes (e.g., car thefts), target locations for CSA are often private areas. Urban myths, which describe sex offenders as lurking around school grounds, remain unsubstantiated by research on offenders' modus operandi. In fact, juvenile offenders have identified places on or near school grounds as one of the least common places where they target children (Kaufman et al., 1994). Research has consistently shown that the majority of CSA crimes occur in the offenders' and victims' homes (Budin and Johnson, 1989; Kaufman et al., 1998; Kaufman et al., 1994; Lang and Frenzel, 1988). This makes considerable sense given evidence that more than 90% of CSA victims are acquainted with their offender, including nearly half of offenders who are family members (Greenfeld, 1997). Identifying the home as a primary CSA target location makes efforts to develop situational prevention strategies a more complex and challenging task. In other words, "hardening" various areas of the home against CSA can be particularly difficult when the most likely perpetrators are family members (both immediate and extended families). It is unrealistic and inappropriate to restrict a child's one-on-one time alone with a primary caregiver who is a member of the family. For this reason, situational prevention in this case would not focus on changing attributes in the physical environment of the home to reduce sex-offending opportunities; rather, it may involve changing those factors within the family that facilitate or create opportunities for offenders to sexually abuse children and teens. Caregivers may utilize information regarding what we know about offenders' modus operandi to alter their behaviors or routine patterns to reduce opportunities for abuse and increase potential offenders' risk of getting caught.

Although extra-familial abuse is less common than intra-familial abuse, it does occur, and the situational prevention model has greater applicability to preventing sexual abuse in these circumstances. For extra-familial offenders (i.e., offenders who were not related to or living with the victim, including strangers), evidence suggests that they often find children in neighborhoods close to their home (Budin and Johnson, 1989; Kaufman et al., 1994) or through organized activities such as sports teams and scouts (Smallbone and Wortley, 2001). While considerably less frequent, evidence suggests that some offenders have perpetrated CSA in vehicles (Kaufman et al., 1994; Lang and Frenzel, 1988) and in isolated places (e.g., parks, wooded areas) (Smallbone and Wortley, 2001). Juvenile extra-familial offenders have reported that parks and playgrounds were critical locations for finding potential victims (Kaufman et al., 1994). These same offenders indicated that they were least likely to find victims in video arcades, movie theatres, and swimming pools (Kaufman et al., 1994). However, regardless of location, modus operandi information regarding features of particular settings can provide crucial data about situations that facilitate crime opportunities for CSA and ways to prevent these situations from arising.

Victims

Numerous situational factors may influence a child's risk of being sexually victimized. The factor that has received some of the greatest attention from researchers and the media is children's lack of sexual knowledge. Since the early to mid-1980s, CSA prevention programs have been adopted by elementary schools nationwide, and have focused on strengthening children's abilities to recognize potentially abusive situations and to resist sexual assault (Reppucci and Haugaard, 1989; Wurtele, 2002). As previously noted, while there has been a reliance on this approach for more than 25 years, there remains no direct evidence that these programs have been effective in preventing CSA (Kaufman et al., 2002). Furthermore, the vast majority of offender reports (78%) indicate that prevention strategies utilized by potential child victims rarely, if ever, stop the abuse from occurring (Barber and Kaufman, in preparation).

Within the context of the home as the primary location for CSA crimes, research has demonstrated that children are at greater risk for CSA if they are living in single-parent households (Creighton and Noyes, 1989; Finkelhor, 1980; Finkelhor and Baron, 1986; Gruber and Jones, 1983; McCloskey and Bailey, 2000). It is also possible that having a parent who works long hours and/or multiple jobs may constitute a CSA risk factor. Likewise, inadequate supervision of children has been identified as a situation that fosters opportunities for both intra- and extra-familial offenders to gain access and obtain time alone with potential victims in their home (Barber and Kaufman, in preparation; Budin and Johnson, 1989; Smallbone and Wortley, 2001). A child's emotional state may also contribute to her/ his vulnerability to CSA. Offenders report seeking out children as victims who are emotionally deprived (Finkelhor, 1984), lonely, troubled, or needy (Budin and Johnson, 1989; Finkelhor, 1986). Research on modus operandi indicates that offenders groom victims by giving them attention and spending a lot of time with them (Kaufman et al, 1996; Kaufman et al., 1994). Berliner and Conte (1990) found that "in many cases, the sexual abuse relationship filled a significant deficit in the child's life . . . the children were troubled and/or their parents were not resources for them" (p. 35). When offenders exploit a child's normal need to feel loved, valued, and cared for by parents, children coming from dysfunctional families become more vulnerable to CSA. Situational factors may contribute to a child's vulnerability for victimization.

Facilitators

Crime facilitators reflect mechanisms that increase the potential for a crime to be enacted (Clarke, 1995). Examples of facilitators for general crimes include guns, cars, and disinhibitors such as alcohol and drugs. Contrary to common perceptions, physical violence and weapons are not generally characteristic facilitators of CSA committed by adult offenders (Conte et al., 1989; Kaufman et al., 1995; Okami and Goldberg, 1992). Discrepancies in physical size and intellectual capabilities between children and adults may make violence less necessary in the case of CSA (Kaufman et al., 1993). Moreover, offenders may recognize that the use of violence may increase a victim's motivation to disclose (Kaufman et al., 1998; Kaufman et al., 1993). Adults' use of authority (i.e., obtaining compliance based on their status as a trusted and/or feared adult), threats, and coercion are among the most common methods used to gain control over victims (Berliner and Conte, 1990; Budin and Johnson, 1989). Although research has shown that juveniles use more overt threats and violence in committing CSA, adult offenders have been found to use more subtle forms of coercion to gain victims' compliance in sexually abusive acts, with facilitators taking on characteristic forms such as bribes and enticements, threats, pornography, and drugs and alcohol (Fehrenbach et al., 1986; Kaufman et al., 1998).

Research has identified bribery as the most frequently used crime facilitator in the time leading up to the onset of abuse. For offenders, gaining victim trust is a critical step in the grooming process. Offenders often gain children's trust and perpetrate CSA by enticing victims with love and attention, money, trips to amusement parks and special gifts such as beer, cigarettes, money, or candy (Conte et al., 1989; Kaufman et al., 1998; Kaufman et al., 1996; Lang and Frenzel, 1988). It is worth noting that the use of alcohol and drugs as CSA facilitators is most commonly associated with extra-familial offenders (Kaufman et al., 1998; Kaufman et al., 1996). Conte et al. (1989) recounted a perpetrator's use of facilitators in grooming a child for sexual abuse. The perpetrator explained that, as an offender, you are "in a position where you are a close friend with someone [*an adult*] who is involved in alcohol and drugs and probably has the attitude that kids are like dogs, just around the house. Someone who has a tight control over kids and where if the kid does anything wrong he'll be severely punished. Being a molester, you can pick on that and start showing the kids extra attention. They'll thrive on it and will become easily manipulated to your control. You can also set it up when the parents trust you and use you as a babysitter. You'll be alone with the kid, and the kid doesn't like his parents" (Conte et al., 1989, p. 298). Evidence suggests that in contrast to strategies used to initiate CSA, offenders more often maintain this abusive relationship and victim silence about the abuse by threatening to withdraw benefits than by actually harming victims (Kaufman et al., 1996).

In grooming the child for sexual contact, research has shown that offenders use pornography as a primary facilitator to legitimize the sexual acts and to gain compliance in sexual activities (Conte et al., 1989; Kaufman et al., 1998; Kaufman et al., 1996). Offenders state that they expose victims to pornography because it extends the "desensitization process," it helps "normalize these behaviors," and it helps "legitimize sexual behavior" (Conte et al., 1989; Kaufman et al., 1998; Kaufman et al., 1996, p. 357). As part of this desensitization process, offenders also report using drugs and alcohol themselves as well as giving them to victims to reduce inhibitions and facilitate participation in the abusive acts (Kaufman et al., 1998; Kaufman et al., 1996). Unlike most other crimes, CSA crime facilitators take on more subtle forms to develop and maintain the façade of a "relationship" with a victim. Research on modus operandi suggests how crime facilitators (i.e., pornography, desensitization to physical touch) are used by offenders in setting up and maintaining the abusive scenario. By understanding offenders' use of crime facilitators within the crime opportunity structure, we can better tailor prevention strategies that reduce the potential for CSA crimes to occur.

Offender-specific Factors

Modus operandi offers a promising avenue for identifying behaviors suggestive of offenders' movement toward sexual perpetration or re-offense. In contrast, many factors related to an offender's individual make-up (e.g., personality factors, demographic characteristics) may be of little value in discriminating them from non-offenders and for guiding primary prevention efforts. In fact, Herman's (1990) conclusion about this population seems to sum up the preventive utility of general personality and demographic profiles: "the most striking characteristic of sex offenders, from a diagnostic standpoint, is their apparent normality." That said, there may be some notable exceptions worth consideration. For example, sexual offending has been associated in the literature with high levels of misogynistic beliefs about women (e.g., rape myths; Bartol and Bartol, 2004; Lonsway and Fitzgerald, 1994), cognitive distortions that include objectifying women and children (Gray and Pithers, 1993; Ward et al., 1997), and sexually-related concerns (e.g., a history of having been abused themselves, sexual arousal to children; Yates, 2003), and inaccurate sexual knowledge (Walbek and Seely, 1999; Wurtele and Miller-Perrin, 1992). Further, factors "outside" of the offender (e.g., probation/parole supervision, freedom of movement, quality of community treatment) may also serve a critical role in determining the "availability" and motivation of the offender to perpetrate CSA. Although primarily a focus of secondary or tertiary prevention efforts, offender-specific factors are a critical component in the situational prevention model and a necessary area of concern when exploring the prevention of CSA (see Figure 1).

Individual Factors

Factors such as deviant sexual arousal, inappropriate sexual beliefs and addiction problems are typically addressed in the treatment setting (Yates, 2003). If an offender is found to have concerns in these areas, interventions may include increased monitoring in the community as well as enhanced treatment requirements. Deviant sexual arousal may be monitored through testing using the penile plethysmograph (PPG – Letourneau, 2002; Marshall, 1999) or visual-reaction time measurement devices (VRT – Letourneau, 2002). The PPG tests penile tumescence while the offender views graphic images of males and females of various ages or listens to audio tapes of various sexual scenarios. VRT tests an offender's sexual interests by monitoring the amount of time he spends viewing clothed images of males and females of various ages. Both tests have been demonstrated to be valid and reliable indicators of sexual deviance (i.e., PPG with deviant arousal and VRT with deviant sexual interest; Letourneau, 2002). Various therapeutic techniques, such as aversive conditioning and covert sensitization, are typically utilized to decrease deviant sexual arousal (Laws, 2001; McKibben et al., 2001).

Addiction problems, as well as continued access to drugs, alcohol and bribes, have also been demonstrated to be associated with increased risk to sexually offend (Hanson and Bussiere, 1998). Research has identified a significantly greater problem with substance abuse among sex offenders as compared to other types of criminals (Looman et al., 2004), and has shown that many sex crimes have some connection to substance use (Kaufman et al., 1998; Kaufman et al., 1996; Peugh and Belenko, 2001). Addiction-specific treatment as well as enhanced supervision requirements, may be key interventions for decreasing the substance abuse problems of offenders and in turn, fostering the prevention of CSA re-offending.

Cognitive distortions reflect the internal processes that offenders' use to absolve themselves of responsibility for their abusive behavior, and these distortions have long been believed to play a significant role in the etiology and maintenance of sexual offending (Yates, 2003). Such beliefs as, "women and children are obligated to sexually satisfy men," and "she never said 'no' so she must have wanted it," allow offenders to blame victims, justify offending behaviors, and minimize the amount of harm offenders inflict on their victims. Offenders have often stated that their child victims enjoyed the sex, and were not fully aware of what was happening to them (and therefore were not harmed), and that both the offender and the child wanted the sexual contact to continue (Lawson, 2003). A 1992 study found that the presence of cognitive distortions was the strongest predictor of criminal behavior (Gendreau et al., 1992). Cognitive-behavioral therapy for sex offenders challenges these distortions and the underlying beliefs and attitudes. Assisting offenders in understanding that they are not able to excuse or justify their abusive acts plays an important role in offender self-management, reducing their risk to re-offend, and promoting community safety (Lawson, 2003; Yates, 2003).

Dynamic risk factors offer a promising approach to understanding immediate concerns that may predispose a CSA perpetrator to re-offend. In contrast to previously relied upon "static" risk factors (e.g., history of offending, offender age), dynamic factors represent changeable areas of behavior that can have important implications for treatment as well as for community supervision (Craissati and Beech, 2003). Dynamic risk factors include cognitive distortions (e.g., attitudes, self-regulation) as well as intimacy deficits and socio-affective functioning (Hanson and Harris, 1998; Thornton, 2002). Offenders' current level of deviancy (or dynamic risk), and therefore their likelihood to re-offend, can be predicted by determining the number and strength of factors present in an individual offender at a particular moment in time (Craissati and Beech, 2003). Five basic dynamic risk factor domains have been identified across several studies. These domains include: (1) Intimacy deficits/social competencies; (2) Social influences (e.g., criminal companions); (3) Pro-offending attitudes; (4) Sexual self-regulation; and (5) General self-regulation (see Craissati and Beech, 2003, for a more thorough explanation). Some of these factors, such as general self-regulation, may be situationally controlled (e.g., arousal when a bus load of elementary aged children enters the McDonalds at which an offender is having lunch) as more cognitive and self-regulatory skills are obtained through treatment of the offender. Collaborative efforts by the offender, his clinician, community partners, and his probation/parole officer can lead to an effective approach to monitoring and controlling dynamic risk factors to create an environment that minimizes offenders' risks of re-offense.

External Factors

Community justice based interventions are designed to limit offenders' freedom of movement and to provide social control through incarceration and community supervision following release from prison. However, over the last few decades, communities have increased their control through community notification systems based upon state laws known as "Megan's Laws" and the institution of mandatory registration for sexual offenders (Beck et al., 2003). Recent technology has also allowed law enforcement to track sex offenders throughout a full 24-hour day with the use of global positioning system (GPS) monitoring devices (Florida Department of Corrections [F.D.C.], 2004; Ko, 2002; Nellis, 2003). This technology provides more accurate monitoring of offenders inside buildings as well as in public. It also allows for immediate, real-time notification of probation/parole violations. This represents a considerable improvement over older electronic monitoring systems that provided information with delays of 24–72 hours. The GPS system allows for 24-hour surveillance rather than the periodic surprise visits typically associated with traditional parole/probation monitoring. GPS monitoring may offer stricter and more constant oversight that may reduce offenders' opportunities to violate probation rules and create situations that could lead to sexual re-offending. Exclusion boundaries can be established so that law enforcement will be notified any time an offender enters a restricted area (e.g., school zones, neighborhood parks, victims' homes). With this system, probation officers also have documentation regarding the whereabouts of offenders, which can be cross-checked if a new crime is committed. This information can help to locate offenders who need to be questioned or arrested, as well. Finally, GPS surveillance may serve as a crime deterrent for newly released offenders.

Other approaches to social control have focused on more proactive systems to reintegrate offenders into the community. The efficacy of these approaches is rooted in research that demonstrates a connection between a lack of social support and sexual offending (Gutierrez-Lobos et al., 2001). Programs known as "Circles of Support and Accountability" (COSA) have demonstrated promising results in reducing sexual recidivism with some of the highest-risk offenders (Hannem and Petrunik, 2004). Developed by the Canadian province of Ontario in the 1990's, COSA is a restorative justice/community protection initiative designed to target high-risk offenders who are released to the community and have little support. Trained volunteers in the community check in with the offender at least once per day and assist the offender with such basic needs as housing and employment. Social systems such as COSA allow for enhanced monitoring of the offenders' activities as well as decreasing their sense of social rejection. Other proactive social interventions have included programs such as STOPITNOW!. This non-profit organization has implemented various public outreach programs, which have included media campaigns to educate the public and a hotline for potential abusers and undetected abusers to call and receive anonymous referrals to local treatment providers (Tabachnick and Dawson, 2000). STOPITNOW! reported that 20 adult offenders and 98 juvenile offenders entered treatment without victims reporting the abuse, perhaps as a result of its community programming (Kaufman et al., 2002).

In considering the role of the offender, it is important to examine aspects of the prevailing context that influence how offender-related factors will be manifested. Referred to as "Subculture Influences" in the situational model (Figure 1), these norms, working assumptions, and preferred practical approaches to dealing with crime will shape the local judicial system, offender supervision and management structure, and clinical treatment networks. A working knowledge of the community's subculture will facilitate the identification and development of systems dynamics that enhance the quality of offender social controls and promote a safer community.

Linking the Crime Opportunity Structure to Offender Specific Factors

The situational prevention model suggests that the presence of crime opportunities and offender-specific factors are necessary precursors for criminal behavior, but may not be sufficient in and of themselves to lead to the perpetration of a crime. As noted in Figure 1, a bidirectional relationship may exist between the crime opportunity structure and offender-specific factors. This relationship reflects not only the presence of crime opportunities, but also offenders' knowledge of these opportunities and offenders' perceptions that these opportunities fit the type of crime that they may be interested in committing. The relationship also points to the need for the offender to have sufficient motivation to commit the crime at the point at which the opportunity is perceived to exist. Clearly, the greater the number of crime opportunity factors present in the environment, the greater the likelihood that an offender will both recognize these opportunities and have the potential of identifying opportunities that fit his propensity to offend. In a similar fashion, the presence of increased numbers of offender-specific risk factors is likely to be associated with higher motivation for offending. To the extent that these factors (i.e., crime opportunities and offender-specific) are present at the same time, one would expect a proportionally higher likelihood of offending behavior.

IMPLICATIONS FOR CSA PREVENTION

The situational prevention model offers insights into potential risks that can increase opportunities for CSA. Risks related to various model components present differential vulnerabilities and require tailored prevention strategies. At the same time, a number of general prevention strategies are likely to be effective in reducing risks. Table 2 provides examples of risks associated with various model components (e.g., lifestyle, physical environment, location) and the types of prevention strategies that may be effective in reducing opportunities for CSA. Prevention strategies described include: screening; supervision; establishing rules; environmental manipulation; providing modus operandi information; community organizing and advocacy; and skills training. The following discussion provides examples of how prevention strategies might be applied to various situational risks. Of course, implementation of these prevention strategies in the community should be preceded by a detailed analysis of strengths

Table 2: Prevention Strategies to Address Particular Situational Risks

Situational Risks → / Prevention Strategies ↓	Lifestyle/Routine Activities	Physical Environment	Victims	Locations	Facilitators	Offenders
Screening	• Babysitters • Organizations	• Identify dangerous neighborhood locations	• Identify children with developmental disabilities	• Child play areas • Teen hang-outs (e.g, Mall)	• Homes of peers for weapons, porno	• Organizational background checks for volunteers and employees • Evaluate offenders based on dynamic risk factors on a regular basis
Supervision	• Babysitters • Older siblings • Checking-in process for teens	• Neighborhood locations requiring closer supervision • Crowded locations requiring greater supervision (e.g., pool, recreation center)	• Provide greater supervision to latchkey children	• Ensure that supervision is provided in homes of peers • Greater supervision in home private areas	• Teach parents to monitor their children's money and purchases	

(continued)

Table 2: *(continued)*

Situational Risks → Prevention Strategies ↓	Lifestyle/Routine Activities	Physical Environment	Victims	Locations	Facilitators	Offenders
Rules	• Walk to/from school in a group • For public transportation • For computer use	• Curfew based on neighborhood • Parts of neighborhood off-limits	• Avoid situations where they are in the neighborhood alone	• Create access rules to home when parents not home • Restrictions on playing in private spaces at home	• Strict access rules for weapons, alcohol/drugs, porno	• Restrict access to child prevalent areas
Environmental Modification	• Have children close bedroom door when changing	• Create safe private spaces in the home (e.g., bathroom locks) • Add outside lights to dwellings	• Children changing route home to busier streets	• Create play spaces in the home that are easy to monitor	• Put locks on guns • Remove porno from house	• Have an offender move to a location further from an elementary school

– 128 –

Table 2: *(continued)*

Situational Risks → **Prevention Strategies** ↓	Lifestyle/Routine Activities	Physical Environment	Victims	Locations	Facilitators	Offenders
Provide Information on Modus Operandi	• Offenders' grooming pattern in daily activities	• Role of the environment in facilitating offenders' perpetration (e.g., dark building corridors)	• Intervene with lonely, needy, neglected children	• Identify high risk locations	• Greater use of porno by teen perps & alcohol by extrafamilial offenders	• Using past offender patterns to develop parole restrictions
Community Organizing & Advocacy	• Organize group of children to walk together to/from school • Organize group of parents to share supervision responsibilities • Advocate for more after-school activities	• Advocate for safe and secure dwellings • Encourage development of safe public play areas	• Empower community members to watch out for children	• Organize neighborhood watch • Advocate for more organized activities	• Advocate for stricter gun control • Stronger penalties for child porno	• Community notification • Community education as part of community meeting

(continued)

Table 2: *(continued)*

Situational Risks → Prevention Strategies ↓	Lifestyle/Routine Activities	Physical Environment	Victims	Locations	Facilitators	Offenders
Skills Training	• Supervision skills for parents • Teach dating skills for teens • Non-violent problem solving skills	• Teach parents	• Teach problem solving • Assertion	• Teach parents/children to recognize characteristics of high risk locations (e.g., isolated)	• Teach drug refusal skills	• Teach empathy anger management, dating skills training

as well as risks and opportunities. This information will provide the specificity necessary to design a comprehensive set of prevention strategies tailored to the particular concerns of the community and related to the populations being addressed.

Screening

Screening represents the process of investigating a person or location to minimize opportunities for CSA and maximize safety. As previously noted, babysitting represents a primary means of accessing potential CSA victims (Kaufman et al., 1998). Screening can be an effective tool in reducing offenders' opportunities for accessing children and young teens in this manner. Parents can be trained to enhance their ability to screen potential babysitter candidates. Training parents to screen babysitters should cover interviewing strategies as well as reference calls. Parental screening can also extend to inquiries about the safety of neighborhood households in which their children play and individuals with whom their children interact. For example, during a brief phone conversation, a mom could ask another parent about the presence of guns and pornography, the other parent's approach to supervision, and how older siblings in the latter's household get along with younger children. They could frame these questions in the context of their own worries about their son getting into things around the house.

Screening outside of the home can reduce crime opportunities in organizations and in neighborhoods, as well as reduce the opportunity for children to interact with identified sexual offenders. Organizational screening typically centers on the recruitment of volunteers and employees to work with youth and families (Wurtele and Miller-Perrin, 1992). Effective organizational screening should include formal background checks augmented by a structured interview process (Wurtele and Miller-Perrin, 1992). Incorporating information about the organization's commitment to children's safety and its policies designed to deter opportunities for CSA can encourage unidentified offenders to seek access elsewhere. City officials and community groups can also screen neighborhoods by reviewing incident reports to identify dangerous locations that require intervention to reduce crime opportunities. Finally, probation and parole officers' screening of their offender caseload can be organized around static and dynamic risk factors to provide critical information to enhance offender placement and supervision (Hanson and Harris, 1998; Thornton, 2002).

Supervision

While screening may often deter or identify individuals who should not be working with children, strategies for enhanced supervision of children and teens offers the benefit of protection over time. Supervision strategies may be developed to be implemented by parents, organizations, professionals, and community members. Parents can provide babysitters with the parameters necessary to keep their children safe. For example, parents can review acceptable and unacceptable discipline strategies with the babysitter, develop a daily schedule, and suggest preferred free time activities. Phone calls home to talk with the babysitter and their children can offer opportunities to ask about the day and how it was spent. Parents can also be coached to vary their schedule and make surprise visits home or ask neighbors or family members to stop by to assess the babysitters' skills and the children's safety. Maintaining regular and open communication with their children will afford opportunities for parents to discuss time spent with the babysitter and how she or he handles various situations. Parental supervision may also need to be adjusted based upon situations that arise in the neighborhood. For example, a parent may notice that a neighborhood teen is paying a great deal of attention to their preadolescent son. By providing more intensive supervision, this parent may be able to better assess the teen's intent and avoid a potentially abusive situation.

Organizational policies should detail not only how to supervise children in their care, but also how to monitor staff to ensure that agency policies are followed. Child protection policies should be shared with parents to increase the potential for identifying breaches in protocol and risks to their children. Community members can also be enlisted and trained to provide supervision for children in their neighborhood, creating a "block watch for children." Furthermore, developing phone lists, asking community members to keep an eye on neighborhood children, and having them contact parents when they observe concerning behaviors, all serve to foster greater child safety.

Rules

When parents cannot be present, the structure that they provide through established rules can help reduce opportunities for CSA. Clear rules about interactions in the home, with neighbors, and in the community may also reduce risks. In establishing rules, consideration should be given to teaching parents and caregivers basic behavioral tenants that enhance their effectiveness (Belsky, 1993; Wurtele and Miller-Perrin, 1992). This may include ensuring that rules are: clear and simple; able to be monitored; applicable in as wide a variety of situations as possible; and reviewed on a regular basis. Rules regarding access to children while they are at home may reduce opportunities for CSA. For example, not allowing friends, neighbors or acquaintances in the home when a parent is not present is a simple, but effective rule that can reduce the opportunity for CSA. Similarly, setting rules that restrict children from going inside neighbors' homes without a parent and limiting visits to friends' homes to occasions when an adult supervisor is present may also have preventive value. Additional rules may place private and isolated areas of the home off limits for play (e.g., bedrooms, basements, garages).

Creating rules regarding neighbors, acquaintances, and other non-family members as well as children's access to high-risk locations in the community may be of value in fending off CSA perpetrators (e.g., "Don't talk with strangers!"; "The park by the river is off limits!"). However, it is important to consider that children may find it difficult to apply rules about particular locations or situations to the broader context (e.g., deciding if a teen they've seen around the neighborhood is "stranger"). Teaching parents to role-play the application of rules to various situations with their children may help them generalize rules to a broader range of situations. In general, it is important to tailor rules and explanations to the age of the child and his/her developmental capabilities. Situations where there is the lure of material gain (e.g., bribes, such as money) or social status (i.e., hanging out with older teens) can also be challenging for children and young teens to resist. Warning children of the potential for offenders (teens or adults) to trick them with bribes or threats is important, but should be moderated with messages describing positive relationships with adults who can be trusted. Parent-child communication is a key factor in establishing effective supervision. Parents should work to maintain their children's trust by discussing a variety of topics with their children on a daily basis. In particular, parents should invite their children to raise difficult issues and strive to be supportive in response. Finally, rules should be reassessed on an ongoing basis and modified as children grow older and situations change.

Environmental Modification

Aspects of the physical environment that increase opportunities for CSA offer prime targets for preventive efforts. In some cases environmental conditions require physical modification, and in other situations they require a change in the use of particular spaces to reduce the risk for CSA. Examples of physical modifications might include: fixing locks on bathroom doors; repairing broken lights on apartment stairwells and in hallways; and locking back and side gates to ensure that visitors are screened at the front entrance of a building. In contrast, changing the use of space to increase safety may be illustrated by switching furniture between two rooms to create a playroom close to the kitchen and living room where it can be more easily supervised. Another example might involve parking cars on the street, rather than in the driveway, to create a play space in a fenced-in area near the front of the house. At the community level, environmental modifications may involve converting a warehouse space for an after-school program or demolishing abandoned buildings to create a ball field. Changes of this nature may increase access to safe play spaces and reduce opportunities for crime.

Providing Information on Offender Modus Operandi

While empirical research over the past 10 years has increased our understanding of offenders' modus operandi, few prevention initiatives have incorporated this information into their programs. Moreover, where patterns of perpetration are included, they tend to lack the detail necessary to adequately describe the complexity of many offenders' patterns of grooming or differences in modus operandi based upon such factors as offenders' age, victim age, victim gender, and offender-victim relationship. Providing more comprehensive descriptions of modus operandi to parents and community members can sensitize them to CSA offenders' sophistication and the types of behaviors they might see with different victim-offender combinations. Information of this nature can also increase parents' awareness of the risks associated with having certain "crime facilitators" in their home (e.g., pornography), as well as allowing them to warn teens of how perpetrators use the lure of alcohol to manipulate them into compliance with sexually abusive acts. Modus operandi information can also be utilized to identify high-risk locations (e.g., vehicles, parks) and environmental concerns (e.g., dark building corridors) that can be addressed to reduce opportunities for CSA.

Community Organizing and Advocacy

Community organizing refers to efforts intended to enhance existing neighborhood strengths through coordination, whereas advocacy reflects focused initiatives designed to foster a particular change. Preventive strategies based on a community organizing framework might include arranging groups of children who can walk together to and from school each day or parents who can share the supervision of children on a rotating basis. CSA may also be prevented through community advocacy for additional after-school programs, safer and more secure dwellings, the development of safer public play areas, and stricter child pornography laws. These approaches can also be used to influence local, state, and federal decision makers, encouraging them to invest in strategies that reduce crime opportunities and create safer neighborhoods.

Skills Training

As previously mentioned, a variety of skills deficits in adolescents, parents, community members, and professionals can increase the potential for CSA to occur. A variety of risks can be addressed with skills training approaches. For example, teaching teens dating skills and parameters for healthy relationships can reduce the potential for sexual violence to occur. Enhancing parenting and supervision skills can help to ensure that adults will know how to establish rules and monitor their children's whereabouts in a fashion that keeps them as safe as possible. Teaching children to be assertive and to communicate with their parents may increase the probability that they will ask for advice and support if they are approached by an older adolescent or adult in a way that makes them uncomfortable. Finally, practicing strategies for refusing offers of drugs and alcohol may prepare a child or teen for an offender who attempts to lure them with promises of sharing a drink or getting high.

FUTURE DIRECTIONS

Applying a situational prevention framework to CSA offers a unique opportunity to examine this challenging social problem from a different perspective. The Situational Prevention Model has demonstrated efficacy in addressing a variety of criminal behaviors. While this model may not be applicable to all forms of CSA, it seems to offer a promising approach to enhancing our understanding of factors that may precipitate some types of CSA. In doing so, it suggests prevention strategies that could be implemented to reduce abuse opportunities and increase resistance to CSA risk factors.

The model proposed in this chapter is rooted in the research literature describing sexual offenders' modus operandi, which therefore offers a strong empirical foundation for the model's formulation. Nonetheless, future research should independently examine the model's conceptualization and test the strength of the relationship between model components. Research should also seek to examine the model's fit for different CSA variants (e.g., adult versus adolescent offenders; stranger versus acquaintance offender-victim relationship). Studies exploring the dynamic relationship between the crime opportunity structure and offender-specific factors may be particularly useful in guiding prevention planning, while current practice involves isolated decisions about offender management and crime opportunities in the community. A systematic investigation into the relationship between these areas may lead to more effective strategies for coordinated interventions. Studies could also elucidate how offender motivation may lead to misperceptions of "crime opportunities" that precipitate perpetration. Identifying this mechanism could lead to strategies that would further reduce offenders' rates of sexual recidivism.

This model also lends itself to the development of a new breed of dynamic prevention programs. Such initiatives would rely on an assessment of community assets and risks (or crime opportunities) and offer a broad array of prevention tools that could be tailored to the specific needs of a given community at a particular point in time. Due to the dynamic nature of communities, and changes in the types of risks and assets present at a given time, a combination of ongoing program evaluation efforts and regular reassessments (i.e., of assets and risks) would ensure that prevention program components were implemented, modified, and discontinued as needed. The flexibility afforded by this sort of prevention approach would also foster the inclusion of a broader group of collaborators (e.g., community members, professionals). Flexible intervention models designed to address the full spectrum of needs have been successful in addressing other forms of child maltreatment (e.g., physical abuse and neglect; see "Project 12 Ways"; Lutzker and Bigelow, 2001) and offer the promise of greater sustainability due to their adaptable nature.

Address correspondence to: Keith L. Kaufman, Ph.D., Psychology Professor and Chair, Portland State University, P.O. Box 751, Portland, OR 97206-0751; e-mail: kaufmank@pdx.edu.

REFERENCES

Anderson, S.C., C.M. Bach and S. Griffith (1981). "Psychosocial Sequelae in Intrafamilial Victims of Sexual Assault and Abuse." Paper presented at the Third International Conference on Child Abuse and Neglect, Amsterdam, the Netherlands.

Barbaree, H.E., W.L. Marshall and J. McCormick (1998). "The Development of Deviant Sexual Behaviour among Adolescents and its Implications for Prevention and Treatment." *The Irish Journal of Psychology* 19(1):1–31.

Barber, M. and K. Kaufman (in preparation). *Sexual Offenders' Perceptions of Preventing Child Sexual Abuse: Efficacy of Prevention Strategies and Advice for Adults.*

Bartol, C. and A. Bartol (2004). *Introduction to Forensic Psychology.* Thousand Oaks, CA: Sage.

Beck, V.S., R.J. Ramsey, J.C. Clingermayer and L.F. Travis (2003). "The Effect of Sex Offender Notification on Community Fear, Perceived Risk of Victimization and Protective Behavior." Paper presented at the annual conference of the Midwestern Criminal Justice Association, Chicago, Illinois.

Beland, K. (1986). *Talking About Touching II: Personal Safety for Preschoolers.* Seattle, WA: Committee for Children.

Belsky, J. (1993). "Etiology of Child Maltreatment: A Developmental-Ecological Analysis." *Psychological Bulletin* 114:413–434.

Berliner, L. and J.R. Conte (1990). "The Process of Victimization: The Victims' Perspective." *Child Abuse and Neglect* 14:29–40.

Berliner, L. and J.R. Conte (1988). *What Victims Tell Us About Prevention?* Chicago: University of Chicago, School of Social Services.

Bickley, J. and A.R. Beech (2001). "Classifying Child Abusers: Its Relevance to Theory and Clinical Practice." *Journal of Offender Therapy and Comparative Criminology* 45:51–69.

Blaske, D.M., C.M. Borduin, S.W. Henggeler and B.J. Mann (1989). "Individual, Family, and Peer Characteristics of Adolescent Sex Offenders and Assaultive Offenders." *Developmental Psychology* 25:846–855.

Breen, M., D. Daro and N. Romano (1991). "Prevention Services and Child Abuse: A National Assessment of the Role of Hospitals, Schools, Districts and

Community-Based Agencies." Unpublished report prepared for the Silkman Foundation.

Briere, J. (1984). "The Effects of Childhood Sexual Abuse on Later Psychological Functioning: Defining a Post-Sexual Abuse Syndrome." Paper presented at the Third National Conference on the Sexual Victimization of Children, Children's Hospital National Medical Center, Washington, DC.

Browne, A. and D. Finkelhor (1986). "Impact of Child Sexual Abuse: A Review of the Research." *Psychological Bulletin* 99:66–77.

Budin, L.E. and C.F. Johnson (1989). "Sex Abuse Prevention Programs: Offenders' Attitudes about Their Efficacy." *Child Abuse and Neglect* 13(1):77–87.

Centers for Disease Control & Prevention [CDC] (1985, December). "Perspectives in Disease Prevention and Health Promotion." *Adolescent Sex Offenders* 34(49):738–741.

Chasan-Taber, L. and J. Tabachnick (1999). "Evaluation of a Child Sexual Abuse Prevention Program." *Sexual Abuse* 11:279–292.

Child Maltreatment (2002). "Reports from the States to the National Child Abuse and Neglect Data Systems." (National Statistics on Child Abuse and Neglect, 2004.) Retrieved on March 9, 2005, from http://www.acf.hhs.gov/programs/cb/publications/cm02/cm02.pdf

Child Maltreatment Report (2001). Washington, DC: Children's Bureau, Administration on Children, Youth and Families.

Clarke, R.V. (1995). "Situational Crime Prevention: Building a Safer Society: Strategic Approaches to Crime Prevention." In: M. Tonry and N. Morris (eds.), *Crime and Justice: A Review of Research* (vol. 29, pp. 91–150). Chicago, IL: University of Chicago Press.

Clarke, R. and R. Homel (1997). "A Revised Classification of Situational Crime Prevention Techniques." In: S.P. Lab (ed.), *Crime Prevention at a Crossroads* (pp. 17–30). Cincinnati, OH: Anderson Publishing Co. and Academy of Criminal Justice Sciences.

Cohen, L.J. and S. Roth (1987). "The Psychological Aftermath of Rape: Long-Term Effects and Individual Differences in Recovery." *Journal of Social and Clinical Psychology* 5:525–534.

Cohn, A.H. (1986). "Preventing Adults from Becoming Sexual Molesters." *Child Abuse and Neglect* 10:559–562.

Collings, S.J. (1995). "The Long-Term Effects of Contact and Noncontact Forms of Child Sexual Abuse in a Sample of University Men." *Child Abuse and Neglect* 19(1):1–6.

Conte, J.R. (1986). *A Look at Child Sexual Abuse*. Chicago: National Committee for Prevention of Child Abuse.

Conte, J., C. Rosen, L. Saperstein and R. Shermack (1985). "An Evaluation of a Program to Prevent the Sexual Victimization of Young Children." *Child Abuse and Neglect* 9(3):319–328.

Conte, J.R., S. Wolf and T. Smith (1989). "What Sexual Offenders Tell Us about Prevention Strategies." *Child Abuse and Neglect* 13:293–301.

Cornish, D.B. and R.V. Clarke (2003). "Opportunities, Precipitators, and Criminal Decisions: A Reply to Wortley's Critique of Situational Crime Prevention." *Crime Prevention Studies* 16:41–96.

Craissati, J. and A. Beech (2003). "A Review of Dynamic Variables and their Relationship to Risk Prediction in Sex Offenders." *Journal of Sexual Aggression* 9:41–55.

Creighton, S. and P. Noyes (1989). *Child Abuse Trends in England and Wales 1983–1987.* London: National Society for the Prevention of Cruelty to Children.

DeFrancis, V. (1969). *Protecting the Child Victim of Sex Crimes Committed by Adults.* Denver, CO: American Human Association.

Design Against Crime Report (April 2000). Retrieved on May 11, 2005, from http://www.shu.ac.uk/schools/cs/cri/adrc/dac/designagainstcrimereport.pdf#search='Design%20Against%20Crime%20Report,%202000'

Ellis, L. (1993). "Rape as a Biosocial Phenomenon." In: G. C. N. Hall, R. Hirschman, J. R Graham and M. S. Zaragozee (eds.), *Sexual Aggression: Issues in Etiology, Assessment and Treatment.* Bristol, PA: Taylor and Francis.

Fehrenbach, P.A., W. Smith, C. Monastersky, and R.W. Deisher (1986). "Adolescent Sexual Offenders: Offender and Offense Characteristics." *American Journal of Orthopsychiatry* 56(2):225–233.

Finkelhor, D. (1994). "The International Epidemiology of Child Sexual Abuse." *Child Abuse and Neglect* 18(5):409–417.

Finkelhor, D. (1992). "Child Sexual Abuse." In: J.M. Last and R.B. Wallace (eds.), *Public Health and Preventative Medicine* (pp. 1048–1051). Norwalk, CT: Appleton & Lange.

Finkelhor, D. (1990). "Early and Long-Term Effects of Child Sexual Abuse: An Update." *Professional Psychology: Research and Practice* 21(5):325–330.

Finkelhor, D. (1986). "Sexual Abuse: Beyond the Family Systems Approach." *Journal of Psychotherapy and the Family* 2(2):53–65.

Finkelhor, D. (1984). *Child Sexual Abuse: New Theory and Research.* New York: Free Press.

Finkelhor, D. (1982). "Sexual Abuse: A Sociological Perspective." *Child Abuse and Neglect* 6(1):95–102.

Finkelhor, D. (1980). "Sex Among Siblings: A Survey of the Prevalence, Variety, and Effects." *Archives of Sexual Behaviour* 9:171–194.

Finkelhor, D. and L. Baron (1986). "High-Risk Children." In: D. Finkelhor (ed.), *A Sourcebook on Child Sexual Abuse.* Beverly Hills, CA: Sage.

Finkelhor, D. and J. Dziuba-Leatherman (1995). "Victimization Prevention Programs: A National Survey of Children's Exposure and Reactions." *Child Abuse and Neglect* 19:129–139.

Finkelhor, D. and G.T. Hotaling (1984). "Sexual Abuse in the National Incidence Study of Child Abuse and Neglect: An Appraisal." *Child Abuse and Neglect* 8(1): 23–33.

Finkelhor, D., G.T. Hotaling, I.A. Lewis and C. Smith (1989). "Sexual Abuse and its Relationship to Later Sexual Satisfaction, Marital Status, Religion and Attitudes." *Journal of Interpersonal Violence* 4(4):379–399.

Florida Department of Corrections (n.d.). "2003–2004 Annual Report: Overview of Community Corrections." Retrieved April 1, 2005, from http://www.dc.state.fl.us/pub/annual/0304/stats/stat_cs.html

Gendreau, P., C. Goggin, F. Chanteloupe and D.A. Andrews (1992). *The Development of Clinical and Policy Guidelines for the Prediction of Criminal Behaviour in Criminal Justice Settings.* (Programs Branch User Report.) Ottawa, Ontario, Canada: Ministry of the Solicitor General of Canada.

Gray, A.S. and W.D. Pithers (1993). "Relapse Prevention with Sexually Aggressive Adolescents and Children: Expanding Treatment and Supervision." In: H. E. Barbaree, W. L. Marshall and S. M. Hudson (eds.), *The Juvenile Sex Offender* (pp. 289–319). New York: The Guilford Press.

Greenfeld, L. (1997). *Sex Offenses and Offenders: An Analysis of Data on Rape and Sexual Assault.* Washington, DC: U.S. Department of Justice, Bureau of Justice Statistics.

Gruber, K. and R. Jones (1983). "Identifying Determinants of Risk of Sexual Victimization of Youth." *Child Abuse and Neglect* 7:17–24.

Gutierrez-Lobos, K., R. Eher, C. Grunhut, B. Bankier, B. Schmidl-Mohl, S. Fruhwald (2001). "Violent Sex Offenders Lack Male Social Support." *International Journal of Offender Therapy and Comparative Criminology* 45(1):70–82.

Haley, J. (1980). *Leaving Home: The Therapy of Disturbed Young People.* New York: McGraw Hill.

Hamburg, M.A. (1998). "Youth Violence is a Public Health Concern." In: D.S. Elliott and B.A. Hamburg (eds.), *Violence in American Schools: A New Perspective* (pp. 31–54). New York: Cambridge University Press.

Hannem, S. and M. Petrunik (2004). "Canada's Circles of Support and Accountability: A Community Justice Initiative for High-Risk Sex Offenders." *Corrections Today* 98:101.

Hanson, K.R. and M.T. Bussiere (1998). "Predicting Relapse: A Meta-Analysis of Sexual Offender Recidivism Studies." *Journal of Consulting and Clinical Psychology* 66:348–362.

Hanson, R.K. and A. Harris (1998). *Dynamic Predictors of Sexual Recidivism.* Ottawa, Ontario, Canada: Department of the Solicitor General Canada.

Hanson, R.K. and A. Harris (1998). *The Sex Offender Need Assessment Rating (SONAR): A Method for Measuring Change in Risk Levels: User report 1998–2001.* Ottawa, Ontario, Canada: Department of the Solicitor General Canada.

Hazelwood, R. and J. Warren (1989). "The Serial Rapist: His Characteristics and Victims: Part 1." *FBI Law Enforcement Bulletin* 11–17.

Herman, D. (1990). "Commentary: Toward Some Operational Principles of Sustainable Development." *Ecological Economics* 2:1–6.

Herman, J.L. and L. Hirschman (1981). *Father Daughter Incest.* Cambridge, MA: Harvard University Press.

Hunter, M. (1990a). *Abused Boys: The Neglected Victims of Sexual Abuse.* New York: Ballantine Books.

Hunter, M. (1990b). *The Sexually Abused Male: Prevalence, Impact, and Treatment, vol. 1.* Lexington, MA: Lexington Books.

Jones, L. and D. Finkelhor (2004). *Explanations for the Decline in Child Sexual Abuse Cases.* (OJJDP Bulletin series.) Washington, DC: U.S. Department of Justice, Office of Justice Programs, Office of Juvenile Justice and Delinquency Prevention.

Kaufman, K., M. Barber, H. Mosher and M. Carter (2002). "Reconceptualizing Child Sexual Abuse as a Public Health Concern." In: P.A. Schewe (ed.), *Preventing Violence in Relationships: Interventions across the Life Span.* (pp. 27–54). Washington, DC: American Psychological Association.

Kaufman, K., E. Daleiden and D. Hilliker (1996). *Examining the Relationship between Child/Adolescent Abductions and Adolescent Sexual Offending.* Final Report to the Office of Juvenile Justice and Delinquency Prevention Grant #3-5411-OH-MC.

Kaufman, K., E. Daleiden and D. Hilliker (1994). *Assessing Adolescent Sexual Offenders: Putting the Pieces Together* (Final Report – Year 2).

Kaufman, K.L., D.R. Hilliker and E.L. Daleiden (1996). "Subgroup Differences in the Modus Operandi of Adolescent Sexual Offenders." *Child Maltreatment* 1:17–24.

Kaufman, K.L., D.R. Hilliker, P. Lathrop and E.L. Daleiden (1993). "Assessing Child Sexual Offenders' Modus Operandi: Accuracy in Self-Reported Use of Threats and Coercion." *Annals of Sex Research* 6:213–229.

Kaufman, K., D. Hilliker, P. Lathrop, E. Daleiden and L. Rudy (1996). "Sexual Offenders' Modus Operandi: A Comparison of Structured Interview and Questionnaire Approaches." *Journal of Interpersonal Violence* 11:19–34.

Kaufman, K., J. Holmberg, K. Orts, F. McGrady, A. Rotzien and E. Daleiden (1998). "Factors Influencing Sexual Offenders' Modus Operandi: An Examination of Victim-Offender Relatedness and Age." *Child Maltreatment* 3(4):349–361.

Kaufman, K., J. Morea, S. Matson, H. Mosher and S. Winchester (2004). *Ethnic Diversity in Sexual Offenders' Patterns of Perpetration: Prevention Implications.* Poster. Los Angeles, CA: Centers for Disease Control Annual Prevention Conference.

Kaufman, K.L., A.M. Wallace, C.F. Johnson and M.L. Reeder (1995). "Comparing Female and Male Perpetrators' Modus Operandi: Victims' Reports of Sexual Abuse." *Journal of Interpersonal Violence* 10(3):322–333.

Kercher, G.A. and M. McShane (1984). "Characterizing Child Sexual Abuse on the Basis of Multi Agency Sample." *Victimology: An International Journal* 9:364–382.

Ko, M. (2002). "Keeping Tabs on Dangerous Parolees." *Report/Newsmagazine* (Alberta edition), 29(3), pp. 27–29.

Kolko, D.J. (1988). "Educational Programs to Promote Awareness and Prevention of Child Sexual Victimization: A Review and Methodological Critique." *Clinical Psychology Review* 8:195–209.

Kolko, D.J., J.T. Moser and J. Hughes (1989). "Classroom Training in Sexual Victimization Awareness and Prevention Skills: An Extension of the Red Flag/Green Flag People Program." *Journal of Family Violence* 4:25–45.

Lang, R.A. and R.R. Frenzel (1988). "How Sex Offenders Lure Children." *Annals of Sex Research* 1:303–317.

Langmade, C.J. (1983). "The Impact of Pre- and Postpubertal Onset of Incest Experiences in Adult Women as Measured by Sex Anxiety, Sex Guilt, Sexual Satisfaction and Sexual Behavior." *Dissertation Abstracts International* 44:917B.

Laws, D.R. (2001). "Olfactory Aversion: Notes on Procedure with Speculations on its Mechanism of Effect." *Sexual Abuse: A Journal of Research and Treatment* 13:275–287.

Lawson, L. (2003). "Isolations, Gratification, Justification: Offenders' Explanations of Child Molesting." *Issues in Mental Health Nursing* 24:699–705.

Letourneau, E.J. (2002). "A Comparison of Objective Measures of Sexual Arousal and Interest: Visual Reaction Time and Penile Plethysmography." *Sexual Abuse: A Journal of Research and Treatment* 14:207–224.

Lisak, D. (1994). "The Psychological Impact of Sexual Abuse: Content Analysis of Interviews with Male Survivors." *Journal of Traumatic Stress* 7:525–548.

Lisak, D., and S. Roth (1990). "Motives and Psychodynamics of Self-Reported Rapists." *American Journal of Orthopsychiatry* 60(2):268–280.

Lonsway, K.A. and L.F. Fitzgerald (1994). "Rape Myths: In Review." *Psychology of Women Quarterly* 18:133–164.

Looman, J., J. Abracen, R. DiFazio and G. Maillet (2004). "Alcohol and Drug Abuse among Sexual and Nonsexual Offenders: Relationship to Intimacy Deficits and Coping Strategy." *Sexual Abuse: A Journal of Research and Treatment* 16:177–189.

Lutzker, J. and K. Bigelow (2001). *Reducing Child Maltreatment: A Guidebook for Parent Services*. New York: Guilford Publications.

Marshall, W.L. (1999). "Current Status of North American Assessment and Treatment Programs for Sexual Offenders." *Journal of Interpersonal Violence* 14:221–239.

McCloskey, L.A. and J. Bailey (2000). "The Intergenerational Transmission of Risk for Child Sexual Abuse." *Journal of Interpersonal Violence* 15:1019–1035.

McCormack, J., S.M. Hudson and T. Ward (2002). "Sexual Offenders' Perceptions of their Early Interpersonal Relationships: An Attachment Perspective." *Journal of Sex Research* 39(2):85–93.

McKibben, A., J. Proulx and P. Lussier (2001). "Sexual Aggressors' Perceptions of Effectiveness of Strategies to Cope with Negative Emotions and Deviant Sexual Fantasies." *Sexual Abuse: A Journal of Research and Treatment* 13:257–273.

Meiselman, K. (1978). *Incest*. San Francisco: Jossey-Bass.

Mercy, J.A. (1999). "Having New Eyes: Viewing Child Sexual Abuse as a Public Health Problem." *Sexual Abuse* 11(4):317–322.

Minuchen, S. (1974). *Families and Family Therapy*. Cambridge, MA: Harvard University Press.

National Clearinghouse of Child Abuse and Neglect Information (2004). "Long-Term Consequences of Child Abuse and Neglect." Washington, DC. Retrieved on April 21, 2005, from http://nccanch.acf.hhs.gov/pubs/factsheets/long_term_consequences.cfm.

Nellis, M. (2003). "News Media, Popular Culture and the Electronic Monitoring of Offenders in England and Wales." *The Howard Journal* 42:1–31.

Okami, P. and A. Goldberg (1992). "Personality Correlates of Pedophilia: Are They Reliable Indicators?" *Journal of Sex Research* 29(3):297–328.

Peugh, J. and S. Belenko (2001). "Examining the Substance Use Patterns and Treatment Needs of Incarcerated Sex Offenders." *Sexual Abuse: A Journal of Research and Treatment* 13:179–95.

Ray-Keil, A.A. (1988). *Intersect of Social Theory and Management Practice in Preventing Child Exploitation.* Seattle, WA: Committee for Children.

Reppucci, N.D. and J.J. Haugaard (1989). "Prevention of Child Sexual Abuse: Myth or Reality." *American Psychologist* 44:1266–1275.

Repucci, N.D., J.L. Woolard and C.S. Fried (1999). "Social, Community and Preventive Interventions." *Annual Review of Psychology* 50:387–418.

Rind, B. and P. Tromovich (1997). "A Meta-Analytic Review of Findings from National Samples on Psychological Correlates of Child Sexual Abuse." *The Journal of Sex Research* 31:237–255.

Rispens, J., A. Aleman and P.P. Goudena (1997). "Prevention of Child Sexual Abuse Victimization: A Meta-Analysis of School Programs." *Child Abuse and Neglect* 21:975–987.

Roth, S. and L. Lebowitz (1988). "The Experience of Sexual Trauma." *Journal of Traumatic Stress* 1(1):79–107.

Russell, D. E. (1995). "The Prevalence, Trauma and Sociocultural Causes of Incestuous Abuse of Females: A Human Rights Issue." In: R.J. Kleber and C.R. Figley (eds.), *Beyond Trauma: Cultural and Societal Dynamics* (pp. 171–186). (Plenum Series on Stress and Coping). New York: Plenum Press.

Satir, V. M. (1983). *Conjoint Family Therapy.* Palo Alto, CA: Science and Behavior Books.

Smallbone, S.W. and R.K. Wortley (2001). "Child Sexual Abuse: Offender Characteristics and Modus Operandi." *Trends and Issues in Crime and Criminal Justice Series* #193. Canberra, AUS: Australian Institute of Criminology.

Tabachnick, J., and E. Dawson (2000, November/December). "Stop It Now! A Four Year Program Evaluation, 1995–1999." *Offender Program Report*, 1(4):49.

Tan, G.G., M.P. Ray and R. Cate (1991). "Migrant Farm Child Abuse and Neglect within an Ecosystem Framework." *Family Relations* 40:84–90.

Thornton, D. (2002). "Constructing and Testing a Framework for Dynamic Risk Assessment." *Sexual Abuse: A Journal of Research and Treatment* 14:139–153.

Tutty, L.M. (2002). "Evaluating School Based Prevention Programs: The Basics." Retrieved on April 5, 2005, from http://www.ucalgary.ca/resolve/violence prevention/English/evaluate.htm

Tutty, L.M. (1994). "Developmental Issues in Young Children's Learning of Sexual Abuse Prevention Concepts." *Child Abuse and Neglect* 18(2):179–192.

Tutty, L.M. (1992). "The Ability of Elementary School Children to Learn Child Sexual Abuse Prevention Concepts." *Child Abuse and Neglect* 16(3):369–384.

Veneziano, C., L. Veneziano and S. LeGrand (2000). "The Relationship between Adolescent Sex Offender Behaviors and Victim Characteristics with Prior Victimization." *Journal of Interpersonal Violence* 15(4):363–374.

Walbek, N.H. and R.K. Seely (1999). "Sex Education and Sexually Explicit Media in Residential Treatment Programs for Sex Offenders." In: B.K. Schwartz (ed.),

The Sex Offender: Theoretical Advances, Treating Special Populations and Legal Developments (pp. 27-1–27-9). Kingston, NJ: Civic Research Institute.

Walker, C.E., B. Bonner and K. Kaufman (1988). *The Physically and Sexually Abused Child: Evaluation and Treatment.* Elmsford, NY: Pergamon Press.

Ward, T., S.M. Hudson and J. McCormack (1997). "Attachment Style, Intimacy Deficits and Sexual Offending." In: B.K. Schwartz and H.R. Cellini (eds.), *The Sex Offender: New Insights, Treatment Innovations and Legal Developments* (pp. 212–14). Kingston, NJ: Civic Research Institute.

Wortley, R. (2001). "A Classification of Techniques for Controlling Situational Precipitators of Crime." *Security Journal* 14:63–82.

Wurtele, S.K. (2002). "School-Based Child Sexual Abuse Prevention." In P.A. Schewe (ed.), *Preventing Violence in Relationships: Interventions Across the Life Span.* Washington, DC: American Psychological Association.

Wurtele, S.K. (1987). "School-Based Sexual Abuse Prevention Programs: A Review." *Child Abuse and Neglect* 11:483–495.

Wurtele, S.K. and C.L. Miller-Perrin (1992). *Preventing Child Sexual Abuse: Sharing the Responsibility.* Lincoln: University of Nebraska Press.

Yates, P. (2003). "Treatment of Adult Sexual Offenders: A Therapeutic Cognitive-Behavioural Model of Intervention." *Journal of Child Sexual Abuse* 12:195–232.

Convergence Settings for Non-predatory "Boy Lovers"

by

Pierre Tremblay

School of Criminology,
University of Montreal

Abstract: *Crime opportunity theorists argue that offender convergence settings rather than criminal groupings provide structure and continuity for offenders seeking like-minded offenders. A convenience sample of offenders violating age-of-consent prohibitions was asked about their interactions with other companions sharing similar dispositions. Self-reported interactions among this subset of sexual offenders were not conducted for the primary purpose of obtaining direct assistance (finding accomplices, for example). For socially isolated pedophiles, the search for "human companionship" was a salient concern, and Internet technology provided a virtual solution to the absence of physical convergence settings. Urban gay villages, on the other hand, have provided a convenient niche for male adolescent prostitution markets. Indeed, interactions among hebephiles interviewed in this study were mainly steered or instigated by male adolescent hustlers searching for providers. In both cases opportunities for interactions among age-of-consent offenders have expanded, and this could partly explain the aggregate increase in reported sex offences. Viewing sex offenders as "social isolates" is thus misleading. The paper argues instead that these convergence settings are best understood as social arrangements originating in a cultural emphasis on self-fulfillment and authenticity.*

INTRODUCTION

West has observed "that an extraordinary upsurge of awareness of sexual abuse of children has occurred in recent years, aided by media presentations of adult recollections of childhood experiences of molestation." (West, 1987). Lieb, Quinsey and Berliner (1998) have documented the "intense legislation and public attention on sex offenders" of the 1990s and the somewhat chilling diffusion in America, as well as in Europe, of both registration and community notification statutes and the increased severity of criminal sentences meted out. It is quite tempting to argue that this upward trend in age-of-consent offences is primarily triggered by improved social support for complaining victims and greater readiness on the part of the police to prosecute (West, 1994). The feminist movement has given a powerful impetus to the current awareness of sexual abuse of children that has occurred in recent years, and to the moral crusades against juvenile prostitution, pornography and child abuse (Okami, 1994). It seems unlikely that this upsurge in public sensitivity would have maintained its momentum without an actual increase in the rate of age-of-consent offences. But why the increase?

Robert Merton's seminal "Social Structure and Anomie" paper (1938) argued that societies or social groups in which individual success is perceived as the ultimate measure of self-worth are more likely to experience higher aggregate levels of property or market crimes (Rosenfeld and Messner, 1998). Merton's basic insight – the "motivational insight" – is that "structural and cultural conditions can set into motion causal processes that motivate members of particular groups or strata to disproportionately engage in criminal behavior" (Chamlin and Cochran, 1997). Modern culture, however, does not simply emphasize monetary success but also, more generally, self-fulfillment. Charles Taylor (1991) suggests that terms like "narcissism," "hedonism," "moral laxism" do not adequately capture "that there is a powerful moral ideal at work here, however debased and travestied its expression might be. The moral ideal behind self-fulfillment is that of being true to oneself" (Taylor, 1991). Trying to explain this moral ideal as simply an expression of self-indulgence is a serious mistake. "The point is that today many people feel *called* to be who they are, feel they ought to do this, and feel their lives would be somehow wasted or unfulfilled if they didn't do it" (*Ibid.*, p. 17). A related theme is that we have come to think of ourselves as beings with "inner depths." "Being true to oneself" is thus not given but requires effort, time, aptitudes as well as a discovery process: "Being true to myself means being true to my own originality, and that is something only I can articulate and discover. In articulating it, I am also defining myself. I am realizing a potentiality that is properly my own. This is the background that gives moral force to the culture of authenticity, including its most degraded, absurd or trivialized forms" (*Ibid.*, p. 29). A third theme is the modern preoccupation that "equal chances allow everyone to develop their own identity, which includes the universal recognition of difference, in whatever modes this is relevant to identity, be it gender, racial, cultural, or to do with sexual orientation" (*Ibid.*, p. 50). The ethics of authenticity has shaped the politics of equal recognition and its implicit assumption that "denied recognition of individual differences can be a form of oppression." It has also increased the perceived seriousness of those offences that could endanger the process by which individuals develop their identity. "Love relationships are not important just because of the general emphasis in modern culture on the fulfillment of ordinary life. They are also crucial because they are the crucibles of inwardly generated identity" (*Ibid.*, p. 49). An attractive feature of this cultural analysis is that it could explain both the current moral and legal crusade against "sexual exploitation of children and adolescents" *and* the concurrent upsurge in the proportion of eligible adults (those attracted to prepubescent or young adolescents) willing or "morally compelled" to actualize their "originality" and express "who" and "what" they are.

The problem, however, is to document how this cultural emphasis on self-worth shapes the behavior of sex offenders. One possibility is that it increases the motivation of such offenders to seek out each other for purposes of mutual assistance and recognition. In his recent review of the co-offending literature, Marcus Felson (2003) recognizes that "crime rates would dwindle if offenders were unable to assist one another," but he suggests that settings rather than criminal groups bring structure, predictability and continuity to offenders' individual efforts to find suitable partners and mentors for their criminal activities. The basic argument is that criminal groupings lack structure or stability for various reasons: criminal careers are either short or subject to voluntary or forceful interruptions; criminal markets provide entrepreneurial opportunities but offer little organizational capacity or stability (Reuter, 1983); and finally, there is little evidence that gangs or networks of offenders show much interest in regulating how exactly individual members go about finding or selecting other offenders as suitable companions in crime (Felson, 2003; Klein, 1995). Yet co-offending patterns are pervasive, and even lone or solo offenders may depend on other offenders for commitment, direction and assistance before or after the offense. Felson's suggestion is that offender convergence settings (street corners, bars, restaurants, parks, school premises, and so on) "provide structure and continuity in the face of individual, group or network instabilities." These settings are:

- *Bounded:* Offenders converge on specific locations rather than areas: even in a "tough neighborhood" there are substantial differences in criminal rates between and within single blocks. Even within criminogenic work settings (garages, scrap yards or bars for example), there are wide disparities in criminal involvement across establishments. Moreover, the same physical location can harbor different behavior settings (a street corner may become an offender convergence setting but only after 9:00 pm).

- *Informal:* Finding a suitable companion requires time to discover affinities, cultivate friendship and trust. Settings where apparent "inaction" or "idleness" are the norm are well suited for "assembling potential co-offenders and getting them ready for criminal action" or exchanges without outside interference.

- *Recurrent:* They persist even if the "roster of participants changes entirely," and allow likely offenders to locate new faces, compare crime scripts, and identify obsolete apprehension avoidance techniques, without outside interference.

- *Safe:* Situational prevention schemes typically target hot spots, which are locations that provide offenders with a large supply of suitable targets (crime attractors). But the accomplice regeneration process requires safe spots, which are settings where offenders meet before and after their illegal activities and screen each other (the "accomplice regeneration process"). In any given locality, there are many settings that may attract offenders, but only a few convergence settings are required for offenders who wish to "meet comfortably."

Analyzing more closely how offenders, even those who commit their crimes without accomplices, go about creating or joining such convergence settings, could provide a promising research strategy for a more precise understanding of how delinquent or deviant subcultures emerge and persist. In this paper I focus on non-predatory offenders who violate age-of-consent prohibitions.[1] Such offenders now represent a large proportion of

incarcerated offenders.[2] I start with offenders who are compellingly attracted to pre-adolescents. Very few males in any given locality or social
group have such an attraction. They are therefore unlikely to experience
much success in locating suitable convergence settings. The first section
describes an innovative solution to this problem. I then examine like-
minded offenders who are attracted to older male adolescents. For them,
access to targets is much easier. But since their main goal is to develop
strong ties with adolescents, how is it that they should develop extensive
ties with other "boy lovers"?

DATA

The paper relies on a prior exploratory investigation[3] in the course of
which I obtained permission from Quebec's federal correctional authorities
to interview inmates that the supervising clinical staff believed to have
been in interaction with other sex offenders prior to their current incarceration. Some of them were interviewed at a regional reception centre, and
others were interviewed in a penitentiary where sex offenders could undergo aversive therapy. I approached a community relapse-prevention
group for sex offenders located in Montreal (L'Amorce) and obtained from
the psychologists supervising this self-help group permission to interview
some of its members. In the process I agreed to join their "administrative
board." As it happened, all of the 17 male offenders interviewed were
unattached singles[4] attracted to boys rather than to girls; some qualified
as pedophiles but most were attracted to adolescents; all subjects were
viewed as non-violent[5] and none of the youths were kin related. All were
repeat offenders but only one had been seriously involved in other kinds
of criminal activities. Only five subjects indicated extensive involvement
with other age-of-consent offenders prior to their incarceration or their
participation in community therapeutic groups. Of course, the purpose of
interviewing this convenience sample of sex offenders was not to derive
any kind of empirical generalizations about such individuals, but rather to
elicit detailed information about the process by which offenders go about
finding other offenders for the purpose of mutual assistance. Mutual assistance may be defined in restrictive terms (the utilitarian search for accomplices) or in general terms (the symbolic search for like-minded
companionship). Mutual assistance should be a salient concern for individuals engaged in the pursuit of highly ostracized illegal activities.[6]

"FEELING LIKE AN ISLAND":
SEARCHING FOR HAVENS

One of the most articulate subjects in the sample was located through indirect referral. As I interviewed one subject[7] in a correctional reception centre, he mentioned having met a fellow inmate who he believed "would be of interest for the research," but who recently had been transferred elsewhere. The first subject agreed that I could mention his name if I managed to interview the former fellow inmate. I then located the latter's institutional whereabouts, told him I had been referred to him, and obtained his consent for an interview. His past record of convictions indicated a mix of property and sexual offences. In 1987, he was working (as a cook) in a hunting resort. The place shut down temporarily because the owner had had a heart attack. The resort's pilot asked him to become the family cook until the resort opened up again. He was also asked to do a bit of administrative work and baby-sit. They had three children, a daughter and two sons, a 12 year old and a 7 year old. The older son was often away and he took care mostly of the younger boy.

> He was not of an age I was predominately attracted to. It was somebody under my normal age – namely 9 to 11. I ended up fondling the young boy. When I realized what I was doing, I knew, if I stayed, it would continue. So I ran with the family's car. I was arrested the same day. The police pulled my file, got suspicious and [I] was prosecuted for 3 charges of sexual contacts. I was sentenced to 7 months in prison.

A number of years later, he ended up working in a Montreal hospital. Because of his skills in teaching sign language, and his religious outlook, he met the secretary of the church he belonged to. The secretary developed a fondness for him. She called him one day and said that a friend of hers needed to go Christmas shopping and asked if he could go to the movie with her son. He did. Progressively the relationship between the mother of the boy and himself developed.

> The mother developed a crush on me. She was looking for an instant-daddy. Because my apartment had been damaged, she offered for me to stay at her place for a couple of days and then asked me to stay longer. So I agreed. A couple of weeks later the boy and I had gotten filthy dirty playing football. I was in the bathtub. The mother knocked on the door, asked me to draw the curtain and put her boy in the bathtub. That did it. The boy, again, was 7 and under my normal age. Sexual contacts and oral sex occurred five or six times.

The child was not knowledgeable but aggressive. I am not justifying myself, just describing the events; anything I did to him, he wanted to do the same to me. Two days before I left, his mother had left the house early. I waited for the boy to get dressed. It was the kind of boy who hates getting dressed. Instead he was jumping on the bed saying "Come lick on this. Come on." That's when I decided to leave. Two days later I took the mother to work and the kid to school. Just before driving him to school, I took pictures of him undressed. I left with the family car and kept it. I got arrested two months later in another province. The car had been reported stolen.

The conviction record of the subject presents a number of characteristics. First, the record shows a continuous fixed deviant inclination, but with nonetheless long spells of abstinence. Second, it shows a combination of property and sex charges that should not be interpreted as an indication of versatility or indiscriminate disposition to commit various crimes. His "joy riding" offences were anything but joyful. Indeed they were indicative of what Lemert (1967:133) described as "the psychic surrender which precedes or attends an almost casual entry into legal custody." Third, the record shows an overall history of frequent changes in residence and jobs. "I am not proud of what I am but I have come to accept it. If I could be born again, I would probably not choose this special attraction. I have *not* come to the conclusion that I am okay and that the rest of society is screwed up but rather that I was not born at the proper time and place." What does not appear in his record, and what the subject will probably not wish to disclose in therapy, is the nature of his extensive interactions with other age-of-consent violators.

He realized that he belonged to a very small minority, but only in the last couple of years before his current arrest and conviction did he realize that it was reachable minority: "I was getting to the point where I was feeling so much like an island that I needed, above anything else, to touch base."[8] Locating this reachable minority happened by chance and not by searching for pornography sites on the Web:

> You hear stories about porno out on the Net so I went searching, very unsuccessfully as it turned out. About a year later, however, I stumbled on what I was looking for completely by accident. I was searching, for purely professional reasons, for children's clothing sites. But one link led to another and as I was going through the links, one of them brought me to *Free Spirits*.

The discovery was eventful: "When I found that link ... it was like ... bang! I recall the day, it was a Saturday." At first he stayed away from the chat rooms and was more attracted by the discussion forums. He was particularly attracted to one of *Free Spirits'* sites, CBLF – the *Christian Boy Lover Forum* – partly because of his strong religious beliefs (although raised as a Catholic in New Brunswick, he now patronizes Anglican churches). "CBLF was a general discussion support group with a religious flavor, whereas boy chat forums are more of the "hey guys, turn to Fox channel for quite a show" variety.

After a year or so, and as he got more and more involved in the chat rooms he asked to become a member of Montreal's Ganymède collective: "I believed I would get arrested but I did it anyway. I was willing to take the risk if I could meet other people whom I could talk with." As it turned out the meeting took place "in a coffee shop by the Basilica in the Old Montreal area, a Friday afternoon in late August." The Ganymède representative was mainly interested in assessing "if my pedophilia attraction was for real."

> Their other concern was to avoid recruiting "radicals." The Montreal group does not advocate physical contact . . . they encourage you to adopt instead a mentoring position. They do not officially encourage you to cross the line. If one is considered to be a militant, he will not be allowed in the group. The group is low profile. It has very strict rules, does not allow trading of pornography, it is only a group of like-minded people that provide mutual support. Within the group, on the other hand you are allowed to be completely yourself. It was a major discovery. The founders of the Ganymède group are three people who met on line. They realized that they were in the same city, founded the group and now it has 50 or 60 members. On average, group members get together once a week for the supper. About 10 to 20 persons attend any given get-together, once a week in the home of one or the other of the founders. At the first meeting, group members presented themselves by their Internet nicknames. I then realized I was meeting the people I had been exchanging with for so long.

As he became part of the group, he chose another Web name and this time kept it. Members attending the weekly get-together were both English and French. Most (about 60%) of the members had a prior record of some sort. "I even met a fellow that had the same case manager in an Ontario prison as I had."

> Within the group the age range of attraction is wide and we joked about the fact that sometimes at the get-togethers the "over-the-hillers" will regroup in one corner of the room, and the "baby rapists" congregate in another corner. But on other occasions members will

divide themselves into French and English-speaking cliques. Whatever the internal in-fighting and individual differences, there is a very strong camaraderie among all members. One particular fellow, a former high school teacher who now works as a free-lance technical writer, got in trouble. He was under police surveillance and had his computer confiscated. Without his computer he couldn't work. So the members arranged that a new computer was brought at his place so that he could continue to work. That sort of thing.

As he got involved in the group, he realized that there were actually two distinct pedophile support groups localized in Montreal: those that belonged to the Ganymède group, and those that belonged to the *Free Spirits* group.

One of the founders of *Free Spirits*, the network that loans sites to all major pedophile support groups (Danish, German, Netherlands), came to Montreal a year and a half ago, after he had been exposed as a pedophile by a reporter who successfully managed a kind of "journalistic sting operation." He used to live in New York, but now lives in Montreal, and moved part of his business activities as well. He is extremely knowledgeable with computers and a certified Microsoft engineer. His computer business is perfectly legal and quite successful. The only thing is that there was the unwritten rule that to work for this company you had to be a member of a pedophile support group.

The *Free Spirits* Internet network that organizes pedophile support groups is itself a non-profit organization. It is self-supporting through the voluntary contributions of its members. This is therefore not a commercial or profit-oriented enterprise. But such a network could not survive long if those who operated and maintained it did not possess the required computer and management expertise and could not rely on the dedication of a large number of individuals.

One employee of the founder's company is a computer programmer by profession; he does technical stuff and is in charge of the maintenance of the whole Free Spirits network. Another member of the Ganymède group is a college teacher and is the group's security expert. When you join the group, one member will come to your place and make the computer safe, especially if you had been trading before. If you have a collection, another member will come over and encrypt the data.

At the time of this arrest, the subject had a 60-megabit collection of pictures. "The detective sat down at my computer. He asked my permission to go into it. I gave him the permission. He never found it. I doubt that most law-enforcement agencies are updated on current encryption programs." Pedophiles' interest in pornography takes many forms. "I, for example, wasn't interested in commercial pornography sites. As I began surfing on the net, at the very beginning, way before learning about *Free Spirits*, I had found lots of pornography sites, but they were always asking me for my credit card, and there was no way I was going to give that and not because I could be traced, but because I am a miser." Moreover much of the pornographic material available on the web was not viewed as desirable. "For a long time the pictures were: a) either low quality, very old black and white pictures – much of it was Russian stuff; and b) more important, if it doesn't look convincing enough that everyone is really enjoying what they are doing, then it didn't interest me and is not worth collecting." The really interesting pictures were not found in the commercial sites but in the newsgroups:

> About 3 or 4 years ago there emerged this fellow who put out multiple series of pictures of the same boy. They were called the *Nathans* or the Nathan collection. This is a collection of 300 pictures of a boy named Nathan. The pictures are spread over a 3 or 4-year period (it begins when Nathan was around 9 and ends when he was 13). The first 60 or 70 pictures start with Nathan fully clothed. In fact, only 20 to 25 pictures portray actual sexual contact scenes. These pictures are extremely rare, hard to find and well guarded.

What made the Nathan series so attractive was that: (i) it was a collection – much like a stamp collection; (ii) it described the evolution of a personal on-going relationship between the photographer and the subject; (iii) the relationship appeared convincingly to be consensual (no violence and no commercial undertone); and iv) collectors had to sort out the pictures in their chronological order. "A big part of the attraction for a pedophile is the ability to establish an enduring one-to-one relationship with a boy. This is may be the reason for the success of the Nathan collection." At the same time, the search for such collections was becoming more and more hazardous: "Before you could find 150 pictures each day from a newsgroup site. Now out of 300 persons posting, 250 of them are hackers, vigilantes or spammers. So now, if you want to download the pictures, you first need to scan the file with a viewer program, and delete the hidden program before downloading." It is also noteworthy that what is perceived by pedophiles as "attractive" is not necessarily "hard core pornography":

There is a TV show on Fox, a sitcom called *"Malcolm in the Middle."* It's about a family that has four sons. What is peculiar of this particular sitcom is that in almost every episode it shows at least one of the boys in under-wear. In the opening episode, two of the boys wrestled on the floor in underwear for about five minutes! When it made its' debut, on Sunday night, all the lines on the Free Spirit network went red hot. "Turn on this! Turn on this!" It got so wild too that even in the Montreal group there was a small clique of people who got together each Sunday night to watch this half-hour TV show. We were wondering which of the three boys would be in his underwear this time. People could talk about the show endlessly throughout the evening.

Much of the work involved in managing the *Free Spirits* network is to ensure that what occurs within the confines of the network remains perfectly legal. This requires extensive self-policing: "The way *Free Spirits* is built allows those who manage it to know exactly who comes into the site, who gets out, where you go and what you post. They have absolutely no qualms to report you to the Internet provider if you engage in illegal trading within the network and ask the provider to have your connection cut off." In any case, illegal operations occur outside the Free Spirits site per se, for example, in the newsgroups such as "alt.pretty boy" or "alt.john." These sites are not under the "jurisdiction" of *Free Spirits*. Similarly, when two individuals meet in a *Free Spirit* discussion or chat forum, what they do after they have left the site is not a matter of concern for the FS webmaster. This overall *Free Spirits* policy is also the policy of the local Montreal Ganymède group. Neither *Free Spirits* nor Ganymède advocate "any physical contact." They welcome those who are attracted to boys and young adolescents, but not those who openly act out their attractions.

> When the particular relationship – the one that got me arrested and convicted – began, I did not advertise to the other group members, although I had mentioned it privately to two other members. But I wasn't allowed to talk about it officially or at the weekly meetings. It's a "you don't tell, and we won't ask" kind of policy. Similarly members can privately show each other collections but not to the whole group. Moreover they are not allowed to trade. In one case we all knew that one of the members had an affair with a 13–14 year old boy but it was all right because it was presented as purely platonic. Very unwisely, this particular gentleman whose relationship with the boy had become in fact quite "physical," took a picture of the boy completely undressed in a very seductive pose and used the

picture to make a Christmas card. Unfortunately, he not only sent the card to a few of his personal friends among the group members but also, inadvertently to all members of the group. As much as the people enjoyed the picture privately, officially they were outraged and indignant – you know what I mean.

Beyond the weekly get-together, special events brought about international reunions.

For the Millennium New Year's party, sixty people came to Montreal from around the world. Asia and Africa were the only continents not represented. One fellow, originally from South America but who now lives in the United States, came up to Montreal with other fellows from Texas and New York. One came from France as he was visiting a friend who lived in Quebec City. Another person was from Australia. The *Christian Boy Lover Forum* (CBLF) also meets once a year, alternatively in Montreal and Washington, because one of the founders of CBLF lives in Washington and the other in Montreal. The Montreal group contributed financially to help out Sharp's costly challenge of the current Canadian child pornography laws and invited him over to give a talk. The talk was quite informative, although he would not be the kind of fellow I would like to include in my personal circle of friends. We also had people from the radical *North American Man-Boy Love Association* (NAMBLA) come over. *Free Spirits* and NAMBLA are two completely different organizations. *Free Spirits* has a low-key outlook and has more affinity with the Danish pedophile support group than with NAMBLA. In fact one of the members of the Danish pedophile support group now lives in Montreal and is also part of the Ganymède collective. NAMBLA representatives were interested in merging the two organizations because of *Free Spirits'* computer expertise and skill in managing web sites. The offer was turned down. NAMBLA's inefficiency in updating on a regular basis their own site is quite obvious you know.

* * *

Web sites such as Free Spirits can be viewed as "convergence settings" in the sense that they provide structure and continuity in face of any given individual, group or network instabilities. Virtual sites have the same attributes as the physical locations contemplated by Felson (2003): they are bounded sites, providing safe, recurrent and informal opportunities for interaction and mutual screening among like-minded offenders. As Felson observed, the number of virtual sites designed for offender convergence is much smaller than those designed from "action" or access to targets.

Thus, crime prevention strategies that attempt to "modify or remove settings so that offenders have trouble finding one another will reduce a wider range of crime problems even though they act upon a smaller number of settings" than conventional crime prevention programs focused on disrupting access to crime targets (Felson, 2003). Identifying convergence settings, on the other hand, does not imply that groups or networks of offenders are unimportant. Indeed, as this example indicates, groups (such as NAMBLA or Ganymède), or networks (such as chat or newsroom participants) are very much active in managing, owning or otherwise inhabiting convergence settings themselves. Nonetheless, continuity (rather than structure) is best viewed as a property of the setting itself rather than as attribute of the groups or networks that occupy it. It is also clear that virtual convergence settings provide a screening mechanism for setting up a variety of private or indoor settings where offenders can actually meet and engage in mutual assistance. At the same time, a special analytical status should be given to those individuals or groups that create, own or otherwise manage convergence settings (such as the Free Spirit site): these groups do not simply join a pre-existing deviant subculture, they actively instigate it.

SEARCHING FOR SUGARS

Whereas pedophiles attracted to prepubescents or pre-adolescents require access to tightly controlled environments (families, schools, summer camps) or generally well-monitored targets (the whereabouts of children are much more controlled in parks, swimming pools, and streets than those of adolescents), pederasts attracted to male adolescents can blend more easily in the urban landscape. But it is a mistake to assume that hebephiles are especially interested in establishing links with like-minded individuals. As one subject observed:

> Of course you could recognize the adults who were looking for youngsters. I myself was not interested in talking to them. Sometimes a guy came to me saying, "There aren't too many people here today," or "They are too young for my taste." But I didn't like to share the youngsters . . . they were mine. Some like to have group sex but not me.

Moreover, interacting with other co-participants increases visibility: "I thought it was dangerous and that I would attract trouble if I interacted too much with the other guys. It wasn't like I was advertising my sexual preferences. Nobody knew about it, except my wife." Their state of mind may also not be conducive for adult interactions: "When I was with a 13 year old boy, I myself talked like a 13 year old kid." Nonetheless, the subject did get to know one market acquaintance, but they did not "cruise together" partly for the above reasons, partly because they were not attracted to the same age group. Another acquaintance also provided him with the use of his apartment, a useful arrangement because it was less expensive than tourist rooms. Nonetheless, he did not wish to be socially integrated in the pedophile milieu. Moreover he did not view himself as homosexual or belonging to the gay community.

Hebephiles occasionally seek out lads, they do not have to invest much time and energy in doing so because the market is there to take care of them and of their money. In a market, sellers (hustlers) are actively engaged in the business of collecting as many customers as possible, and of persuading them to stay on as regular customers or even as privileged "providers." Although M. was mainly attracted to 13- to 15-year-old adolescents, he could also be induced to accept younger boys. "That particular time, I hadn't found anybody appropriate so when this 11 year old boy approached me, I said yes. He was very experienced. We went in a tourist room and the boy was constantly asking if I felt good . . . he was totally devoted to the task of satisfying me." Another subject – Nicolas – provides a detailed account of the male juvenile prostitution market that emerged with the development of the gay village in Montreal. He was 41 at the time of the interview, so his prostitution years (from 12 to 18) covered mainly the 1970s. As he stopped working as a male prostitute, he shifted to the other side of the market and became a very good customer for young adolescents. Indeed the reason why he went to prison – hold-ups in convenience stores – was that he used the money specifically to pay for adolescent prostitutes.[9] A 16-year-old lad arranged the subject's entry into prostitution at age 12.

> At the time, I was hanging around in the Longueuil metro station and I met an older guy – he was about 16 years old – who asked if I wanted to make some easy cash. I asked him if it was dirty money and he said no and that it was simply to go with men and to let them do what they wanted for a half-hour and that I could make $30 or $40. I accepted. My friend showed me the tearoom trade that was going on in a downtown shopping centre – the Complex Desjardins – and said he was working with an escort agency with

deluxe clients. He referred me to the agency and I started working for them at 13. I worked there for 3 years and half. At the beginning I received $50 for a half-an-hour and the agency kept $100. When I was 15, I negotiated a better deal – $70 to $80 for me and the rest for the agency. I never met the agency owner, just the chauffeurs. They picked me up in a limousine and brought me to a fancy motel – the Canada Motel on Taschereau Boulevard. The client paid the agency $150 as well as the motel bill. Sometimes they would bring two or four lads in the same limousine. The chauffeur would park alongside the motel and call the room to say to the client that the half-hour was over. I went with all kinds of clients. Some were physically handicapped, others wanted me to be whipped or to whip me. I had said to the agency that I didn't want to be sodomized. Other lads agreed to do it, but I didn't. Clients who wanted to have anal sex said so and were provided only with those lads that agreed to that.

When Nicolas – the subject's street name – reached 16, he quit the agency for a number of reasons: (i) "If you worked with the agency you were not allowed to have other clients on the side (even if most of us in the agency occasionally violated the rules) and the chauffeurs would interrogate us about whether or not we respected the rules"; (ii) "If I refused to work one night, the sanction was that they didn't give me clients for two or three days"; (iii) "I wasn't making enough money and wasn't free enough." So Nicholas was in the street prostitution scene from 16 to 18 in the gay village in Montreal, on the street corner of Champlain and Alexandre de Sève. "All the lads were homosexual, whereas many of those who were in the agency had girlfriends and were basically heterosexuals moonlighting for the money. Another difference is that we were all on drugs. I mainly sniffed cocaine but others were junkies – shooting themselves with heroine. I also started dancing in the gay clubs (3 months at 16, 3 months at 17)." He quit his extensive involvement in prostitution at 18, mainly because he was sent to prison for 2 years. When he got out of prison, he was 20 years old and quit the prostitution scene, even though, "if you look good there is still a market for prostitutes up to 25 years old." He realized, however, that getting clients was becoming more difficult ("sometimes I had to wait an hour before getting a client").

As he stopped earning his life as a street prostitute or a dancer, he "shifted around" and started living the high life. His idea of the high life was to start the evening by committing a hold-up (in convenience stores), come back to his place, take a shower, put on his jewels, go to the gay village, pick up a lad, bring him to a gay restaurant and pay him a nice dinner and a bottle of wine, and then start making his rounds.

> I liked to flash. Without cash I was nothing. With the cash I was "Nicholas," the guy everyone loved and greeted. All the lads were crazy about me because I paid so well and treated them like the old friends they were in fact. I started by going to a club – the *Track* – from 10 till midnight. Then we would go to *Adonis* from midnight to one clock and then close the night at *Le Taboo*, up to three. I did this over and over again and liked to hang out in the same clubs where people came to know me. A night would cost me $500, and on the weekends around $1,000 paying the lads, the dancers and the coke. I must have committed over 200 hold-ups over the years to finance this life style. For a while I also started selling coke for the bikers. The village was a good place to sell because coke has such a powerful sexual effect.

Finding new hustlers on the scene was not difficult:

> To find the new lads, I went strolling into the St-Laurent and Ste Catherine Amusement Arcades. That's where lads start their prostitution career. It's the best place to find the new ones. Owners were not interested in controlling the traffic because these youngsters were good clients and brought new clients. One owner tried to control the prostitution market but the lads – Blacks, Chinese, Whites – were working for an agency. So two Chinese strong-arm men went to see the owner and simply said that his property would burn if he didn't mind his own business.

Nicolas never got arrested, either as a prostitute or as a client, mainly because he limited the search within the geographical and social boundaries of the gay community and village, although he sometimes recruited young-sters elsewhere. Although currently treated as a "sex offender" at Pinel Institute, he comments:

> I never realized until recently that I had a problem with adolescents. Indeed when they told me I was a "sex deviant." . . . they said I have a sickness . . . yes . . . let me see, the term they used I think was hebephile. I didn't know what they were talking about because in the gay community it is so natural to seek sexual relationships with lads under 18.

Although the prostitution market is organized in such a way as to ensure that entry and exit of sellers and buyers are furtive and quick, often depending on a series of phone or face-to-face contacts at transfer points

(Felson, 1998), cliques do emerge. But these cliques are mainly adolescent-driven and gather around "sugars" or "providers."

> B was a long time friend. He had presented me to C a while back and I knew who he was. But I had not established any particular tie with him. One night, B comes over to my place and starts rambling about the incredible night he had spent with a lad and the marvel of the lad. I had seen him around and the next day I met him at the downtown shopping centre – Complex Desjardins – a favorite meeting ground. So I talk to him and we chat in a café. As we were talking, C comes over. The boy presents me to him, "This is C. This is my man!" So I say, "Congratulations!" C invites us to his place, so I got to know his whole crew of boys. I got to know C more intimately. He knew a lot of boy lovers, but mainly through his lads. He mentioned that a friend of his talked to him about NAMBLA and that he had spent a weekend in the United States at one of their meetings. I went a couple of times with him at the Fullum Street public swimming pool. There he presented me to D, who also knew many of the boys. The lads all knew each other. One boy, in particular, was very interesting for me. We started a relationship. It turned out that he was also a very disorganized fellow, constantly running away from his home or from elsewhere. He also was constantly hustling. So I told him that I didn't want to be simply one of his customers. In fact, I didn't want to be his favorite customer. I was looking for a one-on-one relationship, and I wanted him to love me for my blue eyes only. A guy has a right to have some standards, some kind of ideal. So we broke off and I started dating another of C's lads. But again, the relationship proved unsuccessful. C was a special guy. He didn't mind me dating his crowd. In fact he sort of enjoyed it. "Come and meet them," he would say, "It's fine with me." All the boys knew each other and most of them were into hustling. Basically, they recruited themselves you know. And C was the provider. He was the provider for the whole crew. His place was like a hotel with the lads coming and going. He provided them with hash, with food, with money. His place was their place. He was their provider, their "man." But they were all hustling on their own and C did not receive any tangible benefits from it. So I went from one lad to another. I dated five of C's crew before I started getting fed up with this hustling scene. But it was too late. What was bound to happen, did in fact happen. One of the boys got into trouble, and talked about his sexual relationship with C, me and the others. The police got to know of the lad's friends and we all, except D,[10] got arrested and convicted. The media had their day.

Interactions among hebephiles are largely mediated or organized by the adolescents themselves. They recruit themselves more than they are recruited by the provider. Indeed, providers are elected to that position and encouraged to find other providers as membership in the clique changes or increases. As cliques gather around providers, the odds of arrest, however, also increase. Another subject opened a tattoo shop in eastern downtown Montreal. At the time he had been convicted twice, but only for selling hashish and pot. His two children had turned 18 and were independent. He had divorced his wife a long time ago (she had left with a friend of his). He had another stable relationship for 10 years with another woman, but that was finished. He had always worked: first as a bouncer in the clubs and then as an owner of a poolroom for a number of years.

> Of course, with this kind of business (the tattoo shop), a lot of the customers were boys coming from Mont St-Antoine and Cartier (two juvenile correctional institutions). They had made their own tattoos and of course they did it all wrong. So they came to see me so that I could repair their skin. They looked at me with this look in their eyes and ask if I could fix it with my dick, so what is a fellow to do? The police say it's prostitution, but it isn't. I'll be frank. I love pot, I love hash. I've been stoned since the mid-1970s. The police say I provide the lads with hash in exchange of sex. But I offer a smoke to all of my friends, whether or not I have sex with them. This ain't prostitution. And anyways I am not a paedophile, I just like young lads, you know, 14, 15, 16 years. A friend of mine, he liked them younger and would go to the Arcades. I didn't need to go on Champlain Street. There was always a crowd at my place, two lads in the living room, another in the bedroom. They wanted to be there, I wasn't forcing anybody; they just liked hanging around. We simply had fun. You know how I got this conviction? A lad comes to my shop with his 13 year-old brother. They just want to crash and find a place to sleep. So we go to my place. The younger boy likes me and needs affection; he needs a sugar daddy. This boy was doing prostitution for the past 3 years. He says to me, "If I could have a father, I would like him to be like you," and so on. So the relationship developed for a year or so, he was always around my place. I love the boy. But I have a record. All these juvenile delinquents hang around my shop so the police are after my number. The boy comes from a rotten family and has the social workers on his back. Finally the cops pinch him with a stolen motorcycle and put pressure on him: "You file a complaint against him, or else it's the ticket for the Cartier detention center." There was this educator that the boy liked, and he tries to tell her about our relationship, hoping that she'll be able to stop the pressure. But she uses that to lay a formal complaint against me. Basically they cracked him. What could one expect? He's a young boy. Look, at the courthouse, it was written in the papers, the lad cried and shouted to the court

not to send me to prison. It's not like I assaulted the boy or hurt him. He loved me. And it was mutual.

*   *   *

A side effect of the current cultural emphasis on self-fulfillment has been the emergence of gay villages in many large cities. Such villages can be shown to curtail rather than to attract out-group victimizations (Tremblay et al., 1998), and thus qualify as safe, bounded, recurrent and informal convergence settings for the adult male prostitution market (escort agencies, massage parlors, saunas, hotels, bars, arcades, restaurants). As this market expanded, it also allowed on its margins the growth of a male adolescent hustling market. As the pool of adolescent hustlers expanded, so did the search of privileged customers, the "providers" or the "sugars." Four of the five subjects interviewed who had developed extensive ties with other like-minded offenders could be considered as "sugars." The problem is that male adolescent hustlers are often, as one subject observed, "disorganized lads" who engage not only in sexual promiscuity, but also in other types of imprudent criminal activities. When arrested, their juvenile status provides them with an advantageous plea bargaining leverage in which sugars – a widely despised category of offender – become an enticing asset. Felson (1998) notes that Herbert Gains (1962) coined the term "urban villages" to designate enclaves of vibrant local life and low predatory crime rates. But urban villages can also nurture, precisely because of their vibrant local life, deviant subcultures. One subject expressed his astonishment as being labeled as sexually deviant "because in the gay community it is so natural to seek sexual relationships with lads under 18." At the same time, he also fully realized that extending the search for youths beyond the confines of the gay village increased the odds of arrest. To the extent that norms regulating sexually behavior hold in one local area, and contrary norms govern its surrounding area, we are witnessing what Thorstein Sellin would have viewed as a normative conflict.

CONCLUSION

A noteworthy feature of Felson's analysis of offender convergence settings is that mutual assistance itself is problematic. Indeed, "accomplice depletion is the most natural crime process. To offset depletion, a locality must assist its criminals by providing them suitable settings for finding new recruits" (Felson, 2003). This is why crime rates are not only driven by homeostatic or equilibrium dynamics, but also experience over time significant, irregular, and not easily explained discontinuities (sharp drops, significant increases). Web technologies now provide isolated sex offenders (such as pedophiles) a unique medium to reach one another. Urban gay villages now offer other types of sex offenders (such as hebephiles) the opportunity to seek and find compliant adolescents. Both innovations could account, at least partly, for the aggregate increase in violations of age-of-consent prohibitions reported in the literature. Both innovations are best understood as the means or the social arrangements through which a culture of self-fulfillment and authenticity actually shapes the behavioral routines of such offenders.

Although many convicted sex offenders commit their offences solo, it does not follow that their patterns of interaction with like-minded individuals are irrelevant or that they should be viewed as "social isolates" (Hanson and Scott, 1996). Convergence settings have other functions than supplying accomplices or partners in offending activities: for example raising their spirit and commitment, before and after the offence. Moreover, they are the locus of an elaborate social organization, and this is true for physical as well as virtual offender convergence settings. An interesting feature of the male adolescent prostitution market is that co-offending ties among hebephiles were less of their own doing than steered or instigated by the hustling jingles of adolescents searching for providers. To the extent that interactions among sex offenders are shaped by available convergence settings, they could also become a legitimate target for law enforcement and relapse prevention efforts.

It should be pointed out that exploratory convenience samples are rarely well designed. Whatever tentative value they offer is mainly heuristic. Hebephile subjects interviewed in this research were mainly customers or hustlers, or both, at different periods of their lives. Further research could focus on patterns of interactions among participants who as entrepreneurs, place managers and employees also bring structure to the male adolescent hustling market. It would also be desirable to scrutinize in more detail the learning opportunities provided by offender convergence settings and their impact on participants' subsequent offending. Although convergence settings should increase rates of sexual offending, they could, perhaps, also have an educating, restraining or "prudential" effect on the behavior of individuals violating age-of-consent prohibitions.

Address for correspondence: Pierre Tremblay, School of Criminology, University of Montreal CP 6028 Succ. Centre-Ville, Montreal, H3C 3J7; e-mail: pierre.tremblay@umontreal.ca.

Acknowledgments: Comments and suggestions by Carlo Morselli, Marcus Felson, Richard Wortley as well as the anonymous reviewers of CPS were very helpful. The fieldwork benefit from the support of Alexandrine Chevrel, Line Bernier, Christiane Perreault (Solicitor General of Canada), Bernadette Lamoureux, France Paradis (Philippe Pinel Institute) and Claire Deschambault and Oscar Blais (*L'Amorce*).

NOTES

1. Sexual behavior is socially regulated by constitutive and regulative norms. Regulative norms define the appropriate patterns of erotic behavior, restrict the range of appropriate erotic stimuli (pornography laws) or target "courtship disorders" such as voyeurism, exhibitionism and "toucherism." Constitutive norms define the acceptable domain of erotic partners. Adultery and "sodomy" statutes restrict the range of appropriate range of adult sexual relationships. Age-of-consent prohibitions define what is believed to be the appropriate onset and age differentials of individuals engaged in sexual relationships.

2. For example, a 1995–1996 survey (Ouimet, 1997) of sex offenders convicted in Quebec to a prison (federal) sentence of two years or more indicates that a majority (66%) could be labelled as either paedophiles (38% of their victims were younger than 12) or "hebephiles" (28% of victims belonged to the 13 to 17 age group). Thus, more than half of all federal sex offender inmates could be considered as age-of-consent offenders.

3. The research was funded by the Canadian Ministry of Justice and sponsored by the International Bureau for Children's Rights.

4. Two subjects, not included in this count, were interviewed but dropped from the analysis. They had been convicted for incestuous or quasi-incestuous relationships with their children. The first subject was believed to be involved in the pornography trade. But his pornography

business did not, in fact, include juvenile material, and his current conviction was not related to pornography but to this sexual relationship with his stepdaughter. In the second case, I had met the subject when he had been elected as vice-president of the administrative board of L'Amorce. Following this election, however, he was sentenced to prison. Learning of his whereabouts, and since I was planning to meet other inmates at the same institution, I took advantage of the opportunity to interview him without inquiring about the nature of this current conviction.

5. West (1987, p. 58) documented that the "vast majority of men who are sexually attracted to children are non-violent in their approaches. Signs of fear or annoyance on the child's part would normally make them desist. After all, child lovers are seeking, however inappropriately, an affectionate response and a mutually pleasurable experience." As he observes elsewhere, the legal qualification of "sexual assault" should not be taken as a descriptive or factual attribution since any intimate touching is always categorized as assaults (West, 1994, p. xi).

6. As is often the case in exploratory research endeavors, the major challenge was to find an appropriate analytical framework for making sense of the material elicited in these interviews. The analytical issues raised by Felson's piece on "offender convergence settings" motivated me to do a rewrite of a descriptive research report published elsewhere (Tremblay, 2003).

7. The subject was a teacher and school administrator by profession who combined a distorted courtship disorder ("spanking") with a side attraction to prepubescent youths. He showed me an "erotic story" that had been accepted for publication in a specialized magazine called "*Stand Correct.*" The magazine attracts individuals of both sex who engage in consensual role-playing sado-masochistic sex (on the subculture of this "paraphelia," see Weinberg et al., 1984). Subjects quoted in the paper's first section were English-speaking; those quoted in the section entitled "Searching for sugars" were French-speaking.

8. This echoes Sutherland's observation that the "distress of the solitary thief who is not a member of the underworld society of criminals is illustrated in the following statement by Roger Berton at the time when he was an habitual but not a professional forger: ' . . . I could not rid myself of the crying need for the sense of security which social recognition and contact with one's fellows and their approval furnishes.' " (Sutherland, 1937, p. 204).

9. Property thefts committed by two of the 17 sexual offenders interviewed in this study were intimately connected with their sexual offences. In the first case, the subject's car thefts occurred just after "relapse" and were designed to get him arrested. In this case, armed robberies occurred just before "relapsing" and were meant to pay the lads. Students investigating sex offenders' crime careers should perhaps scrutinize more closely the timing of their non-sexual offences.

10. "When I got out of prison, I met D again. He had gotten out of the city and lived underground in Quebec City for two years, no license, no phone numbers, no reported earnings. He just dived underground and stayed still. It worked."

REFERENCES

Chamlin, M.B. and J.K. Cochran (1997). "Social Altruism and Crime." *Criminology* 35:203–227.

Felson, M. (2003). "The Process of Co-Offending." In: M.J. Smith and D.B. Cornish (eds.), *Theory for Practice in Situational Crime Prevention.* (Crime Prevention Studies, vol. 16.) Monsey, NY: Criminal Justice Press.

Felson, M. (1998). *Crime and Everyday Life.* Thousand Oaks, CA: Pine Forge Press.

Hanson, K.R. and H. Scott (1996). "Social Networks of Sexual Offenders." *Psychology, Crime and Law* 2(4):249–258.

Klein, M.W. (1995). *The American Street Gang: Its Nature, Prevalence and Control.* New York: Oxford University Press.

Lemert, E. M. (1967). *Human Deviance, Social Problems, and Social Control.* Englewood Cliffs, NJ: Prentice Hall.

Lieb, R., V. Quinsey and L. Berliner (1998). "Sexual Predators and Public Policy." In: M.Tonry (ed.), *Crime and Justice: An Annual Review of Research*, vol. 23. Chicago, IL: University of Chicago Press.

Merton, R.K. (1938). "Social Structure and Anomie." *American Sociological Review* 3:672–682.

Okami, P. (1994). "Child Perpetrators of Sexual Abuse: The Emergence of a Problematic Deviant Category." In: D. West (ed.), *Sex Crimes.* Dartmouth, UK: Aldershot.

Ouimet, M. (1997). *Sexual Offences and Offenders.* Montreal: School of Criminology, University of Montreal.

Rosenfeld, R. and S. Messner (1998). "Crime and the American Dream: An Institutional Analysis." In: F. Adler and W.S. Laufer (eds.), *The Legacy of Anomie Theory: Advances in Criminological Theory*, vol. 6. New Brunswick, NJ: Transaction Publishers.

Sutherland, E.H. (1937). *The Professional Thief by a Professional Thief.* Chicago: University of Chicago Press.

Taylor, C. (1991). *The Ethics of Authenticity*. Cambridge: Harvard University Press.

Tremblay P. (2003). "Interracciones Socials Entre Pedofilos Canadienses." In: E. Azaola and R.J. Estes (eds.), *La Infancia Como Mercancia Sexual En América Del Norte*. Mexico: Siglo Veintinuo.

Tremblay, P. (1993). "Searching for Suitable Co-offenders." In: R.V. Clarke and M. Felson (eds.), *Routine Activity and Rational Choice: Advances in Criminology Theory*, vol. 5. New Brunswick, NJ: Transaction Books.

Tremblay P., E. Boucher, M. Ouimet and L. Biron (1998). "Rhétorique de la survictimisation: une etude de cas – le 'village gai.' " *Canadian Journal of Criminology* 40:1–21.

Weinberg, M. S., C. J. Williams and C. Moser (1984). "The Social Constituents of Sadomasochism." *Social Problems* 31:379–389.

West, D. (1994). *Sex Crimes*. Dartmouth, UK: Aldershot.

West, D.J. (1987). *Sexual Crimes and Confrontations: A Study of Victims and Offenders*. Gower, UK: Aldershot.

The Internet and Abuse Images of Children: Search, Pre-criminal Situations and Opportunity

by

Max Taylor[1]

and

Ethel Quayle
Copine Project, University College Cork, Ireland

Abstract: *This paper addresses the issue of Internet crimes against children expressed through the viewing, trade, distribution and production of abuse images of children. It develops an approach to understanding this problem drawing on the rational choice perspective (Cornish and Clarke 1986), and develops a situational or contextual model of the process of engagement with abuse images, emphasising searching as the rate-limiting factor. It further seeks to explore links between the rational choice model and a related cognitive-behavioral model of offending, followed by a discussion of the applications of this to abuse images and the Internet. The concepts of search, pre-criminal situations and opportunities are emphasised as having particular relevance for understanding Internet crimes against children. Whilst the discussion focuses on this relatively narrow area, the issues raised have a broader relevance to understanding how notions derived from rational choice theories might apply to criminal activity involving the Internet, and the new communication technologies more generally.*

Crime Prevention Studies, volume 19 (2006), pp. 169–195.

INTRODUCTION

There is currently great interest and concern about the availability of abuse images of children[2] on the Internet. It is important to note, however, that the trade in abuse images of children is not a new crime: the production and distribution of abuse images of children has probably existed for as long as pictorial representations have been possible (Taylor and Quayle, 2003). What is new, however, is the scale of production and distribution of such images, and this seems to be directly linked to the Internet and its capacity to effect easy and efficient exchange of digital information (in this case digital image and video files). The easy availability of abuse images at low or no cost has both exposed and made possible a degree of sexual interest in children expressed through pornography production and possession that seems to be surprising in its extent.

Whilst the Internet is central to contemporary concerns about crimes involving abuse images, more general issues related to crime and illegal behavior and the Internet are also clearly relevant. The Internet presents a number of difficult conceptual and practical problems in relation to crime and criminal behavior. Its perceived anonymity, the ease of developing social contacts and the capacity to create virtual social groups, its essentially international character and the speed with which digital files can be transmitted, all create an environment that challenges conventional notions of social organization and control. Its capacity to empower marginal communities, and the ease with which enormous amounts of information can be cheaply stored and disseminated, are all often seen as positive elements of the Internet. But those same factors can readily support the emergence of less benign social groups, which can rapidly communicate and interact with each other in ways undreamt of only a few years ago. Association between people, creating complex criminal conspiracies, or involving illegal acts, can rapidly emerge. But such associations may be very transitory, leaving effectively no record other than what appears on the individual's own computers; even this can be easily and permanently deleted.

There have been few explorations of Internet crime from a rational choice perspective (Newman and Clarke, 2003); indeed, criminological and psychological theorizing about crime and the Internet have also been limited. Rational choice theories, however, may offer a number of attractive possibilities to extend our knowledge of this new arena for criminal behavior. The starting point is the emphasis placed by rational choice approaches on locating criminal behavior within its situational and environmental context. Applying these notions to the Internet ought not present any special challenges; however, the environment of the Internet is not that of everyday life. It is bounded by technical limitations that result in a limited virtual world related to and in some senses mimicking, but not necessarily replicating, everyday life.

In the following, an approach is developed to understanding offences related to viewing, trading and distributing abuse images of children using the Internet, emphasizing the significance of the rational choice concepts of search, pre-criminal situation and opportunity. In particular, search is identified as the rate-limiting variable. Links between this approach and a related cognitive-behavioral therapy (CBT) model of offending are also explored. The final section discusses practice issues that follow from this analysis.

CONSTRAINED BEHAVIORAL REPERTOIRES AND THE INTERNET

In all behavioral systems, behavior is determined in the first instance by morphology (the form and structure of an organism). Our structure (physical and psychological) determines what responses we can make to any environmental situation; similarly, we can only respond to environmental properties we are sensitive to. The concept of affordances (Gibson, 1979; Norman, 1988) has been used by Joinson (2003) to describe the process relating the properties of objects and environments to different behaviors, and to draw attention to the fact that some visual environmental cues specify likely behaviors more than others. Given the dominance of visual cues in the experience of the Internet, this is an important point. Whilst the capacity of the organism to respond to visual cues is primarily a function of the quality, nature and capacity of the organism's sensory systems, the response emitted is influenced by what an organism is capable of doing in the situation in which it finds itself, and the affordance and discriminative qualities of visual cues it is exposed to.

In the case of the Internet, the environment is determined by the physical mechanics of communication and the way in which computer applications use those capacities. This, in turn, is determined by the relatively simply designed core structure and interactivity of the network which is collectively termed the Internet, and which is associated with the much more complex applications it supports.

If the Internet is viewed as a communication system, three layers can be identified:

1. A bottom physical layer – the wires, the physical network of data transmission lines, etc. that digital information travels on.

2. A middle code layer – the functional network that makes the network physical hardware run. These are the protocols that define the Internet (TCP/IP[3] for example) and software on which those protocols run.

3. A top applications layer – the content of the Internet and the applications that generate content. This is the material transmitted across the physical layer, using the middle layer protocols that we as users experience when we engage with the Internet.

In user terms, the top layer is the content and applications of the Internet, which the user is aware of and interacts directly with, and which is accessed via the bottom and middle layers that collectively are experienced by the user as the somewhat invisible network. The network defines, in communication terms, what can be exchanged and what is possible; the top layer creates meaning and content through assembling and using digital information accessed through the bottom and middle layers.

The network structures (bottom and middle communication layers) provide a very basic level of service, primarily involving data transport and switching data transmission between points. Intelligent functions related to information processing that are required to provide and run applications are located in or close to devices attached to edges or ends of the network (the top layer) – the term e2e (edge-to-edge) is used to refer to this. The Internet, therefore, is structured to support many independent applications at its periphery or edge, and generally provides only resources of broad utility as network features across applications, while providing to applications usable means for effective sharing of resources and resolution of resource conflicts (Reed et al., 1980). An important quality of this is that any given Internet connection can have multiple simultaneous functions, including overlapping but separate transmission of data.

The e2e quality of Internet architecture has been a significant factor in the development of the Internet, in that it has freed it from proprietary influences, and effectively created the self-correcting system we now have. e2e architecture has also limited the extent of commercial exploitation of network activity, a positive factor of value for many Internet users. However, this same quality of e2e architecture is also a significant factor in limiting the capacity of law enforcement agencies and governments to regulate and control crime on the Internet. Criminal activities such as accessing, storing or trading abuse images, for example, are located at the periphery of the network, dependent on edge capacity, rather than network functioning. The network does not discriminate among kinds of data, or the uses to which data might be put by the end user. Packet switching routing of information (resulting in any given piece of sent data arriving at its destination through potentially a range of routes) means central network monitoring of specific activity across the network is difficult. It is possible to monitor data transmission at low levels in the system, but this presents enormous difficulties related to volume, and in identifying specific targeted data (say from or to a particular source) from the vast amount of other data traffic such mass surveillance will capture. Although this kind of surveillance does take place, it is inefficient and requires immense processing capacity, as well as probably being illegal in many jurisdictions.[4] Targeted surveillance, monitoring and control of a more familiar law enforcement kind, therefore, have to be primarily "edge"-focused, rather than "network"-focused, in targeting the individual user. However at that simple practical level, given the global character of the Internet, and the potential multitude of different legal systems any given network abuse might involve, the difficulties of monitoring and enforcing control and detecting crime are obvious: added to the large number of users online, and the problems of scale this brings, the difficulty in developing effective controls are enormous.

Alternative Internet architectures are possible, giving network functions more capacity and "intelligence" (Lessig, 2001). Proprietary networks, for example, have been, and could be further created that would do this. Such networks would also offer organizations the ability to charge for network access and data transmission (and to generally exploit the commercial potential of the Internet as distinct from services using the Internet), something that at the moment is provided (as far as the user is concerned) for free. But this would cause the loss of much of the Internet's efficiency and its self-correcting capacity, while also greatly adding to costs of data transmission. From the perspective of crime management, however, the problem of e2e architecture is that it effectively places the burden for control of application management and functionality on distributed local computers located at the edge of the network, rather than in a more accessible centralized controllable system. One of the great future challenges for the Internet is maintaining its current decentralized freedom within a context of acceptable control, monitoring and surveillance (Lessig, 2001).

RATIONAL CHOICE THEORIES AND UNDERSTANDING INTERNET CRIME

Cohen and Felson (1979) present a useful starting point to explore rational choice theories and Internet crime when, drawing on notions of routine activity theory, they identify three minimal elements for criminal action:

- a likely offender,

- a suitable target,

- and absence of a capable guardian.

Of these three elements, focusing on access to or availability of suitable targets seems to have proved to be the most attractive for increasing our capacity to exercise some control over the incidence of criminal behavior. This is because it allows a focus on the context in which criminal events take place that can be modified or changed, rather than seeking to change the more distant and complex notions that have to be drawn on to understand "likely offenders" (such as criminal personality, disadvantaged life styles, etc). It also readily leads to initiatives that might create or supplement suitable guardianship. In simple terms, the focus on environmental change to control criminal behavior draws attention to modifying the choices of alternative behavioral options made by the potential offender, rather than seeking to change criminals in some fundamental sense.

Such a target focus reflects the important distinction made by Clarke and Felson (1993) between "criminal inclinations" and "criminal events." Whatever reasons have led an individual to acquire, create or see the emergence of criminal inclinations (caused by, it might be assumed, various social, psychological and perhaps physiological factors), a focus on criminal targets assumes that the necessary preconditions to lead an individual to prepare to engage with a criminal event have occurred. It focuses our concern, therefore, on the process whereby the criminal event is expressed and fulfilled (or not), rather than the past origins of criminal activity, and the process whereby an individual becomes involved in criminal activity. Distinguishing between criminal inclination and criminal event marks an important conceptual advance, enabling a more focused approach to policy and practice through changing events and situations, rather than people; this is a much easier agenda to develop.

If we focus on the target qualities of crime, Cusson (1993) described crime patterns as having three elements:

1. Search

2. Pre-criminal situation

3. Criminal tactics.

Fundamental to this analysis is the assumption of a motivated offender (or the presence of criminal inclination) engaged in developing criminal activity. What follows describes, therefore, the process of engagement with particular criminal events, rather than engagement with crime in a general sense or past influences on the offender that have created his/her criminal dispositions. A further assumption to this approach is that analysis of criminal activity, because it is particular and grounded in its situational context, should therefore be crime-specific (and also person-specific), in that it relates to the context and circumstances of a particular situation.

Search

This first element of Cusson's (1993) analysis refers to the individual looking for a suitable pre-criminal situation that will result in the commission of an offence. This element must be for the individual the first step in the process of the expression of a particular criminal act (as opposed to a propensity to commit crimes). Depending upon the criminal target, the searcher may find a pre-criminal situation easily, may have to find a weak spot in protective systems that will create a pre-criminal situation, or may have to create one. In this latter circumstance, this might, for example, involve enticing a potential victim in some sense, or deliberately engaging with the potential criminal context to shape it into a suitable form (as in the case of Internet seduction of minors, for example). An example of finding weak spots in protective systems might well refer to exploring software options to access computer banking files, or the development of a "back-door" virus that gives access to a target's computer. Finding a target easily may refer to situations involving high-frequency criminal opportunities such as accessing abuse images through Usenet newsgroups, or a commercial website. A critical associated factor as far as the criminal is concerned may be what Cohen and Felson (1979) term "absence of a capable guardian," something which the Internet's e2e architecture makes likely.

Searches may be systematic, or may be the result of chance. In some circumstances, a search may be aided by use of information from secondary sources, such as technical literature, or personal contact with an employee, colleague or friend. It is also reasonable to assume search to be either deliberate, or opportunistic. It might be assumed, for example, that spammers, by indiscriminate distributions of emails advertising illegal or marginally legal web sites, are contributing to opportunistic search by potential criminals.

A particular variant on the search element relates to situations where others may benefit from offending behavior, (i.e. where further or secondary offending behavior committed by someone else is dependent on a particular primary offending behavior). In such circumstances, search may be facilitated by deliberate cues, structures, events and so forth, provided by the individual who gains secondary benefits from the primary offence. An example might be spam offering access to abuse images of children, where one activity (access to illegal images – the actions of a primary offender) is an offence, but commission of this offence benefits the spammer (who is committing offences related to supply and distribution – the actions of a secondary offender). The spammer may well create pre-criminal situations to attract potential downloaders of abuse images.

For Internet offences, the structure of the Internet shapes search activities in a number of senses. This is because "edge" activity is flexible, informal, spasmodic and distributed. Accessing particular locations or activities requires either knowing where to go by knowing an Internet address, or having built into an edge-based application the capacity to recognize individuals, web site presence or applications on the Internet. Unlike the telephone system, for example, there is no explicit "directory" of Internet addresses or services. If you do not know where something is (as in its Internet address) the need to search, for the ordinary Internet user as much as the criminal user, can take two forms; using applications that search the worldwide web for particular sites by key words (such as the Google search facility), or using shared communication applications that have the capacity to identify the presence of individual users on their networks (such as the various proprietary instant messaging applications, or IRC,[5] or the search capacity on p2p[6] networks). Internet searching, of course, takes place from a host computer – the search activity does not require the searcher to physically explore the environment personally. It can also be undertaken without anyone else necessarily being aware of the activity, other than the provider of the search facility.

Pre-criminal Situation

Pre-criminal situations are the set of outside circumstances immediately preceding and surrounding the criminal event and making the offence more or less difficult, risky or profitable (Cusson, 1993). Gottfredson and Hirschi (1990) offer a further definition in terms of "the minimal elements necessary (and collectively sufficient) for a crime to occur."

It is important to distinguish the pre-criminal situation from pre-criminal opportunity; opportunity is a *favorable* situation for committing an offence and makes possible and probable an offence. As Cook (1986) notes, pre-criminal situations that are attractive because of high payoff and low risk are perceived by potential offenders as opportunities. From a rational choice perspective, it is the balance of payoff and consequence that drives choices towards offending and the circumstances in pre-criminal situations may be either favorable or unfavorable. The pre-criminal situation, therefore, is the situation where the potential to commit an offence is present, depending on the activity and response of the offender (which is referred to below as tactics).

The perceived absence of effective capable guardianship in most Internet situations represents a factor that will facilitate the transition from pre-criminal situation to pre-criminal opportunity. However, it is important to stress the perceived rather than necessarily real quality of the lack of effective guardianship. In fact, communication over the Internet, once intercepted or monitored, is very easy to trace, and it is possible to identify user locations, unless active steps are taken to make the user anonymous. This is because core Internet protocols require user and recipient Internet addresses to route data between computers on the Internet.

The identification of a web site that makes available abuse images of children represents the identification of a pre-criminal situation. That is to say, having found the site, if by clicking on a link that gives access to an array of images for downloading, the ingredients for committing a crime are created. The transition from pre-criminal situation to pre-criminal opportunity to criminal act in this case is extraordinarily easy (and illustrates the significance of the concept of affordance), in that it simply requires a click on the link for the crime to take place (the crime of downloading illegal images). Other activities may be necessary to precede the criminal activity (like, for example, giving credit card details in a commercial web site), but the process remains quick, effortless and apparently risk free. Where this process is thwarted, highly motivated offenders may engage in a series of further searches to identify a range of different possible pre-criminal situations, or different routes to the same situation.

For something to be criminal, it has to contravene the law in some sense. However, crimes on the Internet complicate this analysis. In the case of a crime such as residential burglary, for example, the offence and the pre-criminal situation generally occur within the same legal jurisdiction. Thus, there is a clear legal as well as criminological and psychological relationship between the pre-criminal situation and the crime. In the case of pre-criminal situations on the Internet, this may not be the case. Creating an Internet site that makes available abuse images, and enabling someone to access them by charging the fee to a credit card, might be illegal in a particular user's jurisdiction, but may not be illegal in the jurisdiction in which the web-based application is located, or in the perhaps different jurisdiction where credit card transactions are authorized.

This can lead to all sorts of difficulties. For example, in most jurisdictions, possession and distribution of abuse images of children are illegal. However, making available the opportunity to access illegal images in itself may not be illegal in some jurisdictions, or in some circumstances looking at a site but not intentionally downloading images may not be illegal. A critical issue in this case relates to what the offence of possession might mean, and its relationship to looking and downloading. A further issue relates to the proof that might be required to establish whether the crime of possession has taken place, and distinguishing between a crime having occurred versus evidence related to an intention to commit a crime (Gillespie, 2005). Collecting adequate evidence across multiple potential jurisdictions will obviously challenge existing structures. Similar problems can be identified in other specific examples of crimes involving abuse images, such as trading images.

Tactics

Tactic refers to the sequences of choices and actions made by the offender during the criminal event, including use of available means to reach ends in a pre-criminal situation. Tactics are shaped by the pre-criminal situation, and reflect its situational context. What is tactically possible is limited by the structure and form of the environment, its morphology: in the case of the Internet, e2e architecture and the basic communication protocols determine this.

Because the Internet is primarily a communication medium, it is to be expected that criminal tactics will be shaped by the communication potential and capacity that different clients and protocols allow, including social context. The form of exchange of abuse images is an example of this, and the choices and forms of behavior related to exchange are shaped both by the available systems and user requirements. Where real-time activities are concerned in which privacy and secrecy are important factors influencing user choices, as well as perhaps social contact, the form of exchange will be determined by the capacity of applications to effect direct contact between computers (avoiding, for example, access mediated by and potentially monitored by local network servers): IRC has this capacity, as do the various proprietary egroup networks, p2p networks and instant messaging clients. Video networking, because it uses central network servers to managing video streaming and to maintain contact between users, is less secure (central servers can more readily monitor content), and therefore the exchange of "live" video tends to be less of a factor in the exchange of images. On the other hand, direct contact of this kind between computers to exchange digital files or to communicate through text increases the risk of detection or interception, because as noted earlier, TCP/IP protocols require a recipient and sender Internet Address to route digital packets to and from. Monitoring an individual's activity will therefore reveal the addresses of the computers with which the individual is engaged, and these can be used to identify dial-up telephone numbers, or subscriber addresses from the Internet Service Provider (ISP). More public exchange processes which do not involve real-time contact but which allow use of anonymisers to effect security, include the Usenet newsgroups, and proprietary bulletin board systems. Although these allow public access (and therefore limit the capacity to engage in explicit exchange and social contact) they are generally more secure with less risk of monitoring or detection.

Experience suggests that offenders tend to repeat successful offending behavior, and furthermore, one offender tends to repeat successful actions of another where he or she knows about it. Hence we see one element in the similarities and regularities of criminal behavior. However, because the nature of offending behavior is constrained by the criminal situation, so the extent to which it can vary is presumably limited anyway; in the case of the Internet the range of possible behavior is limited, as noted

Figure 1: The Three Strategic Elements of the Offending Cycle for a Motivated Offender: Search, Pre-criminal Situation and Tactics

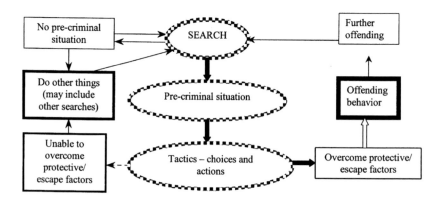

earlier. Most criminal offending behavior, therefore, is not unique, and becomes customary and develops as modes of procedure. An important further factor is that outside of environmental constraints, the critical elements in any criminal behavior that shape its form and content are overcoming protection and escaping detection. The perceived absence of capable guardians on the Internet is clearly a factor here. Given this, the significance of bulletin boards and discussion groups facilitating the exchange of advice as well as images can be clearly seen.

The relationship between search, pre-criminal situation and tactics is diagrammatically illustrated in Figure 1. From this diagram we can identify the central significance of search in the generation of pre-criminal situations and therefore in the commission of criminal acts. Indeed, search might be thought of as the rate-limiting factor on which other activities depend. The potential offender's search strategies are, in part, a function of successful previous search, but also presumably the strategies of search are refined through experience, and may also be influenced by training or communication with other people.

For some offenders search may be a limited and perhaps even a stereotyped activity. For example, we know that some collectors of abuse images of children focus on web sites, and they use search engines, and links from sites they already know, to access further images. If they communicate with others or access bulletin boards, information from such contacts may influence their searching behavior. However, provided these habitual search strategies continue to meet their needs (in terms of access to images) they seem not to extend their behavioral search repertoire. Other offenders focus on p2p systems, accessing files to download through the search capacity of their p2p client, and again seem to develop quite stereotyped forms of search. So long as their needs are met in terms of access to images, these offenders do not need to be innovative or adopt alternative search procedures. However, in circumstances where the sought-for pre-criminal situation is highly specific, unique, or particularly difficult to access, the potential offender may need to develop creative and innovative search strategies. Factors that may complicate this analysis, and drive more innovative search, or even sustain search activities in what might be thought to be a negative decisional calculus, are when in circumstances of high arousal material cannot be accessed, or where the material fails to generate or sustain sexual arousal, or where the social context to the Internet becomes a factor in itself (see Quayle and Taylor, 2003, 2002 for further discussion of these issues). Loewenstein (1996) noted the significance of visceral states (including heightened sexual arousal) on decision making and suggested that such heightened states can impact decision making in three broad ways:

- narrowing attention to factors related to that state;

- reducing time horizons, focusing on short-term factors; and,

- narrowing the focus of attention inwards, where the individual's own needs gain primacy over other decisional factors.

All of these might be expected to influence decision making in search situations involving the Internet and abuse images. In terms of decisional influences on search activities (and perhaps in other situations as well), one significant effect of heightened sexual arousal (and perhaps failure to satisfy sexual arousal), may be an increase in risk taking and a perseveration of search activity even when protective or escape factors cannot be overcome. Loewenstein et al. (1997) suggested that heightened sexual arousal decreased the perception of the cost of sexually coercive behavior (perhaps because the recognition of costs is incongruent with the emotional state [Bouffard, 2002]), and this might also be suggested as a potential factor in Internet situations, especially given perceived lack of effective guardianship, and the related influence of apparent anonymity. Consistent with this, Bouffard (2002) presents evidence that emotional states can influence rational decision making in sexual aggression (see also Carmichael and

Piquero, 2004). From a related perspective, Wright et al. (2004) draw attention to the changing effects of impulsivity as a factor in deterrence of criminal choice, and suggest an inverted "U-shaped" relationship between deterrence effects and crime. It remains to be seen, however, if these same factors influence decision making related to Internet activity and abuse images, but the results are suggestive. They imply that a more complex decisional calculus has to be considered in circumstances of offending involving sexual arousal, but this, of itself, does not necessarily negate the overall analysis. Indeed, such factors might be best accommodated into notions related to imperfections in choice and "bounded rationality" (Simon, 1983) or "bounded decision making" (Güth, 2000).

A failure to identify a pre-criminal situation, or a failure to overcome the protective or limiting qualities of a particular pre-criminal situation will, therefore, result in no offending behavior, and diversion either to doing something else, or engaging in further different search activities for similar (or different) pre-criminal situations. However, the dynamics of this process remain unclear. But what may follow from this is that for some kinds of offending situations, and perhaps for some kinds of offenders, where search strategies are highly structured and limited, changing the situational context in which search takes place and disturbing the search potential will produce immediate changes in the emergence of pre-criminal situations, and hence offending. Internet offences susceptible to rapid rate-changing through impeding search might include access to web site material or Usenet postings. It may also be that for some offenders there are structural rate-limiting factors related to intelligence, experience or other psychological variables that limit or constrain search capacity. The nature and speed of Internet access (in terms of use of broadband or dial-up modem access, for example) may also be a factor.

INTERNET CRIME-RELATED ABUSE IMAGES OF CHILDREN

Having established a broad context, we can now turn attention to understanding the processes whereby offenders become involved in the criminal behavior of accessing and possessing abuse images of children. We should note at the outset that our knowledge in this area is incomplete. However it is clear that there are a number of different ways in which individuals might become involved with abuse images, although the common denominator among them is assumed to be sexual interest in children in some sense (see Taylor and Quayle, 2003). How this sexual interest might be expressed is less clear, and may be quite varied. For example, although it is often assumed that possession of abuse images is related to commission of contact offences against children, the evidence supporting this link is unclear. Some people who possess abuse images are either involved in contact offences, or may become involved as a result of access to abuse images; certainly all producers of abuse images are necessarily involved in contact offences. But there seems to be an unknown, but probably large, group of people who limit their expression of sexual interest in children to possession of images, and furthermore, for some this may be part of a broader array of activities on the margins of Internet life that has little if anything directly to do with sexual interest in children, and may perhaps relate more to other broader sexual interests.

An issue here is to be clear what particular behavior, or set of behaviors, we are concerned with. A crime-specific focus on downloading and trading images, for example, as distinct from behaviors that might be consequential to those actions, such as masturbation, or engagement with sexual fantasy, seems to be necessary. Whilst sexual issues may drive accessing abuse images, the actual activities involved are not in themselves necessarily sexual in character. Indeed, from the perspective of concern here, perhaps our understanding of these kinds of offences and offenders may be improved if we turn attention away from the sexual qualities of these offences, and focus more on the processes whereby offending takes place and the particular behaviors involved. This is not to deny the obvious sexual elements to these crimes, but to do this would serve to place these offences within a broader criminological context, and enable other perspectives (like those drawn from rational choice models) to be brought to bear on improving our understanding.

Quayle and Taylor (2003) sought to do this from a clinical perspective, by presenting a CBT process model of abuse image offending. This model, because it has its roots in a behavior and functional analysis, has clear links with rational choice approaches (see Taylor, 1993). Consistent with the suggestion that process may be an important factor, Quayle and Taylor's model places offending behavior related to abuse images within the broader context of problematic Internet behavior, rather than other forms of sexual offending. The broad outlines of the model can be seen in diagrammatic form in Figure 2 (from Taylor and Quayle, 2003).

The purpose of this model was to place offending within a framework emphasizing behavior, cognitions and emotions, and its focus was the

Figure 2: A Model of Potential Problematic Internet Use (from Quayle and Taylor 2003)

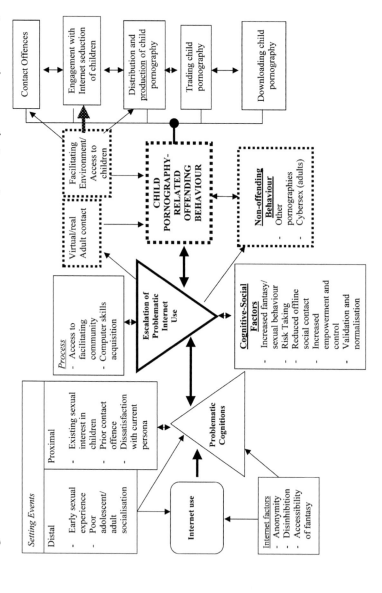

development of systematic therapeutic interventions for Internet offenders, primarily after the offence has been committed, and whilst the offender is in some sense engaged with the criminal justice system, or seeking to avoid engagement with it (see Quayle et al., 2005; Quayle and Taylor, 2004 for details). Whilst offering a functional analysis of the offending process, this model does not explore the situational context as such to offending behavior in the sense addressed in this paper. It is much more concerned with the context to offending, and the capacity to effect behavior change and therefore presumably future offending. It does recognize the obvious central position of offending behavior in the process (within the box labeled "Child Pornography Offending Behavior" in Figure 2), but it does not attempt to examine in detail what this might mean in functional and behavioral terms. The discussion presented in this paper, however, clearly fits within this broader CBT model by providing an account of how we might understand the central elements of that offending behavior as the process of searching for and engagement with criminal opportunities. The process outlined in Figure 1 above therefore elaborates on "Child Pornography Offending Behavior" (reflected in the box in Figure 2) by outlining how that behavior is expressed in terms of the rational choice concepts of search, pre-criminal situations and tactics. The analysis presented here is not dependent on assumptions related to CBT intervention strategies, but clearly it does complement that approach, sharing a commitment to functional analysis.

The two models referred to in this paper therefore represent a broad contextual account of problematic Internet use that may have relevance beyond issues related to abuse images of children. Clinical interventions might draw on the processes represented in Figure 2, but a pragmatic approach to developing systematic management and prevention of current offending behavior on the Internet can supplement that by focusing on the processes outlined in Figure 1. The two approaches (clinical and criminological) complement each other, through the individual focus of the CBT approach (changing the behavioral context in which offending occurs), and the preventative situational emphasis from the rational choice perspective, with both drawing on a functional analysis of the offending behavior.

Quayle and Taylor's (2004) model, although specifically focused on problematic Internet behavior, has elements in common with Ward's (2003) more general pathways model of sexual offending (see also Eccleston and Ward, this volume) and similarly Polaschek and Hudson's (2004) model of rape offending. All make assumptions about process, and all

– 185 –

describe processes of offending that relate to the individual offender's situational context. Although Ward and Polaschek and Hudson do not necessarily frame their accounts in terms of decisional factors, they clearly relate to, and are consistent with, rational choice analyses, in that behavior is seen as related to the contextual and situational framework the individual finds himself in. In addition, recent work on child sex offender treatment emphasizing notions of values and "good life" for offenders (Ward, 2002) may represent a means of further bringing within a treatment framework the decisional calculus envisaged in this analysis in response to search activity. This seems to be suggested by Ward in the following: " . . . one of the reasons individuals commit crimes is that they are perceived to be rewarding in some ways, a criminal lifestyle represents one way of achieving personal goods . . . offenders need to make their own choices and this is guided by a conception of good lives and the belief that it is possible to achieve different ways of living in the world" (Ward, 2002, p. 514).

Recognizing the complementary qualities of these approaches might lead to the development of more coherent strategies for the management of the problem of abuse images and the Internet. Clarke and Felson's (1993) critical distinction between "criminal inclinations" and "criminal events" is relevant here. The development of programs to address "criminal inclinations" or "criminal pathways" is of course relevant when faced with offenders within the criminal justice system, and the need for society to seek protection from them once they are identified. Diminishing "criminal inclinations" might be assumed to have an impact on future offending activity, but necessarily only become relevant once an offence has taken place, and the offender is known. The management of current offending, however, is unlikely to be greatly influenced by such activities, given that deterrence effects seem limited, and current offenders are presumably not known and only fall into the criminal justice and therapeutic networks once they are known through an offence being detected.

Managing ongoing criminal events requires a different perspective, one that does not depend on identifying the deviant qualities of individuals or indeed necessarily catching offenders, but rather focuses on changeable qualities surrounding the criminal event that might limit and influence its emergence. This also implies a focus on prevention in the management of crime, rather than deterrence through apprehending criminals. A focus on the search qualities related to pre-criminal situations in the context of the Internet offers a means of changing the probability of a criminal event being committed, rather than waiting for crimes to be committed, and then either looking for deterrence effects to affect future crime, or seeking to change the criminal. The significance of searching as the rate-limiting factor is particularly important given the limited and constrained nature of the virtual social context of the Internet, and the difficulties for the individual user of navigating the Internet environment, and identifying pre-criminal situations to exploit. An avenue for future exploration will be the examination of pathway models of criminal involvement to explore other ways of conceptualizing search, or identifying other similar rate-limiting points, where intervention in the situational context may allow for changes in offender decisional processes, and thereby changing the probability of offending. For example, efforts to decrease criminal inclinations through self-help strategies (Quayle et al., 2005) might be relevant.

PRACTICE ISSUES

What are the implications of this for practice? One obvious general point is that many of the structures we have to effect control in society in general are largely irrelevant in the Internet environment. Irksome as it may be for governments and law enforcement agencies, the Internet by its very nature cannot be easily centrally monitored or controlled, at least as it is currently configured. Because of the architecture of the Internet, traditional police tactics of mass surveillance through patrolling and monitoring applied to the Internet at the network level to detect criminal activity are likely at best to be very expensive and inefficient; to use Cohen and Felson's (1979) term, capable guardianship is not easily achievable in the current structure at the network level. Furthermore, a failure to recognize crime-specific qualities will even further dilute the effectiveness of initiatives like mass surveillance. Strategies need to be developed that identify specific criminal activities, and then relate initiatives to those activities focusing on the distributed aspects of the Internet environment that can be changed. This effectively means a crime-specific targeting of edge-based user activity. We need to be clear, however, that to be effective, the analysis must be offence-specific. For example, if the concern is with the distribution of abuse images of children, then the first step is to identify the situational factors related to this activity (as distinct from other activities associated with abuse images), which will be determined by the particular way in which images can both be distributed by the offender and accessed by others; different ways of distribution will require different kinds of initiatives. Offender motivations and the influence of heightened emotional states are relevant, but the central element of any offender seeking abuse images remains his or her need to search to identify appropriate pre-criminal situations.

In effecting this within the context of the Internet, a first obvious step is to develop initiatives targeting the various specific search opportunities available to the user, for as we have seen earlier, disrupting pre-criminal search activities will disrupt the capacity of many offenders to engage with suitable pre-criminal situations and therefore reduce offending. Ironically, although the Internet is essentially decentralized, the management of major search facilities is proprietary in nature, and can therefore be readily modified to disrupt such searching (through rejecting inappropriate search terms, for example). However, the challenge is that geographically-distributed private companies rather than states operate search facilities, and many of these companies operate within actual or virtual closed proprietary systems, and some, such as p2p networks, are structured in such a way as to distribute this essentially central capacity through virtual networking.

We can explore this further by taking as an example the problem of abuse images made available through the newsgroups. The Usenet newsgroup network is one of the major sources of abuse images of children on the Internet. Newsgroups appear to the user as a form of publicly accessible bulletin board. Within the thousands of newsgroups available, there are between 10 and 15 groups that make available abuse images of children. Individuals post material to these newsgroups in the form of digital files, which are essentially like email attachments, and subscribers to that newsgroup can download these files. Techniques and services exist to make posting to newsgroups of images (or anything else) anonymous, resulting in the poster being able to act with impunity provided the anonymiser is not compromised. Internet Service Providers (ISPs) can restrict availability of Usenet newsgroups to their subscribers, and indeed most major providers do limit what groups their subscribers can access. However, given the distributed nature of the Internet, the determined searcher can readily find access to what is termed "uncensored news" through providers other than their own ISP, access being either free, or for some small charge to a credit card.

Through addressing the capacity of individuals to search and identify such newsgroups and to interact with them (through impeding search activity and targeted edge-based surveillance of downloading activity from newsgroups), an immediate limit on the distribution of abuse images through this protocol could easily be achieved without interfering with the nature of the Usenet system. To overcome the problems of e2e architecture, however, co-coordinated action by appropriate organizations providing Internet edge access (primarily the ISPs) will be required to achieve this.

The problem of web-based commercial sites selling access to abuse images can similarly be limited by impeding search capacities (through search engines), thus denying potential offenders the opportunity to engage with pre-criminal situations through identifying web sites. In both these circumstances, a further factor that would increase capable guardianship would be for credit card companies to monitor activity, denying authorization for card use and reporting incidents to the police if such sites are accessed or for access to potentially illegal newsgroups. But as above, this will require co-ordinated action among the different organizations involved in either delivery of Internet search capacity or the financial institutions involved in credit card authorization and availability. It will also require a re-orientation of effort away from catching offenders to diminishing the potential to commit crime.

An interesting initiative that may fit within the analysis presented here is Operation Pin, an Internet sting operation launched on 18 December 2003 by the U.K. National Crime Squad. Designed by West Midlands Police, and involving the FBI, Australian Federal Police, Interpol and other police agencies, Operation Pin involved the creation of a web site that purported to offer child abuse images: " . . . Visitors to the sites, which appear to be identical to real pedophile addresses, go through a series of web pages searching for exactly the image they want. When they try to view the picture they will be told they have committed a crime for which they could spend 10 years in jail and that their details have been recorded" (BBC News, 18 December 2003[7]). " . . . The site works by purporting to contain images of child abuse. Users are then led through a series of pages/ sub sites, whilst being prompted the whole time to withdraw from the process. If they choose to continue they will ultimately be taken to a page which will tell them they have entered a law enforcement website, that their actions constitute an offence and that their details have been captured" (media release, Australian Federal Police, 19 December 2003[8]).

Leaving aside the legality of such "sting" procedures, in terms of the analysis presented here, this initiative interferes with search activity through creating a situation of increased threat specifically (in terms of the consequences of progressing through the site) and more generally (in terms of influencing the decisional calculus of potential users in relation to other similar activity). Evidence related to this latter point can be seen in the response to Operation Pin on Internet websites where details of the sting operation were widely publicized, and the addresses of suspect sites were given (with advice to avoid them).[9] The initiative also contributes to a sense of capable guardianship (again as can be seen in comments on the initiative on websites). It is not known how many people in fact entered the site, so it is not possible to judge in that sense its effectiveness; although site entrants were apparently not prosecuted, a police objective may have been the collection of IP addresses, either to act upon later or as an intelligence-gathering exercise. However, these objectives are largely irrelevant to the argument presented here, and judging from web comments it achieved considerable success in the terms presented in this paper.

CONCLUDING COMMENTS

In summary, rational choice perspectives on offending could have a major contribution to make to improve our understanding of Internet crime in general, and specifically in relation to crimes related to the collection and distribution of abuse images of children. Engaging in a crime-specific analysis and focusing on the process of criminal behavior as it relates to the collection of abuse images of children can also offer opportunities to systematically develop effective crime control strategies. Notions related to opportunity, and "searching," as the rate-limiting factor in the creation of pre-criminal situations and opportunities, seem to be particularly relevant to the Internet environment, as does engaging in steps to remedy the absence of capable guardianship.

The analysis presented here may challenge some practitioners to think outside of their accustomed models. But its implementation brings us to the very heart of the problem the Internet presents when seeking to develop coherent crime prevention and control strategies in general, as well as in relation to abuse images of children. Rational choice perspectives give a basis for the development of systematic strategies to address Internet crime problems. However, e2e architecture enables a multitude of individually owned computers and local area networks to engage with and transmit data across the Internet. Such centralized structures that do exist on the

Internet periphery – the Internet Service Provider (ISP), for example, which at a local level draws together multiple users' access to the Internet, or in a different sense, the search facilities such as Google – are private and unregulated companies, sometimes operating across many different jurisdictions and geographical boundaries. The result of this is that in a sense the virtual social structure of the Internet depends not, as we might expect in real world situations, on government or civil society however we might conceptualize it, but on a series of disconnected and at times competitive private companies implementing an array of self-regulatory processes in an array of jurisdictions on the backbone of a complex but largely self-sustaining network.

In part because of this, as well as the inherent structure of the Internet, we see the significance of the absence of the critical factor Cohen and Felson (1979) refer to as a capable guardian. Guardianship implies some form of structured and socially responsible capacity to monitor, deter and in some sense act if necessary; however, it does not necessarily imply government action. But given commercial realities, regardless of social outcomes in terms of the effects on crime, it may well not be in a company's commercial interest to seek to adopt or develop the capable guardian role.

This point is made quite forcibly in the following quotation from an Australian man who was caught in October 2004 in possession of abuse images of children, which came from a web site and which were paid for by credit card.

> I think the fact that VISA card accepted payment and provided access, almost gave it a seal of approval. I am not negating my own guilt, but I cannot understand how credit card companies, who know that these sites are illegal, and they must as they provided my details to the authorities, are able to continue to provide access via their service, and even worse profit from the trade. If credit card companies were faced with strict penalties and an obligation to monitor for illegal sites that their service provides access to, I think it would go a long way to crippling this trade. In fact it is only via a credit card that these sites can be reached. Why should credit card companies, their owners and shareholders be able to claim ignorance to their guilt in providing access to illegal child porn, when this is not an out available to any other offender. They are making fortunes along with the mafias who run these sites. [Personal communication to the authors]

As well as illustrating the issues related to capable guardianship, this quotation, in making reference to "a seal of approval," also gives a rather surprising insight into what seems to be a positive factor in the decisional calculus for this offender.

It may be that our traditional ways of thinking about law enforcement and social control on the Internet (as for example the expression of sovereignty through social control and regulation) will become increasingly irrelevant (for a detailed discussion of this, and its implications for global development, see Castells, 1997). Put in other terms, an implication of the analysis presented here is that whilst we generally see crime as essentially a problem of policing, the solution to the management and reduction of Internet crime may also lie with those who constitute, create and maintain the Internet environment. Perhaps the way forward is to develop socially responsible initiatives and partnerships (Newman and Clarke, 2003) not dependent on governments. Individual companies, company groupings and voluntary organizations need to develop capable guardianship and to target search activities (as in the examples given here) to limit the emergence of pre-criminal situations. This seems to be a realistic way forward if within the context of the current morphology of the Internet we are to see the development of meaningful crime prevention strategies. Thus far, experience suggests that this is unlikely to happen of its own accord, and perhaps we need to explore more effective international means of addressing these problems outside of traditional roles and structures.

Address correspondence to: Max Taylor, Copine Project, Department of Applied Psychology, University College Cork, Ireland; e-mail: M.Taylor@ucc.ie.

NOTES

1. This paper arises from research undertaken whilst the first author held an Irish Research Council for the Humanities and Social Sciences Government of Ireland Senior Research Fellowship.
2. "Abuse images" is a preferred term to use rather than "child pornography," although the latter term may have specific legal meanings in some jurisdictions.

3. *Transmission Control Protocol* and *Internet Protocol*. See http://www.
   yale.edu/pclt/COMM/TCPIP.HTM for discussion of these concepts.
4. ECHELON, the global interception and relay system, is thought to
   do this. At a more local level, the FBI CARNIVORE system similarly
   intercepts local traffic. For a discussion of both, see Nabbali and Perry
   (2003; 2004) and also http://archive.aclu.org/echelonwatch/faq.html.
5. Internet Relay Chat
6. Peer-to-peer
7. http://news.bbc.co.uk/go/pr/fr/-/1/hi/uk/3329567.stm
8. www.afp.gov.au/afp/page/Media/2003/1219childabuse.htm
9. For example, see heh.ca/op_pin/

REFERENCES

Bouffard, J.A. (2002). "The Influence of Emotion on Rational Decision Making in Sexual Aggression." *Journal of Criminal Justice* 30:121–124.

Carmichael, S. and A.R. Piquero (2004). "Sanctions, Perceived Anger and Criminal Offending." *Journal of Quantitative Criminology* 20:371–393.

Castells, M. (1997). *The Information Age: Economy, Society and Culture*, vol. 1–3. Oxford, UK: Blackwell.

Clarke, R.V. and M. Felson (1993). "Introduction: Criminology, Routine Activity, and Rational Choice." In: R.V. Clarke and M. Felson (eds.), *Routine Activity and Rational Choice*. (Advances in Criminological Theory, vol. 5.) New Brunswick, NJ: Transaction Press.

Cohen, L.E. and M. Felson (1979). "Social Change and Crime Rate Trends: A Routine Activity Approach." *American Sociological Review* 44:588–608.

Cook, P.J. (1986). "The Demand and Supply of Criminal Opportunities." In: M. Tonry and N. Morris (eds.), *Crime and Justice: An Annual Review of Research* (vol. 7). Chicago: University of Chicago Press.

Cornish, D. and R.V. Clarke (eds.), (1986). *The Reasoning Criminal: Rational Choice Perspectives on Offending*. New York: Springer-Verlag.

Cusson, M. (1993). "A Strategic Analysis of Crime: Criminal Tactics as Responses to Pre-criminal Situations." In: R.V. Clarke and M. Felson (eds.), *Routine Activity and Rational Choice*. (Advances in Criminological Theory, vol. 5.) New Brunswick, NJ: Transaction Press.

Gibson, J.J. (1979). *The Ecological Approach to Visual Perception*. Boston: Houghton Mifflin.

Gillespie, A. (2005 in press). "Tackling Child Pornography: The Approach in England and Wales." In: E. Quayle and M. Taylor (eds.), *Viewing Child Pornography on the Internet: Understanding the Offence, Managing the Offender, Helping the Victims*. Dorset: Russell House Publishing.

Gottfredson, M.R. and T.A. Hirschi (1990). *A General Theory of Crime*. Stanford, CA: Stanford University Press.

Güth, W. (2000). "Bounded Rational Decision Emergence – A General Perspective and Some Selective Illustrations." *Journal of Economic Psychology* 21:433–458.

Joinson, A.N. (2003). *Understanding the Psychology of Internet Behaviour.* Basingstoke, UK: Palgrave Macmillan.

Lessig, L. (2001). *The Future of Ideas.* New York: Random House.

Loewenstein, G. (1996). "Out of Control: Visceral Influences on Behavior." *Organizational and Human Decision Processes* 65:272–292.

Loewenstein, G., D. Nagin and R. Paternoster (1997). "The Effect of Sexual Arousal on Expectations of Sexual Forcefulness." *Journal of Research in Crime and Delinquency* 34(4):443–473.

Nabbali, T. and M. Perry (2004). "Going for the Throat: Carnivore in an Echelon World – Part 2." *Computer Law and Security Reports* 20:84–97.

Nabbali, T. and M. Perry (2003). "Going for the Throat: Carnivore in an Echelon World – Part 1." *Computer Law and Security Reports* 19:456–467.

Newman, G.R. and R.V. Clarke (2003). *Superhighway Robbery: Preventing E-Commerce Crime.* Cullompton, Devon, UK: Willan Publishing.

Norman, D.D. (1988). *The Psychology of Everyday Things.* New York: Basic Books.

Polaschek, D.L.L. and S.M. Hudson (2004). "Pathways to Rape; Preliminary Examination of Patterns in the Offence Process of Rapists and their Rehabilitation Implications." *Journal of Sexual Aggression* 10:7–20.

Quayle, E. (2005, in press). "The Internet as a Therapeutic Medium." In: E. Quayle and M. Taylor (eds.), *Viewing Child Pornography on the Internet: Understanding the Offence, Managing the Offender, Helping the Victims.* Dorset, UK: Russell House Publishing.

Quayle, E. and M. Taylor (2004 in press). "Sex Offenders, Internet Child Abuse Images and Emotional Avoidance: The Importance of Values." *Aggression and Violent Behavior.*

Quayle, E. and M. Taylor (2003). "A Model of Problematic Internet Use in People with a Sexual Interest in Children." *CyberPsychology and Behavior* 6:93–106.

Quayle, E. and M. Taylor (2002). "Child Pornography and the Internet: Perpetuating a Cycle of Abuse." *Deviant Behaviour* 23(4):331–362.

Quayle, E., M. Taylor, L. Wright and M. Merooga (2005 in press). *Only Pictures? Therapeutic Work with Internet Sex Offenders.* Dorset, UK: Russell House Publishing.

Reed, D.P., J.H. Saltzer and D.D. Clark (1980). *Active Networking and End-to-End Arguments.* http://web.mit.edu/Saltzer/www/publications/endtoend/ANe2ecomment.htm

Simon, H.A. (1983). *Reason in Human Affairs.* Oxford: Blackwell.

Taylor, M. (1993). "Rational Choice, Behaviour Analysis and Political Violence." In: R.V. Clarke and M. Felson (eds.), *Routine Activity and Rational Choice.* (Advances in Criminological Theory, vol. 5). New Brunswick: Transaction Press.

Taylor, M. and E. Quayle (2003). *Child Pornography. An Internet Crime.* London: Bruner Routledge.

Ward, T. (2003). "The Explanation, Assessment and Treatment of Child Sexual Abuse." *International Journal of Forensic Psychology* 1:10–25.

Ward, T. (2002). "Good Lives and the Rehabilitation of Offenders: Promises and Problems." *Aggression and Violent Behavior* 7:513–528.

Wright, R.E., A. Caspi, T.E. Moffitt and R. Paternoster (2004). "Does Individual Risk Deter Criminally Prone Individuals? Rational Choice, Self-Control and Crime." *Journal of Research in Crime and Delinquency* 41(2):180–213.

Situational Prevention and Child Sex Offenders with an Intellectual Disability

by

Frank Lambrick
Disability Services, Victoria, Australia

and

William Glaser
Departments of Psychology and Criminology,
University of Melbourne

Abstract: *Child sex offenders with an intellectual disability (ID sex offenders) have historically been treated far differently from other sex offenders. Due to their lower levels of intellectual functioning they have, for example, been viewed as being more dangerous than other sex offenders. The path to initial conviction of the ID sex offender has typically been characterized by a continuing denial and minimization of their evolving "inappropriate" behaviours, or has in other cases led to an over-reaction, resulting in the implementation of harsh restrictive practices that further entrench the initial behavior. The treatment approach that has been developed at the Statewide Forensic Service (SFS) located in Fairfield, an inner northern suburb in Melbourne, not only involves modified cognitive-behavioural, skills-based and whole-of-life programs, but also places a strong emphasis on the environmental management of this client group. Factors such as the training of carers and significant others in relation to the observation of client*

Crime Prevention Studies, volume 19 (2006), pp. 197–221.

behaviors in the community, and the subsequent redirection of offender behaviour, play an integral role in the treatment process. A comprehensive awareness of these factors and subsequent appropriate action by carers and/or significant others would be a significant crime prevention approach in this population.

INTRODUCTION

Criminologists have tended to cast a jaundiced eye on crime prevention and its practical applications, arguing that preventative programs are often excuses to increase State intervention in the lives of the community's most vulnerable members, for example, young people and minority groups. Yet crime prevention at its most pragmatic level aims "to rely on institutions other than the criminal law and criminal justice" to reduce the damage caused by criminal activities (O'Malley, 1997). It is thus one of the few alternative ways available to protect society from offenders who either will not respond to the sanctions imposed by traditional criminal law or who themselves are likely to suffer major disadvantages from it.

Intellectually disabled (ID) offenders are the example par excellence of this group. They are stigmatized and disadvantaged at every stage of the criminal justice system: they are more likely than most offenders to be apprehended for a crime, confess to it, receive inadequate legal representation, be denied bail, plead guilty, receive a custodial sentence, be harassed and abused in prison, and be denied parole (Glaser and Deane, 1999). On the other hand, paradoxically enough, it is also harder to process them through the criminal justice system. Many of them will, for example, have cases against them dropped because their victims will also be intellectually disabled and therefore unable to give evidence in court. Finally, there are grave risks to the community if an ID offender is placed in traditional criminal justice environments such as prisons, given that for many such offenders with few living skills and limited social networks, prison provides the perfect opportunity to learn anti-social behaviours and acquire a criminal peer group.

Unfortunately, until very recently prevention was seen as being inapplicable to offenders with an intellectual disability, and even more so, for ID sex offenders. They were seen as menaces to society who, because of their intellectual disability, were perceived as being universally cursed with perverse impulses over which they had no control. The only forms of prevention possible were therefore segregation and sterilization (Glaser and Deane, 1999). Yet recent research has demonstrated that ID sex offenders share the same characteristics and are influenced in the same way by their environments as their non-disabled counterparts (Lambrick and Glaser, 2004). Thus, they often plan their offences using deviant fantasies, take advantage of and seek out opportunities where they can victimize others without being detected, respond to precipitants such as pornography or pro-offending attitudes in their family, peer group and community, and display the same rationalizations and minimizations used by non-disabled sex offenders and the community in general to justify their behaviours. They therefore are likely to respond to the preventive strategies discussed in the other chapters in this volume.

More importantly, the case of ID sex offenders can be used to develop the existing theory in this area. Sex crimes against children are rightly regarded with horror and abhorrence by the community. Yet the thinking about it is bedeviled by the problems which attend the planning of programs to prevent sexual violence generally: for example, the overwhelming desire to keep much of this offending private or within the family, the difficulty in challenging social norms and attitudes which encourage it, the problems in selling the advantages of prevention, and the complex ramifications of preventative interventions which will often need to address matters such as family dysfunction, past sexual abuse, social alienation, inequality and substance abuse (Allen, 1995). These considerations are nowhere better epitomised than in the case of sex offenders with an intellectual disability. Thus, planning and implementing programs for them will inevitably produce valuable insights for those tackling the problem on a wider scale.

This chapter firstly examines some characteristics of ID sex offenders and their environment, and then discusses some specific assessment and treatment approaches that might prevent re-offending in this group. It then looks at these approaches in the wider context of current theories that apply public health principles (Basile, 2003) and concepts drawn from preventive criminology, particularly the models of opportunity reduction (Clarke and Homel, 1997) and situational precipitants (Wortley, 1998). Finally, we highlight the lessons that ID sex offenders can teach those who are designing programs to prevent sex offending generally. Because of the ongoing lack of empirical research in this area, in many instances throughout this chapter the authors will draw upon their own experiences as professionals working in this area over many years.

CHARACTERISTICS OF ID SEX OFFENDERS

There is a lack of consensus in the research literature surrounding the characteristics of ID sex offenders and the prevalence of their offending (Lambrick and Glaser, 2004; Lindsay, 2002). This is in part due to the comparative lack of research that has been conducted in this area. Where it has been conducted, the samples have rarely distinguished ID sex offenders who victimize adults from those victimizing children (Lindsay, 2002). This population has only received significant community attention since the process of deinstitutionalization began in the 1980s, which led to the presence in the community of many individuals with an intellectual disability who had previously been locked away for these behaviors (Lindsay, 2002). Studies have subsequently noted an increase in the percentage of offenders with an intellectual disability being sentenced in the criminal justice system (Day, 1993; Lund, 1990).

The research in this area is compromised by methodological problems surrounding the definition of intellectual disability, a term that covers a vast range of intellectual functioning, from the profoundly to the mildly disabled. There is, thus, an enormous variation in cognitive abilities and adaptive behaviour skills in this group of offenders (Lindsay, 2002), and those at the lowest level of intellectual functioning within this range will be far less likely than those who are "high-functioning" to understand legal issues and societal values. Most studies of offenders with intellectual disability, however, make little distinction among the various levels of ability (Lambrick and Glaser, 2004; Lindsay, 2002), and some have included those within the category of "borderline" intellectual functioning (i.e., functioning at just above the cut-off point for intellectual disability) as well, further complicating this issue. Nevertheless the association between offending and intellectual ability seems to be strongest in the borderline range, decreasing as the level of intellectual disability increases (Lindsay, 2002; Simpson and Hogg, 2001a, 2001b).

The characteristics that have been identified in relation to ID sex offenders generally appear to be similar to those of mainstream sex offender populations. They include dysfunctional family backgrounds – particularly having other family members with criminal histories – marital disharmony and separation, violence and neglect and other pathology in multiple family members (Day, 1994, 1993; Lindsay, 2002). Individual factors include difficulties in school, relationship problems, behavioral problems and psychiatric illness (Day, 1993).

Factors that may be more specific to those with an intellectual disability include deficits in sexual knowledge and attitudes, poor relationship skills, confused self-concept, poor peer relations, sexual abuse in childhood, lack of personal empowerment and a subsequent susceptibility to the influence of others (Day, 1994, 1993; Glaser, 1992; Hayes, 1991; Thompson and Brown, 1997). It has also been suggested that ID sex offenders are more likely than non-ID sex offenders to commit offences against a range of victims and are less likely to commit offences that may result in more serious bodily harm to the victim (Blanchard et al., 1999; Boer et al., 1995; Day, 1994, 1993; Hayes, 1991). ID sex offenders may also commit these offences not so much from a basis of sexual deviance, but as a result of a general level of maladaptive functioning due to a poor emotional and social background (Glaser, 1992).

It is important to understand however, that ID sex offenders appear to exhibit much the same patterns of deviant arousal and cognitive distortions as their non-disabled counterparts (Lindsay et al., 2000). There are, therefore, major and obvious implications for preventative work here. Like many other sex offenders who target children, those with an intellectual disability will create their own deviant stimuli, be constantly seeking opportunities to offend, skillfully assess the vulnerability of potential victims, and be able to produce considerable denial, rationalization and minimization of their offending behaviours if detected.

When situational prevention is being considered, the *environment* of the ID sex offender is at least as important in fostering their offending behaviours as their individual characteristics. On the one hand, the settings in which many people with an intellectual disability live tend to restrict their opportunities to offend: these include closely supervised institutional and group home environments, and involvement in community outreach programs, where the staff who "support" them are also able to carefully scrutinize their activities. On the other hand, such settings may make it difficult to recognize offending behaviours, particularly if the victims involved are unable to communicate their distress or are too terrified to do so. Staff and carers are often most reluctant to stigmatize their clients or loved ones with the labels of "pedophile" or "sex offender," will refuse to acknowledge the influence of family or institutional models of deviance on them, and will deliberately ignore or find excuses for even very clear displays of sexual violence.

For example, an ID sex offender with whom both authors have worked over many years committed his index offence while living with his mother in a public housing unit. She had taken in a friend who was a single mother as a temporary boarder. She was aware of her son's offending behavior but ignored the tragic potential that such an arrangement might have. The ID offender stated that he did warn his mother about the risks associated with this living arrangement, but she ignored this warning, to the extent that he was asked to baby-sit the young boy and girl on several occasions. Tragically, he did eventually offend against the young boy while giving him a bath, recording the crime using a video camera secreted in the bathroom cabinet. His ability to both plan and carry out his offenses illustrates the degree of sophistication this group can exhibit in their offending and also how their support network can prevent even the most basic of situational measures from being instituted.

Despite beliefs to the contrary, institutional placements are not effective in preventing this sort of crime. For example, an ID sex offender who had victimized two young girls while living in a community-based unit, was moved into an institutional environment. There he was placed in a mixed gender unit where he was by far the most skilled resident, and he acquired a reputation as being both charming and compliant. The staff came to accept him as being more one of them than simply another resident, and they started giving him duties which should have been their own responsibility. One of these involved bathing a young non-verbal female client, and it was distressingly easy for him to indecently assault her while doing so.

Thus, for ID sex offenders, and particularly for those who offend against children, crime prevention must consider the setting where the offender is living, working, being educated or socializing. In community contexts they may be under a greater degree of control than non-disabled offenders, but they can also be exploited, exposed to more offending opportunities or inducted into deviant sub-cultures. Yet in disability-specific institutional settings they are most likely to be significantly higher functioning than the other residents, and to be afforded a status that provides opportunities for them to victimize lower-functioning peers.

In any highly supervised environment, whether community-based or institutional, interventions may focus on an offender's obviously disruptive behaviours (e.g., stealing from or teasing fellow clients) rather than their more covert sex offending, particularly if they are not offered clinical assessment and treatment oversight. Even within clinically-directed supervised residential programs, ensuring that staff maintain a focus on the more subtle, but much more dangerous, manifestations of offense-specific behavior is often problematic. An ID sex offender with whom both authors have worked over many years has a difficult interpersonal style, but at the same time is highly motivated to engage in his treatment programs. Unfortunately, rather than provide positive reinforcement to this client for his treatment gains, staff tend to focus upon day-to-day behaviors that are at best marginally related to his offending behavior. The resulting conflict, if anything, increases his risk of re-offending.

Finally, there is a small but worrying group in this population who need a very complex and wide range of preventative interventions which extend well beyond manipulation of their environment. They often deliberately use their disability to take attention away from their deviant sexual activity, for example by feigning poor communication skills in order to sidetrack discussion of their behaviors and by exaggerating their disability in order to evoke sympathy from the courts and other criminal justice agencies. In the authors' experience, these individuals are often able to reside independently in the community, actively maintaining their offense-specific and -related activities with very little consequence. Unfortunately, this particular group of individuals exploits a still widely held notion that this group is not responsible for their actions and therefore should not be accorded the responsibility expected of others.

RELEVANT ASSESSMENT AND TREATMENT MODELS

Environmental management perspectives have historically been utilised with ID sex offenders, although more recent interventions have been criticized for placing too great an emphasis on intrapersonal factors with this population (Demetral, 1994; O'Connor, 1997). Demetral (1994) maintained that while intrapersonal factors were important components of the treatment process, the quality of the external environment of the participant determined the level of generalization of these factors across their day-to-day environments. Demetral (1994) conceptualized the external environment as comprising the multiple problems of ID sex offenders that arise from and are maintained by the inter-relationship between the offenders and their external milieu. Demetral was of the opinion that while skills can be taught in treatment sessions, their generalization across the ID offenders' day-to-day environment was dependent upon the quality of their external environment. For example, the degree to which an ID sex offender experiencing stress is able to utilize coping skills taught in treatment sessions will be dependent upon the quality of their support network.

O'Connor (1997), like Demetral (1994), was also of the opinion that interventions were too focused on the intrapersonal dimension of the offender, perhaps due to the emphasis upon cognitive-behavioural techniques in the intervention process. She considered that environmental factors such as employment and social network quality had a significant impact upon the long-term outcome of intervention. O'Connor (1996) outlined a problem-solving approach, based upon the work of Nezu and Nezu (1989), that also incorporated applied behavior analysis as a framework for assessment and treatment with this population. The assessment comprised four main factors: internal control; external control; social environmental; and biological. Intervention was subsequently guided by the outcomes of the assessment in each of the four factors. The importance of a case management approach to co-ordinate the support is emphasized in this model, particularly from a long-term structured-support perspective. Case managers were considered to be in the best position to monitor the ID offender's progress and intervene around those environmental factors that may increase the ID offender's risk presentation (O'Connor, 1997).

Two treatment models have been developed at the Statewide Forensic Service (SFS) to assist ID sex offenders to comprehend the process of assessment and treatment, and to operationalize the generalization of skills across day-to-day environments. Both of these models reinforce and reflect themes of taking responsibility for behaviors and relating to others in a pro-social manner. The first model is the "old-me/new-me" model, which has been derived from Haaven et al.'s (1990) approach. This approach used an individual poster, outlining those aspects of the self that comprised offense-specific and -related features or "old-me," as well as those that comprised an offence-free life style, and acquisition of positive, or "new-me" skills. The SFS has developed this concept further by simplifying it to symbolic images that are recognized around most of the world and by the inclusion in the model of the concept of "freedom" in a visual format. This format provides for a more visual and concrete comprehension of the old-me/new-me concept and facilitates its generalization across differing environments. The model is used to structure peer feedback and ensures that feedback and redirection by carers, treatment providers and significant others who are supporting the client are consistent (Lambrick and Glaser, 2004).

The second model is the Positive Sanctions Model, which is based on the premise that all clients have access to daily core activities and services, regardless of their behavior. In order to obtain less restriction and supervision, clients are required to participate in individual and group treatment and demonstrate "new-me" behaviors within day-to-day environments. Client participation in all program areas is evaluated using a numerical rating, ranging from 0 to 5. The scores obtained by the client are subsequently averaged over the individual treatment plan review period. Depending upon the environment in which the client is located, the average rating will determine their "phase" level. Each phase level determines the degree to which clients have access to community-based activities. The basic phase is the most restrictive, with the client having limited and highly supervised community access, what are regarded as "core activities." Clients have access to these core activities regardless of their behavior. In using this model, all clients are initially placed in this phase, along with those clients who consistently average a poor program participation rating. Subsequent higher phases reflect increasing levels of community access and decreasing levels of staff supervision. The aim of this concept is to facilitate in clients a greater awareness of their progress in treatment, which in turn fosters peer feedback.

The concurrent use of the old-me/new-me model and Positive Sanctions Model, at least in the experience of SFS, provides an ongoing positive pressure on clients to actively and pro-socially engage in their treatment program. Client access to community-based activities is dependent upon their participation in treatment programs and the demonstration of pro-social behavior within their day-to-day environments. Peer feedback is encouraged through the simplified language of the old-me/new-me model and through the observational learning perspective provided by other clients who have gained greater access to increased community-based activities. Supervised community-based activities provide the opportunity for staff to assess client utilization of – and the efficacy of – strategies developed within treatment programs. Clients in turn gain increased and less supervised community access as they demonstrate greater degrees of internal control while engaging in these activities.

PREVENTION OF SEXUAL CRIMES AND
ID SEX OFFENDERS

Two models have been developed in the literature for addressing the prevention of sexual violence: the public health model (Allen, 1995; Basile, 2003) and models based on situational factors, particularly opportunity reduction (Clarke and Homel, 1997) and situational precipitator reduction (Wortley, 2001). Both models incorporate distinctive approaches. The public health model sees the sex offender as similar to a micro-organism, carrying the "disease" of sexual violence, whose growth and/or access to potential victims must be curtailed in some fashion. By contrast, situational crime control measures such as those proposed by Clarke and Homel (1997) and Wortley (2001) view the offender as a rational agent who is usually able to compare the benefits of committing a crime (e.g., gaining sexual satisfaction) against the costs (e.g., being detected). Wortley (2001) argues further that situational factors may also either provide or reduce the motivation to commit crimes. In both the public health and the situational models, however, interventions which directly impact on the setting of the criminal activity are of primary importance, although the public health model tends to place more emphasis on an offender's innate pre-dispositions to offend and on preventing the development of these.

The Public Health Model of Prevention

In public health practice, particularly public mental health practice, there are three levels of prevention. At the primary level, the aim is to prevent the onset of the condition, for example, in people with a disability, eliminating factors which might produce or exacerbate disability, such as poor antenatal care, inadequate parenting skills or environmental toxins. Secondary prevention consists of the early identification and prompt treatment of a condition in order to limit its prevalence and duration: in the disability field, measures include early detection of children with developmental delay and early interventions such as correcting communication deficits and specialist childhood development programs. Tertiary prevention programs focus on reducing the extent and duration of residual defects or disabilities: for people with an intellectual disability, such programs will include appropriate educational, vocational and accommodation services and help with accessing these.

Unfortunately, for many people with an intellectual disability, "prevention" has acquired somewhat sinister connotations, being used to justify serious threats to their rights, health and safety (e.g., abortion of foetuses with congenital abnormalities, forced sterilization of disabled people during their reproductive years, and segregation from the rest of the community) (Glaser, 1996). By contrast, measures aimed at reducing sexual violence have traditionally focused on victims, especially women (e.g., programs helping women to avoid and resist rape and other forms of sexual abuse). But given the potential for an offender to victimize literally hundreds of people, it seems more logical to focus on programs for offenders or potential offenders (Basile, 2003).

The areas of need for primary prevention are unfortunately obvious in this group and have been mentioned already: disrupted and dysfunctional family backgrounds, educational, relationship and behavioral problems, deficits in sexual knowledge and attitudes, poor socio-sexual skills, poor impulse control, poor self-concept and criminogenic influences from family, peers and others. All of these are eminently amenable to interventions, which are often easy to implement. Unfortunately, the barriers to such implementation include not only a lack of resources, but the stigmatizing attitudes of care givers and the community in general. For example, an obvious intervention such as sex education for people with an intellectual disability continues to generate enormous unease and controversy (Thompson and Brown, 1997).

By contrast, secondary and tertiary-level interventions can be readily incorporated into the assessment and treatment models discussed above. These fit quite comfortably into the public health model, particularly with their focus on diminishing the harmfulness of an individual offender as a "disease transmitter." They also are consistent with the developmental approach adopted by many professional workers, with the disabled utilizing preventive measures such as the old-me-new-me model, which facilitates the efforts by families, care givers and professional staff to help those with a disability develop appropriate skills to minimize the impact of their disability on their lives and the lives of others.

However, applying the public health model to ID sex offenders presents two major obstacles. First of all, the role of the wider community in promoting the "spread" of the "disease" of sexual violence is minimised or even ignored: e.g., the persistence of rape myths, hostile attitudes towards women and children, work place sexual harassment, professionals ignoring or not recognizing signs of child sexual abuse (see Basile, 2003). ID sex offenders are, if anything, even more susceptible to these influences than their non-disabled counterparts because of their limited opportunities to acquire appropriate sexual skills, knowledge and attitudes.

A second major problem with the public health approach is that it tends to downplay the importance of the interaction between the offender and the environment. Like all other offenders, ID offenders generally will only offend if the opportunity arises and if they are exposed to a setting which somehow motivates them to offend. While the public health model acknowledges the importance of such offender-environment interactions (e.g., by ensuring that an offender has skills to avoid opportunities for offending), it offers only a limited guide as to the specific interventions which might be successful. To consider these in a systematic fashion, we need to turn to the situational prevention models proposed by Clarke and Homel (1997) and Wortley (2001).

Situational Crime Prevention and ID Sex Offenders

Regardless of an individual perpetrator's propensity to offend, our experience with those with a disability matches the observations of those working with non-disabled offenders: he offends mainly when the extended networks that are known to him and who know his history, unwittingly or otherwise, present opportunities for him to offend. This clinical impression is supported by research conducted by Smallbone and Wortley (2000), which concluded that child sexual abuse overwhelmingly occurs in circumstances where the perpetrator is related to or knows the victim. On the other hand, the label of disability often renders offenders less risky than other offender populations, at least within the state of Victoria, Australia. Those assessed and registered as having an intellectual disability in Victoria are more closely monitored than most other offender groups due to their greater support needs. There is, thus, an opportunity for support workers such as case managers, carers and outreach workers, if sufficiently trained around specific risk factors, to provide an informed observational and reinforcement role (Lambrick, 2003).

Opportunity Reduction

Clarke and Homel's (1997) classification of situational crime prevention techniques focuses upon the alteration of immediate environments in order to reduce opportunities for crime. This model is based upon a rational choice perspective, which views potential offenders as actively deliberating the costs and benefits of engaging in the offense, prior to making a decision as to whether to engage in the offense or not (Wortley, 2001). There are four basic strategies outlined in this classification structure: increasing the perceived effort involved in crime; increasing the perceived risks; reducing the anticipated reward; and inhibiting the rationalizations that facilitate crime. While people with an intellectual disability have traditionally not been regarded as "rational agents" (as noted above), these strategies can in fact be applied successfully to this group.

ID sex offenders are readily deterred by any measures which *increase the perceived effort* that they must put into committing their crimes. One simple but very effective measure is to ensure that their residential placement in the community is far from (i.e., more than reasonable walking distance from) facilities such as schools, parks, playgrounds or other locations frequently accessed by children.

This group also responds well to measures which *increase the risks perceived by them* of committing their offences. Relevant strategies include concrete but detailed descriptions re-enforced by pictorial representations of locations where anti-loitering laws would apply, explanations of the requirements that those applying for employment in child-related fields will need to undergo police record checks, and most importantly of all, the monitoring of their activities by informed support staff and carers.

ID offenders respond to measures which *reduce the rewards they might anticipate* for their offending activities. While victim empathy is difficult to instill in them, they can develop an understanding of the adverse consequences for themselves. Thus, although imprisonment itself may have little deterrent value – due to its provision of a structured, predictable routine and basic comfort such as food and shelter with very little effort required of the offender personally – the deprivations associated with imprisonment may be of more immediate relevance. One offender known to the authors, for example, declared that he was very happy with prison life and the activities of a typical day in prison, but subsequently confessed that he would not like to go back there because he did not like the taste of the bread served at meals. ID sex offenders also need to be made aware of their higher risk of detection by police due to, firstly, their often inefficient ways of committing their crimes and secondly, the fact that they are often "known to the police as regular offenders."

Finally, an opportunity-reduction approach justifies assisting offenders (and those involved with them) to *inhibit their rationalizations* for offending. As we have seen, the old-me/new-me model stresses that it is only after an offender recognizes his old-me thoughts, feelings and behaviors, and moves on to practising new-me thoughts, feelings and behaviors, that he can truly achieve freedom and the post-treatment goals that he expects in life. That message is reinforced not only during the phase of formal treatment, but also repeatedly during post-treatment follow-up involving a variety of agencies and carers.

Unfortunately, the Clarke and Homel (1997) model, while correctly emphasizing the importance of environmentally-based interventions for this population, still seems to give only limited attention to the rather more complex and often reciprocal interactions between the offender and his environment. Thus opportunity reduction provides only a partial answer to the problems of:

1. *Unlearning maladaptive behaviors*: particularly those which are easily triggered or prompted by frequently-encountered environmentally stimuli (e.g., depictions of children in advertising and popular culture, particularly in a sexualized way);

2. *Generalising newly acquired skills and learning*: a difficult task for offenders with an intellectual disability, particularly when they progress through treatment and start gaining increased access to the community; and,

3. *Maintaining motivation*: especially in an already stigmatized and devalued group of offenders who may see themselves as gaining very little reward despite very sincere attempts to comply with the onerous restrictions on their lifestyle demanded by participation in a treatment program.

Of course, these are problems faced by any sexual offender targeting children, whether disabled or not. They are, however, of particular significance in the group with an intellectual disability because of both their cognitive limitations and their devalued and disadvantaged place in society. Recently, for example, a client known to the authors managed to successfully complete the application process for a job as a cleaner in a high school, despite the authors' warnings. His motivations may well have included that of his deviant sexual arousal involving children, but he was also desperately keen to mark out a place for himself in the community as a non-stigmatized regular employee. Predictably enough, he did not obtain the position when the appropriate police record checks were performed; in one sense this result is an instance of successful crime prevention, but at another level, by highlighting his own powerlessness and stigmatisation of him as a sex offender, it possibly could have decreased his motivation to comply with ongoing treatment.

Situational Precipitators

These sorts of problems might be better addressed by Wortley's (1998) two-stage model of situational crime prevention. His classification complements the opportunity-reduction approach of Clarke and Homel (1997). Wortley (2001) pointed out that:

> whereas the term opportunity reduction assumes the existence of a motivated or at least ambivalent offender who is ready to give in to criminal temptations, it is argued that the motivation to commit crime may itself be situationally dependent. [Wortley, 2001, p. 63]

Wortley's (1998) two-stage model recognizes that firstly, situational forces exist which precipitate criminal conduct and control of them may entirely avert the subsequent commission of a crime. It is only when criminal behavior is initiated that the offender will rationally consider the costs and benefits of the opportunities for crime commission which are presented. Furthermore, excessive control of precipitating factors may preclude the use adequate opportunity-reduction strategies or, alternatively, there maybe excessive control at the opportunity-reduction stage. Both of these "feedback loops" will, paradoxically enough, lead to the commission of a crime (even though seemingly adequate crime prevention strategies are in place). For example, for ID offenders an important precipitating factor is the presence of child pornography, or indeed depictions of children generally. This may be sufficient for the offender to then actively search for opportunities to commit crimes (i.e., attempt to target vulnerable child victims). Stringent restrictions on an offender's ability to access depictions of children may, however, be ultimately counterproductive, because as they gain more freedom to move around in the community, offenders may not learn how to appropriately handle material such as "junk mail" catalogues depicting children in underwear. Similarly, not allowing an offender to have any contact with children may prevent them from learning how to deal with situations in which they might accidentally encounter children, such as when going to the movies. Their level of risk can really only be assessed by well-supervised and graduated exposure to the relevant situational precipitants and opportunities for criminal behavior. Yet it has to be acknowledged that offenders from this group often take a very long time to learn appropriate new-me skills for dealing with situations and opportunities, and these restrictions on their activities may need to be maintained for periods of months or even years while such learning is taking place.

Wortley (2001) postulates four ways in which situational factors might precipitate criminal responses: they might *prompt* an individual to perform criminal behavior; they can exert social *pressure* forcing an individual to offend; they can *permit* potential offenders to carry out crimes by weakening moral and other prohibitions; and they can *provoke* an offender to commit a crime through for example arousing him emotionally. Each of these situations may be controlled in at least four different ways. For example, prompts to offending maybe limited by controlling triggers such as pornography, providing reminders of offending potential, reducing inappropriate imitation by restricting access to models of criminal activity, and setting positive expectations that an offender will behave pro-socially in particular circumstances.

Unfortunately, the *prompts* encouraging re-offending in an ID sex offender are everywhere. Every suburb or town has schools, parks and child-care centres, every letter box receives junk mail advertising children's sleepwear, and every milk bar and convenience store sells child-attracting items such as sweets and ice-creams. The treatment approaches with this group thus place a heavy emphasis on the offender's day-to-day environment, and the identification and management of seemingly innocuous precipitants for the old-me thoughts, feelings and behaviors which inevitably lead to offending. This process begins under conditions of high supervision, gradually leading to lowered levels of supervision, as the ID offender demonstrates increasing levels of internal control.

Thus, *triggering* factors such as depictions of children in store catalogues are initially considered as contraband. Such material is confiscated, and in a supervised setting ID sex offenders are not allowed to watch children's television programs, access photographs of children in magazines, and so on. As they gradually progress to less supervised environments, ID sex offenders learn how such materials involve a high risk to them and develop alternative visual fantasy scripts to replace the viewing of such inappropriate materials. ID sex offenders also learn the timing and location of high-risk activities in the community (e.g., visiting a fast food restaurant after school hours). Under supervision they are taught when and where it is appropriate that such visits take place.

Various techniques are used to provide *reminders* to ID sex offenders of appropriate behaviors, emphasizing visual cues or symbols. The treatment model described earlier uses the old-me/new-me model to develop visual prompts to remind ID sex offenders of various scenarios, their consequences, and ways of dealing with them. Each offender at SFS develops and rehearses his own pictorial relapse prevention plan, focusing on the offence pathways and strategies to prevent recidivism which are unique to them. The offender can refer to this plan repeatedly, long after he completes the treatment process (James et al., 2000).

Figure 1 is an example of an individual "cue card" used by an ID sex offender to control his exposure to a trigger. It pairs a self-talk statement (enabling self-control) with a visual image that is meaningful to him and which reflects key elements of the old-me/new-me model, so that the green new-me figure in the image is in control of the red old-me figure. The small size of these cue cards enables them to be carried in the offender's pocket at all times. They eventually assume symbolic power in themselves: offenders at a more advanced stage of treatment report that they are able to re-direct themselves in high-risk situations simply by touching the pocket or wallet in which the cue card has been placed.

Inappropriate imitation is a major problem for this group who, as noted above, often have little incentive to unlearn old-me deviant behaviors. Furthermore, as has also been noted, the general community environment of an sex ID offender is awash with inappropriate models of and rationalizations for their offending behaviour, including sexualized depictions of children, portrayals of other criminal activity (particularly domestic violence) and glorification of violence generally (e.g., as a means of settling disputes).

It is thus crucial to ensure that staff, carers, family members and other important people in an ID sex offender's life model appropriate behaviors. In some cases this may necessitate dramatic shifts in an offender's social networks. The mother of an ID sex offender known to us encouraged him to assault staff and to generally resist treatment. Ultimately, tight restrictions had to be placed on her visits and it was only after these were

Figure 1:   Example of an Individual "Cue Card" Developed with an ID Offender in Treatment

NEW ME TELLS OLD ME WHAT TO DO!

©Statewide Forensic Service 2002

in place that the offender was able to understand the nature and impact of her destructive influence and could then negotiate more appropriate but limited contact with her.

There is still, however, the potential for inappropriate imitation by offenders of each other. This can be minimised by *setting positive expectations*. Both the old-me/new-me model and the Positive Sanctions Model described previously aim to motivate the offender to engage in pro-social behaviour. The Positive Sanctions Model, in particular, selectively rewards those offenders who demonstrate compliance to the program and new-me behaviors. Such positive reinforcement is particularly important for people with an intellectual disability being treated in residential environments where, traditionally, staff attention has tended to focus on negative and "attention-seeking" behaviors.

ID sex offenders at SFS are also expected to act pro-socially and cooperatively in other areas of their lives, for example in completing household tasks, their day-to-day interactions with others and observing household rules. The "pay-off" here is that they are able to achieve some choice in determining household and community access activities. This focus upon co-operation, decision making and choice within the residential environment assists in setting up a sense of positive expectation amongst residents, providing an experiential model for future co-operative relationships in post-treatment environments.

Unfortunately, such positive expectations are often not rewarded when ID sex offenders move into the community. Those with an intellectual disability still face a major lack of educational, pre-vocational, vocational and accommodation options. Because most offenders in this group experience only a "mild" level of intellectual disability, they are "too smart" for more traditional services catering to disabled people, where in any case, clients functioning at a lower level of intellectual disability may present as potential "targets" for these offenders. The ID sex offenders are also however "too dumb" for other programs catering for people with other types of disability or disadvantage (e.g., the mentally ill) (Lambrick, 2003). They are thus left with the challenge of maintaining an offence-free lifestyle where they have little meaningful daytime activity or opportunity for positive social experiences.

Wortley (2001) has suggested that offenders may be pressured to offend by *inappropriately conforming* with deviant group norms, *inappropriately obeying* crime-condoning authority figures, *not complying* with pro-social rules, and *adopting the anonymity* of the crowd as an excuse for behavioural disinhibition. As we have noted, the old-me/new-me and Positive Sanctioning Models encourage an ID sex offender to take personal responsibility for his behaviors and recognize when he needs to take action in high-risk situations, even when people important to them seemingly approve of his remaining in such situations.

The challenge remains, however, to educate families and carers to the fact that high-risk environments not only increase an ID sex offender's danger to the community, but also place unfair and unreasonable stresses upon them. In our experience, too many families and carers insist on exposing an offender to small children on home visits, with the excuse that the offender needs to "keep in touch" with the extended family or needs lots of "cuddles" from them.

ID sex offenders at SFS are also encouraged to be "their own person" in other ways, such as being encouraged to buy their own clothing – sometimes against the wishes of family members who don't want the offender "wasting" money which he should be contributing to family finances – following up individual interests and hobbies (within the limits of the program), and buying their favourite foods.

According to Wortley (2001), situations which encourage offending behaviors may often distort their moral implications by allowing the offender to rely on ambiguous rules and behaviors that can be guided by that situation, and also to abrogate responsibility, ignore the consequences, or de-humanize their victims. These are of course, classic problems encountered with all sex offenders who use complex cognitive distortions to deny, minimize or justify their behaviors at various levels.

As we have seen, the cognitive distortions of ID sex offenders are very similar to those of non-disabled offenders. Cognitive distortions within this population are addressed in group and individual sessions utilizing the framework provided by the old-me/new-me model. ID sex offenders are encouraged to take responsibility for their actions, using the key principles of control, honesty, respect and trust, and they themselves take responsibility for reminding themselves of their treatment objectives using techniques such as cue cards.

As we have already noted, an awareness of the consequences of old-me behaviors remains a crucial part of treatment in this group. Years after intensive treatment has formally ceased, individual offenders report to us that they are still deterred in high-risk situations by using cue card statements such as "kids mean gaol" or "25 years if I offend again." By contrast, offenders as we have also already seen, find it difficult to empathize with their victims, and thus the "humanizing" of their victims is only a limited part of treatment.

Provocation, according to Wortley (2001), comprises adverse environmental factors which induce stress and then "provoke an anti-social response, particularly some form of aggression." Provocations include frustration, crowding, invasions of one's own territory and environmental irritants such as high temperatures, air pollution, noise, cigarette smoke and poor lighting. Many of these environmental factors in the authors' experience have also been shown, not surprisingly, to precipitate disturbed behavior in people with an intellectual disability, both offenders and non-offenders, particularly in institutional settings. All too often, however, these basic considerations have been ignored, usually when an ID offender commits or threatens to commit some spectacular crime, resulting in his being placed in a highly restricted setting beset by the environmental hazards just described. We know of cases of literal "one-person prisons" where, predictably enough, a bored, socially isolated offender existing in conditions of significant sensory deprivation, with his every movement monitored and supervised, experiences a major escalation of the behaviors, leading to a vicious cycle of a further tightening of the restrictions and further behavioral deterioration.

At SFS, two clients in the last few years have absconded and subsequently re-offended. Although these were only two isolated instances, compared to the otherwise successful treatment of dozens of other high-risk offenders, the resultant media publicity, formal enquiries and other responses have now produced considerable anxiety amongst residential and operational staff. This, in turn, has lead to increased resistance to implementing community access for other residents, thus compromising the treatment process and, paradoxically enough, rendering other ID sex offenders more dangerous because they are unable to learn skills for self-management in real-life settings. Similarly, the requirement for increased staff ratios demanded for those who accompany offenders into the community following these absconding incidents, appears to have heightened the ID offenders' own anxiety about their own high risk and also about their potential to be scapegoated themselves by vengeful community members.

An obvious lesson here is that the more control an offender has over his environment, the more he will want to protect and keep it stable. This is particularly important for offenders in this group who are under some form of surveillance and supervision for much of their waking lives. One simple yet profoundly useful technique developed by the program to ensure this is the "green book," a notebook (appropriately coloured green) which is a sort of personal clinical file largely retained by the offender. The offender is responsible for taking it with him at all times and presenting it to any clinician, staff member or service provider with whom he has contact. In it are written notes regarding clinical progress, important incidents in the offender's life, learning and vocational activities and so on.

Both new-me and old-me behaviors are noted and, most importantly, the offender is told exactly what is being written about him and who will be reading the material involved.

As well as serving as an important avenue of communication through the often complex web of professionals involved in the ID sex offender's care, the green book also reminds the offender that he controls, in a large part, the communications regarding him, and must maintain the honesty and integrity to fulfill this task. Remarkably enough, the offenders overwhelmingly have risen to this challenge; of approximately 150 offenders issued with a Green Book so far, only one has tried to destroy it (indeed, we are more fearful of an offender risking inappropriate access to his personal details by inadvertently leaving their Green Book on the bus!).

CONCLUSION

There is no perfect model of crime prevention for ID sex offenders. This is probably an advantage for practitioners in the area: an eclectic use of the models which are available helps to highlight different and changing areas of need for this most complex group. For example, the public health model is useful in developing strategies for early prevention which may well need to start in early childhood, including sexuality and human relationships education, support for disadvantaged families struggling to cope with a disabled child, and more assertive monitoring and interventions for children with a disability who are at risk of physical and sexual abuse. By contrast, the opportunity-reduction model exposes the stereotype of the person with an intellectual disability who supposedly cannot control his or her innate perverse instincts and emphasizes the importance of planning interventions which recognize the ability of most ID sex offenders to plan their abuse of children in a deliberate fashion, much like their non-disabled counterparts. Finally, Wortley's (2001) model incorporating situational precipitants emphasizes that, for this stigmatized and disempowered group, too much control over their offending activities may be just as criminogenic as too little.

This group of offenders however poses challenges over and above the requirements of practical crime prevention. These offenders ultimately provide the litmus test for any theory of crime prevention itself. The sad fact is that for most offenders, if crime prevention fails, communities can and will resort to the traditional controls provided by the criminal justice system. Imprisonment, for example, may be harsh, costly, and ineffective in reducing long-term recidivism, but it does incapacitate the offender, at least while he is in custody, and it may deter. Yet such dispositions are simply not an option for most ID offenders. For example, an Australian survey of judicial officers' attitudes to intellectual disability confirmed world-wide findings that magistrates and judges remain reluctant to impose traditional sanctions on those they saw as being, at best, only partially responsible for their actions, and who were likely to suffer unduly in the criminal justice system (Cockram et al., 1992; McGillivray and Waterman, 2003). Prevention therefore remains the only way to deal with offending and re-offending by this group.

The challenge is not so great as to be insurmountable. Many of the obstacles, as we have seen, involve biased attitudes and stereotyped thinking relating to the disabled. The intervention programs we have described obviously are not perfect and will require continuing modifications and improvement for many years to come. But they consistently stress that change is possible. Old-me is not "bad me," "mad me" or "dumb me": it is simply a collection of thoughts, feelings and behaviors which are not immutable or uncontrollable and which can and must be changed so that the offender, despite the heavy burdens of disability and disadvantage, can live a happier and more productive life. The task is a difficult, but not impossible one: developmentally it is at least as important as all the other tasks which we set our clients with a disability, such as learning to walk, talk, socialize, cook, clean and budget. If we ourselves can adopt a new-me approach to the needs of this group of offenders, we may well be pleasantly surprised at what they can achieve.

Address correspondence to: Frank Lambrick, Senior Clinician – State-wide Forensic Service, Disability Services, PO Box 137, Fairfield VIC 3078, Australia; e-mail: Frank.Lambrick@dhs.vic.gov.au.

REFERENCES

Allen, S. (1995). "Sexual Assault Prevention Program: New Direction in Violence Prevention." Australian Crime Prevention Council (On-line). Available at: www.acpc.org.au/CONF95/Allen.htm

American Psychiatric Association. (2000). *Diagnostic and Statistical Manual of Mental Disorders, 4th edition, text revised.* Washington, DC: Author.

Basile, K.C. (2003). "Implications of Public Health for Policy on Sexual Violence." *Annals of the New York Academy of Science* 989:446–463.

Blanchard, R., M.S. Watson, A. Choy, R. Dickey, P. Klassen, M. Kuban and D.J. Ferren (1999). "Pedophiles: Mental Retardation, Maternal Age and Sexual Orientation." *Archives of Sexual Behaviour* 28(2):111–127.

Boer, D.P., J. Dorward, C.M. Bauthier and D.R. Watson (1995). "Treating Intellectually Disabled Sex Offenders." *Offender Treatability* 7(3):30–33.

Clare, I.H.C. and G.H. Gudjonsson (1993). "Interrogative Suggestibility, Confabulation and Acquiescence in People with Mild Learning Disabilities (Mental Handicap): Implications for Reliability During Police Interrogations." *British Journal of Clinical Psychology* 32:295–301.

Clarke, R.V. (1995). "Situational Crime Prevention: Everybody's Business." *Australian Crime Prevention Council* (On-line). Available: www.acpc.org.au/CONF95/Clarke.htm

Clarke, R.V. and R. Homel (1997). "A Revised Classification of Situational Crime Prevention Techniques." In: S.P. Lab (ed.), *Crime Prevention at the Crossroads.* Cincinnati, OH: Anderson.

Cockram, J., R. Jackson and R. Underwood (1992). "Perceptions of the Judiciary and Intellectual Disability." *Australian and New Zealand Journal of Developmental Disabilities* 18:189–200.

Day, K. (1994). "Male Mentally Handicapped Sex Offenders." *British Journal of Psychiatry* 165:630–639.

Day, K. (1993). "Crime and Mental Retardation: A Review." In: K. Howells and C. Hollin (eds.), *Clinical Approaches to the Mentally Disordered Offender* (pp. 111–144). Chichester, UK: Wiley.

Demetral, G.D. (1994). "Diagrammatic Assessment of Ecological Integration of Sex Offenders with Mental Retardation in Community Residential Facilities." *Mental Retardation* 32(2):141–145.

Glaser, W. (1992). "A Comparison of Intellectually Disabled and Non-Disabled Sex Offenders." *Proceedings of the 12th Annual Congress of the Australian & New Zealand Association of Psychiatry, Psychology and Law*, 243.

Glaser, W. and K. Deane (1999). "Normalisation in an Abnormal World: A Study of Prisoners with an Intellectual Disability." *International Journal of Offender Therapy and Comparative Criminology* 43(3):338–356.

Haaven, J., R. Little and D. Petre-Miller (1990). *Treating Intellectually Disabled Sex Offenders: A Model Residential Program.* Orwell, Vermont: The Safer Society Press.

Hayes, S. (1991). "Sex Offenders." *Australia and New Zealand Journal of Developmental Disabilities* 17(2):221–227.

James, R., M. Leslie and N. Lancaster (2000). *Prevention of Relapse for Offenders and Maintenance Programs (PROP and PROP Maintenance).* Melbourne, Australia: Disability Services Division, Victorian Department of Human Services.

Lambrick, F. (2003). "Issues Surrounding the Risk Assessment of Sexual Offenders with an Intellectual Disability." *Psychiatry, Psychology and Law* 10(2):353–358.

Lambrick, F. and W. Glaser (2004). "Sex Offenders with an Intellectual Disability." *Sexual Abuse: A Journal of Research and Treatment* 16(4):381–392.

Lindsay, W.R. (2002). "Research and Literature on Sex Offenders with Intellectual and Developmental Disabilities." *Journal of Intellectual Disability Research* 46(1):74–85.

Lindsay, W.R., D. Carson and E. Whitefield (2000). "Development of a Questionnaire on Attitudes Consistent with Sex Offending for Men with Intellectual Disabilities." *Journal of Intellectual Disability Research* 44:368–374.

Lund, J. (1990). "Mentally Retarded Criminal Offenders in Denmark." *British Journal of Psychiatry* 156:726–731.

McGillivray, J., and B. Waterman (2003). "Knowledge and Attitudes of Lawyers Regarding Offenders with Intellectual Disability." *Psychiatry, Psychology and Law* 10(1):244–253.

Nezu, A.M. and C.M. Nezu (1989). *Clinical Decision Making in Behaviour Therapy: A Problem Solving Perspective*. Champaign, IL: Research Press.

O'Connor, W. (1997). "Towards an Environmental Perspective on Interventions for Problem Sexual Behaviour in People with an Intellectual Disability." *Journal of Applied Research in Intellectual Disabilities* 10(2):159–175.

O'Connor, W. (1996). "A Problem-Solving Intervention for Sex Offenders with an Intellectual Disability." *Journal of Intellectual and Developmental Disability* 21(3):219–235.

O'Malley, P. (1997). "Introduction." In: P. O'Malley and A. Sutton (eds.), *Crime Prevention in Australia: Issues in Policy and Research* (pp. 1–11). Melbourne, Australia: The Federation Press.

Simpson, M.K. and J. Hogg (2001a). "Patterns of Offending Among People with an Intellectual Disability: A Systematic Review. Part 1: Methodology and Prevalence Data." *Journal of Intellectual Disability Research* 45(5):384–396.

Simpson, M.K. and J. Hogg (2001b). "Patterns of Offending Among People with an Intellectual Disability: A Systematic Review. Part II: Predisposing Factors." *Journal of Intellectual Disability Research* 45(5):397–406.

Smallbone, S. and R. Wortley (2000). *Child Sexual Abuse in Queensland: Offender Characteristics and Modus Operandi*. Queensland Crime Commission and the Criminology Research Council.

Thompson, D. and H. Brown (1997). "Men with Intellectual Disabilities Who Sexually Abuse: A Review of the Literature." *Journal of Applied Research in Intellectual Disabilities* 10:140–158.

Wortley, R. (1998). "A Two-Stage Model of Situational Crime Prevention." *Studies on Crime and Crime Prevention* 7(2):173–188.

Wortley, R. (2001). "A Classification of Techniques for Controlling Situational Precipitators of Crime." *Security Journal* 14(4):63–82.

Is Risk Management Enough? Approach and Avoidance Goals in the Treatment of Sex Offenders

by

Lynne Eccleston
Department of Criminology, The University of Melbourne

and

Tony Ward
School of Psychology, Victoria University of Wellington,
New Zealand

Abstract: *The focus of this chapter is the relationship between situational risk in sex offenders and the "good lives" model of rehabilitation. It briefly reviews situational theories of offending and the risk management approach to sexual offending. It acknowledges that standard rehabilitation and treatment approaches to sexual offenders concentrate on changing internal implicit theories and controlling external situational conditions related to their offending behavior. It suggests that the treatment of sexual offenders places too much emphasis on avoidance goals and seeking a range of primary negative goods in their environment, and argues that rehabilitation involves more than accepting environmental influences. A balance must be achieved between risk management and need fulfilment to ensure that approach goals and primary goods are more effective. It goes on to propose a "good lives model" for the treatment of sexual offenders in which* *individuals might be equipped with the necessary internal and external conditions to secure primary human goods in adaptive ways to reduce their situational risk of offending.*

INTRODUCTION

The treatment and rehabilitation of child molesters have undergone several paradigm shifts in the last century ranging from medical models influenced by psychodynamic theory, to the more recent Risk-Needs model of offender rehabilitation (Andrews and Bonta, 1998; Laws, 2003). According to the medical model, child molesters, and other sex offenders, were thought to suffer from a major mental illness that increased their susceptibility to committing sexual offenses, and that rendered them relatively resistant to treatment (Laws, 2003). Most therapists today acknowledge that psychodynamic approaches, which focus on helping child molesters gain insight into the causal mechanisms of their antisocial behaviors, are ineffective.

Increasingly, practitioners were informed by the rehabilitative promises offered by the "what works" framework. Andrews and Bonta (1998) identified three principles that they recommended should be incorporated into any successful offender rehabilitation strategy – *risk, need* and *responsivity* (Howell et al., 1999). In essence, this emerging philosophical shift towards rehabilitation contained elements of risk reduction or risk management, and advocated the development of prison and community programs that focused specifically on criminogenic needs. Emphasis is placed on tapping dynamic offender attributes that, when changed, are associated with reductions in recidivism, and ultimately less community harm (Andrews and Bonta, 1998; Ward and Brown, 2003). The treatment of sexual offenders in the last two decades has therefore focused on reducing the psychological and social deficits associated with each individual's offending (Ward and Mann, 2004). Best practice informs us that sexual offending in child molesters can be reduced by targeting cognitive distortions and deviant sexual preferences. The expectation is that by identifying and managing dynamic risk factors (e.g., antisocial attitudes and deviant sexual arousal) offending rates will be reduced.

Within the risk-needs framework, the dominant treatment model for sexual offenders culminates in relapse prevention (RP). In recent years several clinicians and researchers have argued that the treatment of sexual offenders should be based on understanding the process whereby an individual relapses into another sexual offense (e.g., Pithers, 1990). It has been suggested that there are clear patterns evident in the behavior of child molesters which translate into distinct clusters of cognitive, affective, and behavioral offence variables (Ward et al., 1995). For example, a lapse can include various *offence precursor activities*, such as deviant fantasizing about children, accessing pornographic materials, or cruising for potential victims in locations where children congregate (Laws, 2003).

There are many possible causal factors related to sexual offending, and research has shown that prior sex offense convictions are a good indicator of future recidivism among child sex offenders (Andrews and Bonta, 1985). It is also becoming increasingly apparent that a history of criminal versatility may also increase a child molester's chance of future reconviction for non-sexual as well as sexual offenses (Hall and Proctor, 1987; Smallbone et al., 2003). Marshall (1997) reminds us that most risk factors emanate from a desire to offend or result from a pattern of well-practiced offending. Some are distant causal factors, including early developmental experiences such as a history of childhood abuse, that result in sexual offending against children in adulthood. Other situational factors are more immediate or proximal, such as being intoxicated, or due to technological advances that create new opportunities for crime, for example access to Internet child pornography. For many child molesters, early adverse factors in the offender's life have led to etiologically significant risk factors, and transitory emotional, situational, and state factors that in adulthood intensify the immediate precursors to offending. For example, persistent alcohol abuse can reduce inhibitions and control mechanisms that would otherwise prevent offending behavior (Marshall, 1997). Similarly, a heightened emotional state, such as anger or high levels of stress, increases the immediate risk to offend (Pithers et al., 1989). One of the most important precursors to offending is whether the offender is in a suitable situation and has the opportunity to commit a sexual offense, such as by being alone with a child and/or holding a position of authority, such as a parent, teacher or scout leader (Ekblom and Tilley, 2000; Marshall, 1997; Ward and Hudson, 2000). Models of the relapse process thus set out to provide a rich description of the cognitive, behavioral, motivational and contextual risk factors associated with a sexual offense. Theory at this level typically includes an explicit temporal factor and focuses on proximal causes or the "how" of sexual offending, and the presence of situational risk factors.

Although the *risk management model* (Andrews and Bonta, 1998) has dominated current rehabilitation policy, and great advances in offender rehabilitation have been achieved within the "what works" framework, some high-risk child molesters continue to recidivate despite participating in programs that specifically target their criminogenic needs and deviant sexual preferences. Moreover, Wortley and Smallbone (this volume, chapter 2), posit that in addition to targeting an individual offender's criminogenic risk and needs, acts of child molestation can be prevented even further if the criminogenic features of the crime scene itself are modified to reduce the risk of an offense.

Importantly, within current rehabilitation models, treatment goals are primarily designed to reduce and manage risk, but they neglect to enhance the quality of offenders' lives (Ward, 2002). Ward (2002) argues that in the next phase of offender rehabilitation it will be possible to capitalize on the strengths of the risk management perspective by locating or embedding it within a more constructive, strengths-based capabilities approach – the good lives model (GLM) of offender rehabilitation. According to the GLM, risk factors are viewed as obstacles that erode individuals' capacity to live more fulfilling lives. Essentially, risk factors function as indicators or markers that an individual's pursuit of primary human "goods" (a concept discussed below) is compromised in some way. That is, the internal and external conditions necessary to achieve valued outcomes may be missing or incomplete. Thus the therapeutic focus should be on implementing offenders' good-lives conceptualization rather than simply managing risk by changing internal implicit theories and controlling external situational conditions. The modification of criminogenic needs, or dynamic risk factors in the offender's environment, will occur as a consequence of implementing a good-lives plan. In other words, the GLM has a *twin focus* to offender rehabilitation – "goods" promotion and risk management – and it explicitly argues that focusing on one of these two aims in the absence of the other is likely to result in poorer quality treatment. That is, the GLM is an ecological perspective that explicitly incorporates the external in two ways: (a) the particular capabilities or skills imparted to offenders will be selected on the basis of whether their possession will enable them to achieve a good or better life within the environment in question (e.g., friendship as opposed to romantic intimacy skills); and, (b) the environment may be directly modified to help individuals avoid or escape from "high-risk" situations (e.g., restrict access to children).

In this chapter we discuss the notion of the relationship between situational risk in child molesters and the good-lives model of rehabilitation. We provide a brief overview of selected theories of situational offending, namely, Routine Activities Theory and Rational Choice Theory, and the risk-needs model of offender rehabilitation, focusing on the key areas of risk management versus treatment. In particular, we suggest that current strategies place too much emphasis on child molesters' avoidance goals and we posit that rehabilitation involves more than managing environmental influences. We propose that offenders' needs – criminogenic and non-criminogenic – are integrated into a more holistic rehabilitation framework based on Ward's (2003, 2002) good-lives model. Furthermore, we contend that rehabilitation models for child molesters need to be mindful that sexual offending lies within an ecological niche that predisposes child molesters to offend – an integration among their social and cultural environment, their personal circumstances and their physical environment (Ward, in press). We argue that to treat sexual offenders effectively they must be equipped with the necessary internal and external conditions to secure primary human goods in adaptive ways to reduce their situational risk of offending.

SITUATIONAL THEORIES OF OFFENDING

Overview

Historically, theorists of criminality have tended to focus on enduring characteristics such as personality, cultural differences, or group affiliation, to understand differences between offenders and law-abiding members of society. During the last few decades greater emphasis has been placed on situational factors, such as targets and opportunities for crime (Cohen and Felson, 1979; Cook, 1986; Hindelang et al., 1978). Situational approaches to offending seek to explain the relationship between offender and victim, and why specific crimes are committed, in an attempt to inform policy decision making and crime control strategies (Sommers and Baskin, 1993). In general, situational theorists aim to describe the nature and statistical distribution of criminal opportunities, and how offenders' decisions are related to the situations they encounter (Cohen and Felson, 1979; Cook,

1986; Gabor, 1986; Hindelang et al., 1978). Crime is not perceived as a random occurrence; instead, it is possible to predict high-risk times, places, and persons based upon individual choices that escalate an offender's propensity to engage in risk and criminal behavior.

Routine Activities Theory

Routine activities theory (Cohen and Felson, 1979) proposes that three key factors must be present for a crime to occur – a likely offender, a suitable target, and the absence of a capable guardian (Ekblom and Tilley, 2000; Palmer, 2003). The theory states that it is also important to consider how the key factors are integrated in an environmental context to gain a deeper understanding of how criminal behavior eventuates. According to routine activities theory, a criminal event occurs when it is married with criminal opportunity and triggered by the "immediate precursors" of crime. Borrowing from Ekblom and Tilley's (2000) guidelines, which describe how opportunity optimizes a criminal event, a hypothetical scenario of the key elements in a situational criminal act of child molestation would involve:

- a vulnerable and attractive *target of crime* (e.g., a young child known to a sex offender) in a vulnerable *target enclosure* (e.g., the offender's home);

- the *absence* of willing and able *crime preventers*, who make crime less likely by *shaping the situation or influencing the offender* before the criminal event (e.g., parents arranging for the sex offender to babysit for the child despite the child's protestations), by *intervening* during the event, or by *reacting* after it (e.g., hearing child's account of the molestation and then failing to inform the police), the anticipation of which deters the offender, and the realization of which may prevent the next crime;

- the presence of unwitting, careless or deliberate crime promoters – making crimes more likely by *shaping the situation or influencing the offender* (e.g., parents aware of sex offender's history and leave the child alone with the offender), by *intervening* during the criminal event (e.g., encouraging or enabling the offender to offend), or by *reacting* after (e.g., conveying approval for the offender);

- a *wider environment* favorable for the offender and crime promoters and unfavorable for crime preventers (e.g., offender takes the child away for the weekend to an unknown destination), and one that may attract the offence (e.g., secluded cottage in the country) or motivate it (e.g., offender has taken other children there previously); and,

- a potential *offender* who is criminally predisposed, motivated, and *adequately resourced* for crime (e.g., offender has groomed the child, has organized the accommodation, and plans to use alcohol in the criminal act).

Routine activities theory certainly has a part to play in providing insight into some of the high-risk environmental factors that, when present, can elevate an offender's chance of committing an act of child molestation. Situational crime prevention, in essence creating safe environments, means increasing guardianship to protect vulnerable children. In today's society of working parents and single-parent families, increasing numbers of children are either left unsupervised in their homes or placed in the care of baby-sitters. Given that 32% of child molesters strategically use babysitting to ensure time alone with a child (Wortley and Smallbone, op. cit.), this is clearly a situational issue that requires close scrutiny. Instead of parents leaving vulnerable children with questionable guardians, governments could establish formalized guardianship programs by providing assistance and funding for after-school supervised care for children.

Rational Choice Theory

Rational choice theory builds on opportunity theories and posits that crime is a calculated and deliberate event. Criminal *involvement* is the entire process through which individuals become involved in offending, whereas criminal *events* are the decisions that offenders make in specific situations prior to committing an offense. Essentially, offenders are rational actors who make choices and decisions to maximize their benefits and minimize their losses. Decisions are made based on considerations of risk, effort and reward (Cornish and Clark, 1986; O'Grady et al., 2000). Theorists have applied this model to a wide variety of offenses, including drunk driving and sexual assault, in an attempt to comprehend why an individual makes a rational choice to commit a criminal act (Nagin and Paternoster, 1994).

According to the theory, a child molester's decision to offend is influenced by whether the opportunity (driving past a school), environment (school playground, park), and target (an unguarded child) are optimal for success, and whether the risk of detection is low (lack of witnesses). These factors are susceptible to change, and are dependent on the situational context and type of offense (O'Grady et al., 2000). To illustrate, a child molester deliberately goes to a busy shopping mall to watch young children and sees a young girl who appears to be alone (opportunity). His decision to abduct the child will be based on the presence or absence or situational risk factors such as whether:

- the child is really alone or temporarily separated from her parent or guardian;

- the child's guardian is actively searching for the child and may return at any moment;

- the offender is surrounded by a crowd of people who could be alerted by the child's cries;

- the offender notices surveillance cameras in operation and fears being caught on tape; and,

- the shopping mall is regularly patrolled by security officers.

In the above scenario, a child molester is far more likely to offend if the child is alone or unsupervised by a guardian near an exit without any witnesses, and there is an absence of surveillance cameras and security officers. The costs and benefits involved in committing an offense therefore are both material (e.g., going to prison) and intrinsic (e.g., being labeled a "child molester" and facing social disapproval) (Palmer, 2003). In essence, rational choice theory proposes that offending is an interactional process whereby the offender reacts cognitively to the environmental opportunities for crime that occur in a given situation (Palmer, 2003).

Rational choice theory, however, is limited in that it assumes that an offender is capable of being a "reasoning criminal" and making rational informed decisions. Conversely, as Palmer (2003) reminds us, many offenders have flawed social cognitive skills and deficits which may impact on their ability to make a rational decision. Typically, many offenders are opportunistic and impulsive. For example, in the above scenario a child molester's attention may be drawn to an unsupervised child in the shopping mall. He grasps the opportunity to abduct the child and impulsively picks her up and runs out of the shopping mall. At that moment he has little or no consideration that the offense will be recorded by the surveillance cameras, thereby increasing his risk of apprehension (lack of rational decision making).

SEXUAL OFFENDING AGAINST CHILDREN - SITUATIONAL AND PSYCHOLOGICAL FACTORS

Mischel (1968) posits that sexual offending may best be understood as the end result of specific interactions between an individual offender's psychological factors (dispositional) and situational factors. A high-risk situation for a child molester is defined as a circumstance in which the individual's attempt to refrain from a particular behavior (ranging from loitering outside a school to becoming intoxicated prior to the offence) is threatened. These high-risk situations vary from individual to individual depending on their lack of supportive resources and level of vulnerability (Witkiewitz and Marlatt, 2004). For example, Tom has a history of dysfunctional adult relationships, exhibits fragile self-esteem, and is socially isolated. He may therefore, in the absence of an adult relationship, be more likely to seek out a child to meet his intimacy needs (dispositional). He may, for example, volunteer as a sports coach or scout leader, thereby increasing the situational opportunity to meet a vulnerable child.

Manipulating the environment to gain access to a child (situational) is just one element in an act of child molestation – the offender's transient internal state combined with specific external situations has the potential to increase or decrease the risk of an offense taking place. To illustrate, in the above scenario Tom is angry that his adult partner has left him and he is feeling lonely (internal state). He finds he is sexually aroused by a 14-year-old girl in his scout group (internal state) and masturbates to pornography (external situation) while fantasizing about the girl (internal state). Tom enacts his fantasy by taking the girl on a weekend camp (external state) and takes a supply of alcohol (external state) with him with the intention of "relaxing" the girl prior to committing the sexual act that takes place while both parties are intoxicated (internal state).

One of the most consistently observed situational risk factors among adolescent and adult child molesters is the abuse of, or the use of, an intoxicating substance to facilitate an offense (Langevin and Lang, 1990; Lightfoot and Barbaree, 1993; Rada, 1976; Travin and Protter, 1993). Langevin and Lang (1990) found that 56% of child molesters were alcoholics according to the Michigan Alcoholism Screening Test (Selzer, 1971), and 18% had a drug abuse problem evidenced by their scores on the Drug Abuse Screening Test (Skinner, 1982). In fact, alcohol abuse might exacerbate negative emotionality, for example loneliness, and intimacy deficits that elevate a child molester's risk of offending (Looman et al.,

2004). Nonetheless, although substances can be used by a child molester to induce intoxication (transient internal state), a great deal of planning is required to ensure that substances are readily available (external situation) to ensure the offense is successful.

Pithers et al. (1989) developed the concept of an offence chain to explain sexual offending behavior. First, the offender possesses certain personality and circumstantial factors that, combined with a certain life-style, provide the background to the offense behavior. Second, the offender experiences dysphoria in response to feelings of deprivation or loss, or resulting from conflict or stress. In a dysphoric state (transient internal state) the offender is more vulnerable to entering a high-risk situation, which may lead him to a potential victim. In essence, the internal barriers and controls that could prevent a sexual offence are drastically reduced. Third, the offender lapses into behavior that places them at risk of committing a sexual assault, such as fantasizing about sexual contact with children (Barbaree and Seto, 1997). The offender is then at greater risk of manipulating his external situation to ensure that he has access to a vulnerable child.

Importantly, research has identified some key individual risk factors that place child molesters and other sexual offenders at increased risk of offending. Many of these factors are internal states such as low self-esteem, loneliness, depression, and negative emotionality (Looman et al., 2004; Marshall et al., 2000; Marshall et al., 1999). In particular, Marshall (1997) reported that child molesters suffered from extremely low self-esteem, and Pithers et al. (1989) found that 61% of child molesters reported a significant reduction in self-confidence directly prior to their offence. Cognitive distortions also are an important and immediate precursor to sexual offending (Pithers et al., 1989) including empathy deficits, denial and minimization, pro-offending attitudes and beliefs, and shifting responsibility to others, or to situational factors (Marshall, 1997).

Ward (in press) theorized that there are three sets of causal factors that, when combined, help to explain why sexual offenders exhibit psychological vulnerabilities that predispose them to offending – biological factors (genetics/evolutionary), the offender's ecological niche (social, cultural and personal circumstances), and three neuropsychological systems (motivational/emotional, action selection and control, and perception and memory systems). A child molester's behavior has consequences that maintain and/or entrench his vulnerability factors due to the impact on his environment and his psychological functioning. Sexual offending occurs when distal and proximal factors are married and interact dynamically. A child's genetic predisposition and social learning experiences significantly impact on his/her developing brain and the three interlocking neuropsychological systems eventuate. An individual's exposure to developmental adversity (sexually abused as a child), poor genetic inheritance (intellectually disabled child molester), or biological insult (post traumatic stress disorder) can threaten the integrity of the three systems. In essence, vulnerable individuals are more likely to function in maladaptive ways: for example, a man may sexually offend against children when his adult relationships deteriorate and he experiences overwhelming levels of stress.

In addition to understanding the psychological causal mechanisms of sexual offending, therapists must also consider external factors, such as whether a man who offends against children is a *situational* or *preferential* child molester. A consideration of the offender's internal states integrated with the external risk factors help to formulate individual treatment plans to reduce recidivism. For example, strategies to target the treatment needs of a *situational* child molester (social misfit, insecure and lonely, lack of capacity to achieve agency, use of substances and acts impulsively) would necessarily be different from strategies targeted at a *preferential* child molester (sexual preference for children, need to inflict pain, has not developed alternative strategies for achieving sexual intimacy, corruption of agency achieved through sexual domination of a child) (Ward and Mann, 2004).

THE RISK-NEEDS APPROACH TO OFFENDER REHABILITATION

A number of best practice principles have emerged to dominate offender rehabilitation policies based on the "what works" literature (Andrews and Bonta, 1998). The authors propose that recidivism rates are reduced when offender psychotherapy and programs are based on *risk, need* and *responsivity*.

The *risk principle* matches an offender's risk level with the amount of treatment warranted: thus high-risk individuals should receive more treatment (Hollin, 1999). In Victoria, child molesters are exposed to a tiered-treatment approach depending on the level of risk. The *need principle* suggests programs should target criminogenic needs, or offender characteristics directly related to recidivism. Ideally, criminogenic needs should be detected for each type of crime (e.g., sexual, violent or drug-related crimes) rather than simply for crimes in general. For example, Hanson and Harris (2000) identified a number of criminogenic factors that should be targeted in sexual offending programs, including deviant sexual arousal, intimacy deficits and loneliness, and difficulties with emotional regulation. Since sexual offenders are heterogenous by nature, it is imperative that in therapeutic programs child molesters should be separated from, for example, rapists, to effectively target their specific treatment needs. The *responsivity principle* ensures that program content makes sense to those for whom it was designed. In other words, will offenders be able to understand the content of the program and subsequently change their behavior? Factors that may impede learning could include gender, learning styles, ethnicity, and treatment motivation (Andrews and Bonta, 1998).

Taking into account the best practice principles of Andrews and Bonta (1998) and McGuire (2001), the notion of risk management and criminogenic needs has received the most attention in the rehabilitation of child molesters. Criminogenic needs are dynamic attributes of offenders and their circumstances that, when changed, are related to reduced rates of recidivism (Andrews and Bonta, 1998). Examples include pro-offending attitudes and values (e.g., acts of child molestation are not perceived as morally wrong), aspects of antisocial personality (e.g., impulsiveness), poor problem-solving ability, substance abuse, high levels of hostility and anger, and contact with criminal associates (e.g., pedophile networks) (Andrews and Bonta, 1998). Thus, criminogenic needs represent a subset of factors predictive of recidivism. Other risk factors include static or unchanging factors such as gender, age, and offending history (Andrews and Bonta, 1998). Although static factors play an important role in determining initial levels of risk, they play less of a role in guiding treatment. Static factors are unlikely to reveal whether a person has changed as a result of the treatment, or whether an offender is likely to re-offend. Conversely, dynamic risk factors (i.e., criminogenic needs) can inform therapists about the impact of treatment on an individual's level of risk and also indicate where change has occurred.

Relapse Prevention

The major form the risk-needs model takes in the sexual offending domain is that of relapse prevention (RP), which was adapted from research on addictive behavior (Marlatt, 1985; Marlatt and George, 1984). Based within a cognitive-behavioral framework, the strategy involves: (1) identifying high-risk situations in which the individual is likely to relapse; (2) teaching skills to help the individual to identify these high-risk situations and to avoid them; (3) identifying lapses as pre-offence behaviors that do not constitute full-fledged relapses but which constitute approximations to risky behavior and which may act as a precursor to a relapse (e.g., deviant fantasizing, purchase of pornography, or cruising for potential victims); (4) teaching the individual to recognize a lapse; and, (5) teaching the individual various coping strategies which can be accessed in response to both high-risk situations and lapses to reduce the risk of a relapse (Laws et al., 2000; Pithers, 1997, 1990).

Theorists working with the RP model have identified clear patterns in the behavior of child molesters which translate into distinct clusters of cognitive, affective, and behavioral offense variables (Ward et al., 1995). Models of the relapse process set out to provide a rich description of the cognitive, behavioral, motivational and contextual risk factors associated with a sexual offense (Ward and Hudson, 2000). The focus of RP typically includes an explicit temporal factor and targets the proximal causes or the "how" of sexual offending against a child. Treatment aims to ensure that individuals acquire skills to cope with risk factors in a non-abusive manner. The different stages of an individual's offense process are typically linked to distinct treatment strategies (Ward and Mann, 2004). RP necessitates that the offender adopts a person-centered approach to his own rehabilitation by recognizing his risk factors and enacting strategies to prevent recidivism, but successful RP also relies heavily on applying situational controls to ensure that the offender avoids high-risk situations. Situational controls are particularly important when child molesters are released into the community on parole and are expected to abide by their RP plan. Parole officers have a key role to play in applying situational controls and ensuring the RP plan is maintained. During supervision they can, for example, monitor the offender's movements and ensure that he stays away from locations frequented by children that might cue fantasies of children and precipitate offending behavior.

Realistically, however, in RP child molesters who are attempting to maintain new behaviors are often faced with the challenge of balancing contextual cues and potential consequences. There are potentially multiple influences that can trigger and function within high-risk situations (Barton, 1994; Kauffman, 1995). In effect, a self-organizing process facilitates the interaction among background factors (e.g., family history, history of abuse, victimization issues, and presence/absence of social supports), physiological states, cognitive processes (e.g., self-efficacy, outcomes expectancies, motivation, empathy deficits), and coping skills (Craissati et al., 2002; Witkiewitz and Marlatt, 2004).

Although the RP model has remained dominant for practitioners working with sexual offenders, Laws (2003) has recently noted that RP has effectively escaped evaluation. Laws argues that despite the highly positive results reported by Pithers et al. (1989), they have consistently reported highly positive results, they have neglected to compare their RP-based program with a more standard treatment model or against an appropriate control group (see Laws, 2003, for a more thorough critique of RP). Interestingly Hanson and Harris (2000) comment that sexual offenders often lack the necessary motivation to successfully participate in RP interventions, and that some offenders engage in crime patterns that fail to match the standard RP format, such as possessing enduring antisocial attitudes and engaging in covert planning. Moreover, Ward (2002, Ward and Stewart, 2003a, 2003b, 2003c) has proposed that treatment strategies to remove deficits or risk factors consistent with the RP model are unlikely to motivate child molesters sufficiently to engage in treatment, and that the RP model also neglects to pay attention to the issue of psychological agency and personal identity.

Limitations of the Risk-Needs Model

Although the risk-need model has a great deal to offer in that it provides a theoretically sound and empirically defensible framework to guide offender rehabilitation, the theory does have some weaknesses associated with each of its key principles that we believe affect how it can effectively conceptualize treatment, especially for child molesters (Ward and Brown, 2003).

Firstly, within Andrews and Bonta's (1998) theory, *risk* and *need* are inter-related concepts since criminogenic needs are perceived as dynamic risk factors. In essence, it is proposed that low-risk offenders have few, if any, criminogenic needs compared to high-risk offenders. Although Ward and Brown (2003) acknowledge that marrying risk and need simplifies offender rehabilitation in the sense that it focuses interventions on risk management and reducing recidivism, they argue that estimates of risk should not always determine the type and extent of criminogenic needs that are addressed in treatment. This is because there are a number of possible relationships between them which would not be captured by the high risk-high need, low risk-low need assumption. For example, it is possible that sexual offenders who are assessed as low risk may display high needs, or clinical problems. These needs may not be criminogenic needs, but could still require therapeutic attention and have an impact on rehabilitation (e.g., depression, anxiety, relationship problems, etc). More importantly, without appropriate coping skills or supports in place, a child molester's non-criminogenic needs could elevate his risk from low to high if these needs are not adequately addressed.

It is also possible to be confronted with sexual offenders who are considered high risk, but who exhibit low needs. These individuals could have distinct and well-defined problems that place them at risk of recidivism, but they do not display a *wide range* of problems. A high-risk low-need child molester, for example, can have deviant sexual preferences, but he possesses good social skills and demonstrates no obvious interpersonal or self-regulatory deficits (Ward and Siegert, in press). Therefore, in effect, the relationship between risk and need is more complex than that proposed in the risk-need model. Ward and Brown (2003) argue that to allocate sexual offenders correctly into treatment programs, it is essential that the range and severity of an individual offender's clinical problems are known, in combination with a clear understanding of the complex relationship between risk, needs and sexually criminal acts.

A second problem with the risk-need model is its assumption that high-risk offenders do better if they are treated more intensively because they have a greater number of needs, that medium risk offenders do better with moderate amounts of treatment and so on. Ward and Brown (2003) posit that this assumption is questionable in some cases. For example, some sexual offenders may have a small number of intense or severe needs (low need), such as psychotic symptoms, or sexual abuse trauma, that require *prolonged* treatment to shift. Other sexual offenders may have a wide range of needs (high need) of varying intensity or severity – addressing several needs in a *shorter* duration may address other needs. For instance, a child molester's low self-esteem is also related to other treatment targets – such as, social competence, loneliness and intimacy deficits – enhancing self-esteem can facilitate changes in these other critical areas.

Thirdly, Ward and Brown (2003) argue that the notion of always basing treatment on risk management is problematic as it implies that the major task of rehabilitation is to reduce the chances of harm to the community, which is best achieved by focusing on eliminating or modifying pro-criminal factors (criminogenic needs). However, basing a treatment model on risk factors alone is insufficient as it is "too reductionistic, too negative, and not sufficiently attuned to the psychological reality of individuals' everyday lives" (Ward, 2002a, p. 178). Therefore, rehabilitative policies based on a risk management model need to be supplemented by additional policies which also focus on *enhancing* positive capabilities (i.e., non-criminogenic needs), rather than just focusing on a sexual offender's skills deficits. For example, a treatment goal that focuses on the *acquisition* of relationship skills for a child molester is more useful than one that simply aims to *reduce* intimacy deficits. Ogloff (2002) supports this notion by intimating that the needs of offenders often extend beyond the criminogenic factors that have been found to be directly related to offending behavior.

In summary, according to the risk-needs model, interpersonal dynamic needs – such as low self-esteem, anxiety, personal distress, or group cohesion – are not considered significantly predictive of recidivism (Andrews and Bonta, 1998). We believe that this is a major flaw in the risk-needs model. In essence, the risk-needs model fails to allow for the complexities, such as individual strengths and non-criminogenic needs, that also place child molesters at higher or lower risk of recidivism. We would argue that it is equally important to target these interpersonal dynamic factors as well as criminogenic needs so that we can meet a child molester's fundamental psychological needs, increase well-being and self-worth, and secure primary human goods in socially acceptable ways.

We contend that in order to be responsive to sexual offenders' needs, it is imperative that we look beyond recidivism rates to recognize the various obstacles preventing child molesters from living balanced and fulfilling lives (Ward and Stewart, 2003a). Offender rehabilitation must therefore encompass a holistic approach that can offer offenders concrete possibilities for living worthwhile lives based on individual abilities, circumstances, interests, and opportunities, to ultimately culminate in lasting lifestyle changes and reduced recidivism rates. This notion will be explored in more detail in the next section.

THE GOOD-LIVES MODEL OF OFFENDER REHABILITATION

Despite the undoubted virtues of the risk management model, it is imperative that rehabilitation must focus on more than risk factors alone if we are serious about teaching child molesters to achieve a balanced lifestyle that helps them to secure psychological and human needs (Ward, 2002a;

Ward and Stewart, 2003a). Arguably, risk models of rehabilitation place too much emphasis on avoidance goals and neglect approach goals. In essence, RP focuses on ensuring that offenders are removed from high-risk negative situations (a strategy that may be difficult to enforce), instead of creating positive changes in offenders' environments to minimize the temptations of future offending. Any therapeutic approach based on a risk management model therefore needs to be supplemented by additional theories which also focus on *enhancing* positive capabilities (i.e., non-crimi-nogenic needs) rather than just *suppressing* dysfunctional ones. In this way, both the interests of the community and the best interests of sex offenders are considered (Birgden, 2002). This does not mean abandoning the hard earned gains of the risk-need model, but rather extending its scope and conceptual focus (Ward, 2002a).

Ward and Stewart (2003a, 2003b) offer a new theoretical model, known as the *enhancement* or *good lives* model (GLM). A major advantage of the GLM is that therapeutic interventions with child molesters focus on the internal and external conditions of individuals that include, but go beyond, their criminogenic needs. In the GLM, risk factors are viewed as obstacles that erode sexual offenders' capacity to live more fulfilling lives. Essentially, risk factors function as indicators or markers that an individual's pursuit of primary human "goods" is compromised in some way. That is, the internal and external conditions necessary to achieve valued outcomes may be missing or incomplete. Ward has written extensively elsewhere on the GLM: therefore, for the purposes of this chapter we will summarise the main concepts (for a more thorough exploration of the GLM, see Ward, 2002a, 2002b; Ward and Brown, 2003; Ward and Stewart, 2003a, 2003b).

"Primary goods" are actions, states of affairs, characteristics, experi-ences, and states of mind that are viewed as intrinsically beneficial to human beings and are therefore sought for their own sake rather than as means to some more fundamental ends (Deci and Ryan, 2000; Emmons, 1996; Schmuck and Sheldon, 2001). Primary goods are viewed as objective and tied to certain ways of living that if pursued involve the actualization of potentialities that are distinctively human. Individuals can, therefore, be mistaken about what is really of value and what is in their best interests; human goods are not simply individual preferences or desires. Primary goods emerge out of basic needs, while instrumental or secondary goods provide concrete ways of securing these goods, for example, certain types of work, relationships, or languages. A good life becomes possible when an individual possesses the necessary conditions for achieving primary goods, has access to primary goods, and lives a life characterized by the instantiation of these goods (Ward and Stewart, 2003a). Theoretically, if the negative situational conditions that precipitated an act of child molestation (e.g., deviant peer networks, access to Internet child pornography) are replaced with positive conditions, such as support by friends and family to pursue healthier activities, the offender has a much greater chance of rehabilitation. The attention to situational variables in effect provides the sexual offender with more adaptive secondary goods and therefore the (external) resources to secure access to primary human goods. Of course, it may still be necessary to equip the individual concerned with the skills and capabilities (i.e., internal conditions) to effectively utilize these resources if he is to actually achieve a good life.

The primary aim of the GLM rehabilitation theory is to enhance human well-being and quality of life, which is partially determined by an individual's basic needs. Importantly, adverse developmental experiences could lead a child molester to lack the skills necessary (internal conditions) to establish robust interpersonal adult relationships, which results in social isolation and problems with intimacy, and further compounds psychological and social deficits. A child molester's ecological niche (genetic/developmental/socio-cultural) thereby increases his vulnerability factors and contributes to the etiology of sexual offending by ensuring he has access to potential victims, and by creating the specific circumstances that exacerbate his psychological deficits (Ward, in press). It is possible however, that an individual may commit a sexual offense against a child under some circumstances when psychological vulnerabilities or deficits are absent. For example, individuals who have never sexually offended will commit rape in a war due to powerful social and cultural influences. Similarly, an act of child molestation may be based in the ecological niche rather than the person; therefore, a crime of opportunity occurs when the individual "suspends" his ethical values and morals. As we have argued, the presence of internal and external obstacles in a child molester can be extremely damaging, and they result in impaired social and psychological functioning, and ultimately, a less fulfilling life (Ward, 2002a, 2002b; Ward and Stewart, 2003a, 2003b, 2003c).

Therefore, according to Ward and Stewart (2003a, 2003b), strict adherence to Andrews and Bonta's (1998) model overlooks vital non-criminogenic issues, with the enhancement model better encapsulating sexual offenders' diverse needs. Rehabilitation should, therefore, focus first on identifying a child molester's internal and external obstacles (criminogenic factors) that prevent him from meeting his fundamental needs (e.g., personal and vocational skill deficits, maladaptive attitudes and beliefs, inadequate social supports). Hence, in the GLM, criminogenic needs function as markers that there is a problem in the way a child molester is obtaining human goods, which is directly related to the individual acting in an antisocial way against children. However, to stop here would mean that treatment would merely focus on what is wrong with the individual rather than what is required to live a different kind of life (Ward, 2002a; Ward and Stewart, 2003a, 2003b, 2003c). Many vulnerable offenders relapse because they lack the life skills to avoid risky situations and may be unaware that they can live a better life.

The next step in creating positive change and reducing risk, therefore, is the construction of a well-designed individual treatment plan that will equip a child molester with the necessary conditions to meet basic needs in different, more prosocial ways, and ultimately to live a more balanced and fulfilling life (e.g., close relationships, rewarding employment, leisure time, self-respect, a sense of meaning and purpose, agency, creativity, relatedness, etc.).

This "good life" should be realistic for a sexual offender, encompassing his capabilities, temperament, interests, skills, deep commitments, and support networks. Strategies should therefore be employed to help child molesters achieve agency and mastery in non-sexual situations, and to achieve appropriate secondary goods of sexual satisfaction and sexual intimacy to achieve successful relatedness with adults. Other treatment goals include problem solving and decision making, skills of self-directedness, emotional management and self-control strategies.

Although the enhancement model may seem radical, it has gained some support in contemporary literature. Firstly, there is ample evidence from motivational psychology (goal theory and research), personality psychology, social psychology, evolutionary theory, moral philosophy, and philosophical anthropology that human beings seek primary human goods (Ward, 2002a, 2002b). In particular, Deci and Ryan (2000) have recently developed the Self-Determination Theory of Needs, which states that human beings are inherently active, self-directed organisms who are naturally predisposed to seek the needs of *autonomy, relatedness* and *competence*. They argue that these needs outline the conditions essential for psychological well-being and fulfilment, and that individuals can only flourish if they are met. The failure to meet these three basic needs will inevitably result in psychological distress and maladaptive lives (Ward, 2002b).

Maruna's (2001) recent research on desistance from crime is further support for the enhancement model. In this research, Maruna compared the self-narratives of 30 desisting ex-offenders with a carefully matched sample of 20 active, or persisting offenders, and 15 offenders who did not belong to either category. Results revealed no differences in the personality traits of the desisting and persisting offenders – both exhibited more deviant, anti-authority, rebellious profiles than normal adults. However, the difference appeared to reside in the offenders' construction of their lives. Persistent offenders appeared to live their lives according to a *condemnation script*. They saw themselves as victims, and believed that the structure and tone of their lives was set in stone. Thus, they exhibited a poor sense of self-efficacy and felt powerless to change the fate that was set out for them. Their reason for engaging in antisocial behavior was an attempt to restore some sense of personal control over their lives. Conversely, desisting offenders lived their lives according to a *redemption script*. These offenders essentially saw themselves as good people who had become corrupt or overwhelmed by external influences, with a criminal lifestyle giving them some power over their bleak circumstances. However, by discovering their true selves (i.e., skills, abilities, roles, traits, etc), establishing a sense of empowerment and control over their life, and learning to give something back to the community, their family and other offenders, these individuals were able to create a new identity distinct from their criminal lifestyles. In a sense this new identity involved the offender making sense of his earlier crimes and experiences, and creating a bridge between his undesirable life and the adoption of new ways of living (Ward, 2002b).

It can therefore be said that child molesters who are serious about relinquishing an offending lifestyle in order to seek primary goods or valued outcomes, and the securing of these goods, are thought to be crucial components of successful rehabilitation – the essence of the enhancement model. We posit that it is not entirely possible to shift individuals from an antisocial lifestyle to a prosocial one by simply utilizing the principles of the risk-need model alone. Essentially, a child molester must make a rational choice that the benefits of achieving a "good life" far outweigh the benefits of continued offending behavior. To promote this shift towards a better life, we need to also promote certain values or human goods by adopting the conception of good lives into a rehabilitation framework

(Ward, 2002a, 2002b). In simple language, this means that offender rehabilitation should encompass a holistic approach that involves addressing the factors that relate to child molesters' sexual offending behavior (i.e., criminogenic needs), *as well as* addressing their psychological distress (i.e., non-criminogenic needs), in order to instil in them the skills, knowledge and resources to live different kinds of lives.

Implications for Treatment and Rehabilitation

Treatment programs based exclusively on risk management and relapse prevention are essentially focused on avoidance goals, and as such, do not provide the opportunity for child molesters to develop greater levels of satisfaction and well-being (Emmons, 1996; Mann et al., 2002). Arguably, standard risk-needs models that focus on changing individuals or controlling situational risk factors do not pay enough attention to goals and competencies. By focusing on risk reduction, it is true that a sexual offender's risk may be managed, but at what price? In effect, his environment may be controlled to such an extent that he may be isolated from friends, be denied access to meaningful employment and recreational activities, and struggle with identity and self-agency issues (Ward and Stewart, 2003). Ward has outlined several principles that underlie the construction of a treatment program for sexual offenders (Ward and Mann, 2004). They are:

- Many child molesters have experienced adverse developmental experiences as children, and have not had access to the opportunities and support necessary to achieve a coherent Good Lives plan.

- Consequently, child molesters lack many of the essential skills and capabilities necessary to achieve a fulfilling life.

- Sexual offending may be an attempt to achieve desired human goods but the child molester does not possess the skills or capabilities necessary to achieve them. Alternatively, sexual offending can eventuate from an attempt to relieve the sense of incompetence, conflict or dissatisfaction that arises when an individual is unable to achieve valued human goods.

- The absence of certain human goods – agency, inner peace, and relatedness – seems to be more strongly associated with sexual offending.

- The risk of sexual offending may be reduced by assisting child molesters to develop the skills and capabilities necessary to achieve the full range of human goods, with particular emphasis on agency, inner peace, and relatedness.

The aims of GLM treatment therefore are best understood as "approach goals," which are defined in terms of what an offender will achieve and gain, rather than in terms of what they will cease to think or do (Emmons, 1996; Mann, 2000; Mann et al., in press). Treatment should therefore be seen as an activity that should *add to* a child molester's repertoire of personal functioning, rather than a strategy to simply *remove* a problem or *manage* problems, such as controlling the situational risk factors. Sex offender treatment for this specific group should only place restrictions on activities that are highly related to the problem behavior and should instead aim to promote normal levels of functioning. Thus, a man who molests children due to intimacy deficits and failed relationships with adults should not be discouraged from attempting to develop an intimate relationship with an appropriate adult partner. Rather, he should be supported and encouraged to join social activities or groups that will increase his opportunities to develop age-appropriate relationships.

Initially, the specific activities of a GLM-based treatment programme for child molesters appear to fit standard treatment protocols; however, there is a major difference – the goal of each intervention component is explicitly linked to the GLM theory. Ward's treatment model is intrinsically a more holistic treatment perspective, based on the notion that the best way to reduce risk in a child molester is to teach him the skills to live a more fulfilling life by helping him to achieve agency and mastery so that he can choose to control his situation. In this way relapse into offending is no longer a considered option.

Within the GLM model therapy is tailored to individual sexual offenders while still being administered in a systematic and structured way. Child molesters are only exposed to those activities that are specific to their individualized treatment plan, such as targeting intimacy deficits, or building up the areas where skill, knowledge or ability already exist or are potentially achievable. A key aim in treatment therefore is to focus on a better fit between therapy and a child molester's specific issues, abilities, preferences, and contexts. The objective is to develop a stronger therapeutic alliance and increase responsivity based on mutual respect and trust, and the GLM assumptions about the value of persons, and their pursuit of primary goods.

As we have discussed previously, risk factors are regarded as internal and external obstacles that impede an individual's ability to implement a

GLM in a socially acceptable and personally fulfilling manner. Thus, we have adopted a twin focus with the GLM that incorporates the strengths of relapse prevention and adds the capabilities approaches to treatment. We acknowledge that it is important to initiate situational controls to ensure that child molesters do not relapse, however we contend that controlling a risky situation is not enough – offenders instead must be encouraged to initiate moves towards positive situations. The ultimate therapeutic aim is to motivate offenders to rationally choose a positive lifestyle. In the GLM approach, the goal is always to create new skills and capacities within the *context* of individuals' good lives plans and to encourage fulfilment through the achievement of human goods.

CONCLUSION

In this chapter we have outlined the good lives model of offender rehabilitation and discussed its application to child molesters and situational risk. The GLM is a strengths-based approach which proposes that the major aim of treatment is to equip child molesters with the necessary internal and external conditions required to implement a good lives plan in their particular set of circumstances. In the GLM, risk factors are viewed as distortions in these conditions and are not expected to provide the sole focus of rehabilitation. Instead there is a twin focus on establishing good lives and reducing risk. In essence, this shift from antisocial to prosocial lifestyles should encompass a holistic approach – i.e., one that involves addressing the factors that relate to offending behavior (i.e., criminogenic needs), *as well as* addressing offenders' psychological distress (i.e., non-criminogenic needs) – in order to instil in them the skills, knowledge and resources to live different kinds of lives.

Importantly, although all human beings have the same basic needs, the environment in which they strive to attain these human goods is influenced dramatically by the ecological niche they encounter. Since human beings are contextually-dependent organisms, rehabilitation should always consider the match between a sexual offender's characteristics and the environment he is asked to function in optimally to reduce risk and achieve human needs. The GLM recognizes that our concept of self begins with intrinsic activity and an organismic integration process (Deci and Ryan, 2000). As human beings we possess innate tendencies to engage in fulfilling and satisfying activities that define our sense of self and how we function in our environments. The one thing humans require to thrive as individuals is to become involved socially to learn from others and explore the boundaries of their capabilities (Doyal, 2001).

We would argue that the best way to lower sexual offending recidivism rates against children is to equip child molesters with the tools to live more fulfilling lives rather than to simply develop increasingly sophisticated risk management measures and strategies. It is simply inadequate to control a child molester's situational risk by ensuring that he avoids risky environments such as schools, playgrounds or shopping malls. GLM's holistic approach, for example, could provide a child molester with alternative external conditions, such as establishing support networks to engage in age-appropriate adult activities. To illustrate, a child molester who has coached a junior football team to gain access to potential victims should be encouraged to pursue his love of sport and coach adult football. In this way, he will maintain a sense of mastery and agency but without placing himself at situational risk of offending. By coaching adult football he increases his social networks with adults and has a greater chance of forming appropriate relationships that may fulfil his intimacy needs, and increase his self-esteem. In our view, this theory has the conceptual resources to provide a comprehensive guide for therapists in the difficult task of treating child molesters and making society a safer place.

Address correspondence to: Lynne Eccleston Ph.D, Department of Criminology, University of Melbourne, Victoria 3010, Australia: e-mail: lecc@unimelb.edu.au.

REFERENCES

Andrews, D. A. and J. Bonta (1998). *The Psychology of Criminal Conduct*. Cincinnati, OH: Anderson Publishing Co.

Barbaree, H.E. and M.C. Seto (1997). "Pedophilia: Assessment and Treatment." In: D.R. Laws and W. O'Donohue (eds.), *Sexual Deviance: Theory, Assessment and Treatment* (pp. 152–174). New York: The Guilford Press.

Barton, S. (1994). "Chaos, Self-Organization and Psychology." *American Psychologist* 49:5–14.

Birgden, A. (2002). "Therapeutic Jurisprudence and "Good Lives": A Rehabilitation Framework for Corrections." *Australian Psychologist* 37:180–186.

Cohen, L. and M. Felson (1979). "Social Change and Crime Rate Trends: A Routine Activity Approach." *American Sociological Review* 44:588–608.

Cook, P. (1986). "The Demand and Supply of Criminal Opportunities." *Crime and Justice* 7:1–27.

Cornish, D.B. and R.V.G. Clarke (1986). *The Reasoning Criminal: Rational Choice Perspectives on Offending*. New York: Springer-Verlag.

Craissati, J., G. McClurg and K. Browne (2002). "Characteristics of Perpetrators of Child Sexual Abuse Who Have Been Sexually Victimised as Children." *Sexual Abuse: A Journal of Research and Treatment* 14:225–239.

Deci, E.L. and R.M. Ryan (2000). "The 'What' and 'Why' of Goal Pursuits: Human Needs and the Self-Determination of Behavior." *Psychological Inquiry* 11:227–268.

Doyal, L. (2001). "The Moral Foundation of the Clinical Duties of Care: Needs, Duties and Human Rights." *Bioethics* 15:520–535.

Ekblom, P. and N. Tilley (2000). "Going Equipped." *British Journal of Criminology* 40:376–398.

Emmons, R.A. (1996). "Striving and Feeling: Personal Goals and Subjective Well-Being." In: P.M. Gollwitzer and J.A. Bargh (eds.), *The Psychology of Action: Linking Cognition and Motivation in Behavior* (pp. 313–337). New York: Guilford.

Gabor, T. (1986). *The Prediction of Criminal Behavior: A Statistical Approach*. Toronto: University of Toronto Press.

Gollwitzer, P.M. and J. A. Bargh (eds.). *The Psychology of Action: Linking Cognition and Motivation to Behavior*. New York: Guilford.

Hall, G.C.N. and W.C. Proctor (1987). "Criminological Predictors of Recidivism in a Sexual Offender Population." *Journal of Consulting and Clinical Psychology* 55:111–112.

Hanson, R.K. and A.J.R. Harris (2000). "Where Should We Intervene? Dynamic Predictors of Sexual Offense Recidivism." *Criminal Justice and Behavior* 27:6–35.

Hindelang, M.J., M.R. Gottfredson and J. Garofalo (1978). *Victims of Personal Crimes*. Cambridge, MA: Ballinger.

Hollin, C. R. (1999). "Treatment Programs for Offenders: Meta-Analysis, 'What Works' and Beyond." *International Journal of Law and Psychiatry* 22:361–372.

Howells, K., A. Day, S. Byrne and M. Byrne (1999). "Risk, Needs and Responsivity in Violence Rehabilitation: Implications for Programs for Indigenous Offenders." Paper presented at the Best Practice Interventions in Corrections for Indigenous People Conference, Adelaide, 13–15 October.

Jarjoura, G.R. (1996). "The Conditional Effect of Social Class on the Dropout-Delinquency Relationship." *Journal of Research in Crime and Delinquency* 33:232–255.

Kaufman, S. (1995). *At Home in the Universe: The Search for Laws of Self-Organisation and Complexity*. Oxford University Press: Oxford.

Langevin, R. and R.A. Lang (1990). "Substance Abuse Among Sex Offenders." *Annuals of Sex Research* 3:397–424.

Laws, D.R. (2003) "The Rise and Fall of Relapse Prevention." *Australian Psychologist* 38:22–30.

Laws, S. M., T. Hudson and T. Ward (eds.), (2000). *Remaking Relapse Prevention with Sex Offenders.* Thousand Oaks, CA: Sage.

Laws, D.R., S.M. Hudson and T. Ward (2000). "The Original Model of Relapse Prevention with Sex Offenders: Promises Unfulfilled." In: D.R. Laws, S.M. Hudson and T. Ward (eds.), *Remaking Relapse Prevention with Sex Offenders: A Sourcebook* (pp. 3–24). Thousand Oaks, CA: Sage.

Lightfoot, L.O. and H.E. Barbaree (1993). "The Relationship Between Substance Use and Abuse and Sexual Offending in Adolescents." In: H.E. Barbaree, W.L. Marshall and S.M. Hudson (eds.), *The Juvenile Sex Offender* (pp. 203–224). New York: Guilford Press.

Looman, J., J. Abracen, R. DiFazio and G. Maillet (2004). "Alcohol and Drug Abuse Among Sexual and Nonsexual Offenders: Relationship to Intimacy Deficits and Coping Strategy." *Sexual Abuse: A Journal of Research and Treatment with Sex Offenders* 16:177–189.

Mann, R.E. (2000). "Managing Resistance and Rebellion in Relapse Prevention." In: D.R. Laws, S.M. Hudson and T. Ward (eds.), *Remaking Relapse Prevention with Sex Offenders* (pp. 187–200). Thousand Oaks, CA: Sage.

Mann, R.E., R. Becket, D. Fisher and D. Thornton (2002). "Relapse Prevention Interview." In: D.M. Doren (ed.), *Evaluating Sex Offenders: A Manual for Civil Commitment and Beyond* (pp. 201–209). Thousand Oaks, CA: Sage.

Mann, R.E., S.D. Webster, C. Schofield and W.L. Marshall (in press). "Approach Versus Avoidance Goals in Relapse Prevention with Sexual Offenders." *Sexual Abuse: A Journal of Research and Treatment.*

Marlatt, G.A. (1985). "Relapse Prevention: Theoretical Rationale and Overview of the Model." In: G.A. Marlatt and J.R. Gordon (eds.), *Relapse Prevention* (pp. 3–70). New York: Guilford.

Marlatt, G.A. and W.H. George (1984). "Relapse Prevention: Introduction and Overview of the Model." *British Journal of Addiction* 79:261–273.

Marshall, W.L. (1997) "Pedophilia: Psychopathology and Theory." In: D.R. Laws and W. O'Donohue (eds.), *Sexual Deviance: Theory, Assessment and Treatment* (pp. 152–174). New York: The Guilford Press

Marshall, W.L., D. Anderson and Y. Fernandez (1999). *Cognitive Behavioral Treatment of Sexual Offenders.* New York: Wiley.

Marshall, W.L., G.A. Serran and F.A. Cortoni (2000). "Childhood Attachment, Sexual Abuse and Their Relationship to Adult Coping in Child Molesters." *Sexual Abuse: A Journal of Research and Treatment* 12:17–26.

Maruna, S. (2001). *Making Good: How Ex-convicts Reform and Rebuild Their Lives.* Washington, DC: American Psychological Association.

McGuire, J. (2001). "What Works in Correctional Intervention? Evidence and Practical Implications." In: G. A. Bernfeld, D. P. Farrington and A. W. Leschied (eds.), *Offender Rehabilitation in Practice: Implementing and Evaluating Effective Programs* (pp. 25–43). Chichester, UK: John Wiley & Sons.

Mischel, W. (1968). *Personality and Assessment.* New York: Wiley.

Nagin, D. and R.Paternoster (1994). "Personal Capital and Social Control: The Deterrence Implications of a Theory of Individual Differences in Criminal Offending." *Criminology* 32:581–602.

Ogloff, J.R.P. (2002). "Offender Rehabilitation: From 'Nothing Works' to What Next?" *Australian Psychologist* 37:245–252.

O'Grady, W., M. Asbridge and T. Abernathy (2000). "Illegal Tobacco Sales to Youth: A View From Rational Choice Theory." *Canadian Journal of Criminology* January:1–20.

Palmer, E.J. (2003). *Offending Behaviour: Moral Reasoning, Criminal Conduct and the Rehabilitation of Offenders.* Devon, UK: Willan Publishing.

Pithers, W.D. (1997). "Maintaining Treatment Integrity With Sexual Abusers." *Criminal Justice and Behavior* 24:34–51.

Pithers, W.D. (1990). "Relapse Prevention with Sexual Aggressors: A Method for Maintaining Therapeutic Gain and Enhancing External Supervision." In: W.L. Marshall, L. William and D. Laws (eds.), *Handbook of Sexual Assault: Issues, Theories and Treatment of the Offender* (Applied Clinical Psychology, pp. 343–361). New York: Plenum Press.

Pithers, W.D., L.S Beal, J. Armstrong and J. Petty (1989). "Identification of Risk Factors Through Clinical Interviews and Analysis of Records." In: D.R. Laws (ed.), *Relapse Prevention With Sex Offender* (pp. 77–87). New York: Guilford Press.

Rada, R.T. (1976). "Alcoholism and the Child Molester." *Annuals of the New York Academy of Science* 273:492–496.

Schmuck, P. and K.M. Sheldon (2001). *Life Goals and Well-Being.* Toronto, Ontario: Hogrefe & Huber Publishers.

Selzer, M. (1971). "The Michigan Alcoholism Screening Test: The Quest for a New Diagnostic Instrument." *American Journal of Psychiatry* 127:1653–1658.

Skinner, H.A. (1982). "The Drug Abuse Screening Test." *Addictive Behaviors* 7:363–371.

Smallbone, S.W., J. Wheaton and D. Hourigan (2003). "Trait Empathy and Criminal Versatility in Sexual Offenders." *Sexual Abuse: A Journal of Research and Treatment* 15:49–60.

Sommers, I. and D.R. Baskin (1993). "The Situational Context of Violent Female Offending." *Journal of Research in Crime and Delinquency* 30:136–162.

Travin, S. and B. Protter (1993). *Sexual Perversion: Integrative Treatment Approaches for the Clinician.* New York: Plenum Press.

Ward, T. (in press). "Towards a Unified Theory of Sexual Offending." In: T. Ward, D. Polaschek and A.R. Beech (eds.), *Theories of Sexual Offending.* Chichester, UK: John Wiley.

Ward, T. (2002). "Good Lives and the Rehabilitation of Offenders: Promises and Problems." *Aggression and Violent Behaviour* 7:513–528.

Ward, T. and M. Brown (2003). "The Risk-Need Model of Offender Rehabilitation: A Critical Analysis." In: T. Ward, D.R. Laws and S.M. Hudson (eds.), *Sexual Deviance: Issues and Controversies.* Thousand Oaks, CA: Sage.

Ward, T. and S.M. Hudson (2000). "Sexual Offenders' Implicit Planning: A Conceptual Model." *Sexual Abuse: Journal of Research & Treatment* 12:189–202.

Ward, T., K. Louden, S.M. Hudson and W.L. Marshall (1995). "A Descriptive Model of the Offense Chain for Child Molesters." *Journal of Interpersonal Violence* 10:452–472.

Ward, T. and R. Mann (2004). "Good Lives and the Rehabilitation of Offenders: A Positive Approach to Treatment." (in press). In: A. Linley and S. Josephs (eds.). *Positive Psychology in Practice* (pp. 598–616). Chichester, UK: John Wiley.

Ward, T., & Siegert, R. J. (in press). "Toward a Comprehensive Theory of Child Sexual Abuse: A Theory Knitting Perspective." *Psychology, Crime, & Law.*

Ward, T. and C.A. Stewart (2003a). "Criminogenic Needs and Human Needs: Theoretical Model." *Psychology, Crime, & Law* 9:125–143.

Ward, T. and C.A. Stewart (2003b). "Good Lives and the Rehabilitation of Sexual Offenders." In: T. Ward, D. R. Laws and S. M. Hudson (eds.), *Sexual Deviance: Issues and Controversies* (pp. 21–44). Thousand Oaks, CA: Sage.

Ward, T. and C.A. Stewart (2003c). "The Treatment of Sex Offenders: Risk Management and Good Lives." *Professional Psychology: Research and Practice* 34:353–360.

White, R. and F. Haines (2003). *Crime and Criminology: An Introduction* (2nd ed.). Oxford, UK: Oxford University Press.

Witkiewitz, K. and A. Marlatt (2004). "Relapse Prevention for Alcohol and Drug Problems: That was Zen, the is Tao." *American Psychologist* 59:224–235.

Strategies Adopted by Sexual Offenders to Involve Children in Sexual Activity

by

Benoit Leclerc

Julie Carpentier

and

Jean Proulx, Ph.D.
School of Criminology, University of Montreal
Philippe Pinel Institute of Montreal

Abstract: *The aim of the present study was to determine whether offenders who adopted a manipulative or a coercive strategy to involve their victim in sexual activity could be distinguished from those who used a non-persuasive strategy. Four categories of factors were considered: 1. Offender characteristics; 2. Characteristics of the criminal activity of the offender; 3. Victim characteristics; and, 4. Situational factors. Two hundred and twenty-six subjects who had sexually abused at least one child of 13 years old or younger were included in this study. Data were obtained from a semi-structured interview conducted with the offenders, and from official sources of information, such as police reports and victim statements. The results of polytomous logistic regressions suggest that prior offending achievement, victim age and the presence of deviant sexual fantasies 48 hours before the crime are related to the adoption of a manipulative strategy. Implications of these results for the elaboration of prevention measures are discussed.*

Crime Prevention Studies, volume 19 (2006), pp. 251–270.

INTRODUCTION

Because empirical knowledge about the strategies adopted by sexual offenders against children is crucial to prevention programs (Repucci and Haugaard, 1989), several descriptive studies have been conducted in recent decades (e.g., Berliner and Conte, 1990; Elliott et al., 1995). Typically, however, these studies did not analyse the *modus operandi* at all the stages of the crime-commission process, that is, from offenders' first contact with their victims to the ultimate attempts to maintain their victims' silence. Although Kaufman (1991) and his colleagues developed an instrument (*Modus Operandi Questionnaire*) to systematically investigate all stages of modus operandi among sexual offenders against children, very few data are available concerning factors related to the type of strategy adopted by adult offenders to involve children in sexual activity.

Proulx and his colleagues did report results about this particular modus operandi stage. Specifically, Proulx et al. (1999a) reported that extrafamilial sexual offenders adopted two main offending pathways: coercive and non-coercive. These pathways matched the positive- and negative-affect pathways found by Ward et al. (1995) on a number of characteristics like offending strategy and the presence of deviant sexual fantasies prior to the offence. Results of these studies showed that the presence of deviant sexual fantasies before the offence was associated with the adoption of non-coercive strategies. Moreover, Proulx et al. (1999b), working with a larger sample of extrafamilial sexual offenders against children, reported that non-coercion was more prevalent with male victims, and coercion more prevalent with female victims. Further, it was found that non-coercion was adopted in cases of non-acquaintance offender-victim relationships (e.g., strangers). In another study, sexual offenders who worked with or did volunteer work with children and adolescents (e.g., school teachers, coaches) were found to often use non-coercive strategies to gain victims' trust and co-operation, and maintain their victims' silence about sexual contacts (Leclerc et al., 2005).[1]

Despite the value of these results, very few data are available concerning the factors related to the type of strategy adopted by offenders to involve their victim in sexual activity. Proulx and his colleagues reported that characteristics related to the victim, offender-victim relationship and the presence of deviant sexual fantasies play an important role in the choice of offending strategies. However, due to some methodological limitations (small sample size, few variables considered), the results of these studies do not allow firm conclusions to be drawn, and must be considered preliminary. Moreover, the use of an alternative, non-persuasive strategy by sexual offenders of children was not considered in these studies.

Non-persuasive strategies may be conceptually distinguished from both coercive and manipulative (non-coercive) strategies. Sexual offenders against children who adopted a non-persuasive strategy are opportunistic offenders. One offender reported:

> I would wait at night and go in their room. When I could see they were sleeping, I would touch their penis. If they would get awake and resist or tell me to stop I would stop and tell them to not tell anyone and that I would not do it again. If they would not show any resistance, I would go further and masturbate them . . . I would sexually touch a child almost every night.

Another offender explained that:

> Most of the days, I would simply go in a park and sit on a bench watching children play. Children are curious so most of them would come and see me, asking me questions and so on. After some times, I would wait for a child to stay with me and when I would find an opportunity to sexually touch him, I would do it. I would not use a particular strategy . . . I do not know why . . . it was stronger than me . . . I was like a drug addict that could not stop himself from smoking a joint. . . . If I wanted to go further and masturbated them and so on, I would wait to be in an isolated place in the park for sure . . . only one young girl resisted by saying no to me so I stopped and told her I would not do it again. I never tried to touch her again because there were so many other opportunities. . . . They were between 3 and 8 years of age and the older was about 10 years old.

These offenders wait for an opportunity to sexually abuse their victims, but do not try to persuade them in the first place. Although they may have deviant sexual fantasies and plan their offence, this type of crime does not rely on the offenders adopting specific strategies to persuade their victims. Furthermore, strategies like physical force or violence could be used if the child is resisting and the offender wants to go further anyway, but if the child is receptive the offender may not need to use particular strategies to involve him in sexual activity. Therefore, an opportunity may be sufficient for sexually abusing a child, particularly with younger children. In fact, younger children are more vulnerable and may not realize the sexual nature of particular physical contact when being touched by an offender (Berliner and Conte, 1990).

THE RATIONAL CHOICE PERSPECTIVE

The rational choice perspective on criminal behavior (Clarke and Cornish, 2001; Cornish and Clarke, 1986) is the basic framework for the present study. The most important assumption of this perspective is that crime is a rational, purposive behavior and that the choices offenders make during criminal events are voluntary. This perspective views offenders as individuals who commit crimes in an attempt to satisfy their need for rewards such as money, sexual intercourse, elevated status, and excitement (Clarke and Cornish, 2001). Despite the fact that offenders exhibit limited rationality (Johnson and Payne, 1986), they nevertheless attempt to minimize their risks of being apprehended and maximize their gains. For instance, sexual offenders of children have been found to say that they would select the most friendly and receptive child and that they take into account the possibility of being caught (Conte et al., 1989).

According to Clarke and Cornish (2001), the rational choice perspective offers a dynamic picture which views offending as much more present-oriented and situationally influenced than does other criminological theories. It also "pays as much attention to the causal role of immediate situational variables as to more remote variables such as family background and upbringing" (Clarke and Cornish, 2001, p.33), which is necessary to advance our understanding of offending. Thus, the strategies offenders adopt to reach their goals may depend on their personal background or experiences, the characteristics of the victim, and situational factors. For this reason, this investigation of the strategies adopted by offenders to involve their victim in sexual activity analysed the role of characteristics related to offenders, their criminal activity, their victim, and situations.

Aims

The main goal of the present investigation was to determine the relative importance of characteristics related to offenders, their criminal activity, their victim, and situational factors on the type of strategy adopted by sexual offenders to involve children in sexual activity. A more specific goal was to establish whether these factors could help predict the adoption of a manipulative or coercive, rather than a non-persuasive strategy. A further question was whether characteristics related to offenders, their criminal activity, their victim, and situational factors differ in cases involving offenders who adopted a non-persuasive strategy compared to cases involving offenders who adopted a manipulative or a coercive strategy. It may be that offenders who adopted a non-persuasive strategy did not have to use a more sophisticated strategy, because, for example, of the characteristics of the victim (e.g., younger children).

Method

Participants

The sample consisted of 226 adult males who had been convicted for a sexual offence against a child of 13 years old or younger. During their incarceration between 1995 and 2000, they were assessed at the Regional Reception Centre of Ste-Anne-des-Plaines, Quebec, a maximum-security institution of the Correctional Service of Canada, where they underwent a six-week assessment of risk level and treatment needs prior to transfer to another institution.

The mean age of the participants was 45.1 (range, 18–78 years; SD = 11.77) and most of them (72.1%) had completed grade school (n = 163). Nearly half of the participants (43.8%) had at least one prior sexual offence(s) (n = 99). The mean age at commission of first sexual crime (including non-contact and unreported sexual crimes) was 30.3 years old (SD = 10.42), and two-thirds of offenders (66.8%; n = 151) were considered to have had a high previous success rate of offending without being caught (labelled "prior offending achievement").[2] The mean age of the victims was 8.6 years (SD = 3.11), and more than half of the victims (68.6%; n = 155) were female.

Relatively few offenders said that they had premeditated their crime (20.8%; n = 47), while 42.9% (n = 97) had been living with the victim at the time of the crime, 38.1% (n = 86) had an extrafamilial relationship with the victim, and 31.9% (n = 72) had deviant sexual fantasies 48 hours before the crime. Almost a third of offenders sexually abused their victim only at night (29.2%; n = 66), but half of the group did so both day and night (50.9%; n = 115). Finally, while many offenders (40.7%; n = 92) adopted a manipulative strategy to involve their victim in sexual activity, a minority (12.4%; n = 28) used a coercive strategy, and nearly half (46.9%; n = 106) used a non-persuasive strategy.

Procedure

The method of collecting these data has been described in a study of a subset of the present sample (Proulx et al., 1999a). All data used in this study were gathered through a semi-structured interview conducted with each participant and from official sources of information (e.g., police reports, victim statements). The participation in this study was strictly voluntary. Each participant signed a consent form stating that the information would be used for research purposes only.

Measures

Interrater agreement was measured on the basis of 16 interviews conducted jointly by two raters (the principal research assistant and the first author). Ratings were done independently following these interviews, which were conducted by one interviewer in the presence of the other. The mean kappa was .87, which represents very strong agreement. Examples of questions included asking participants if they had been living with their victim at the moment of the crime, had planned to sexually abuse their victim, and had fantasies involving sexual contacts with their victim 48 hours before the crime.

In this study, four types of data were gathered: 1) Offender characteristics (age, highest school diploma obtained); 2) Criminal activity of the offender (age at commission of first sexual crime, prior sexual offence(s) including non-contact and unreported sexual crimes, and prior offending achievement); 3) Victim characteristics (age, gender); and, 4) Situational factors (the time of day the crime was committed, living with the victim at the moment of the crime, type of offender-victim relationship, premeditation of the offence, and presence of deviant sexual fantasies 48 hours before the crime, that is, fantasies involving sexual contacts with the victim). All of these variables were dichotomous (0 = absence, 1 = presence), except for time of day, which had three possible values (0 = day, 1 = night, 2 = both day and night), and three continuous variables (age of the offender, age at commission of first sexual crime, age of the victim).

The dependent variable in this analysis was the type of strategy used to sexually abuse a child, that is, the most common strategy adopted by offenders to sexually abuse their victim. Initially, this variable consisted of eight categories: 0 = seduction (n = 58); 1 = money and gifts (n = 16); 2 = playing with the victim (n = 13); 3 = trickery (n = 3); 4 = intoxicating the victim with alcohol-drugs (n = 2); 5 = acting on the victim (n = 106);

6 = threats of coercion or violence (n = 8); 7 = physical force (n = 20). *Acting on the victim* refers specifically to situations in which the offender acted directly on his victim without using any particular strategy in order to involve him/her in sexual activity. In other words, without trying to persuade the victim in the first place, the offender committed his crime when he had the opportunity to do so, using a non-persuasive strategy. The above categories were subsequently regrouped into three broader categories: 1) manipulative strategy, that is, bribing or tricking the victim (categories 0 to 4); 2) coercive strategy, that is, verbally or physically forcing the victim (categories 6 and 7); and, 3) non-persuasive strategy, that is, the absence of any particular strategy (category 5).

RESULTS

Statistical Analyses

Hierarchical polytomous logistic regressions were conducted to distinguish which type of strategy was adopted on the basis of the characteristics of the offender, his criminal activity, his victim, and situational factors. Since we wanted to distinguish offenders who used a non-persuasive strategy from other offenders, the analyses consisted of comparisons between adopting a manipulative and a non-persuasive strategy and between using a coercive and a non-persuasive strategy. Polytomous logistic regression allows the inclusion of any kind of independent variables (continuous, dichotomous, ordinal) and does not assume a normal distribution (Hosmer and Lemeshow, 2000). Moreover, to ensure a logical temporal sequence (Cohen and Cohen, 1983) in the crime event analyses, we used a hierarchical type of analysis and considered the four types of characteristics in the order listed above (offender, criminal activity, victim, situational factors).

Following the recommendations of Hosmer and Lemeshow (2000), the bivariate relationships between each independent variable (the four types of characteristics) and the dependent variable (the three types of strategies) were analysed first. Then, variables with a p-value of 0.25 or higher were excluded and the polytomous logistic regression was conducted with remaining variables.

Each time a block was entered, the independent variables which were not statistically associated with the dependent variable were excluded, which ensured the most parsimonious model (see Hosmer and Lemeshow,

2000, p. 92). In other words, independent variables which did not improve the ability to predict the dependent variable were withdrawn. This allowed the identification of the independent variables that made a unique contribution to the prediction of the dependent variable. As stated by Hosmer and Lemeshow (2000): "The rationale for minimizing the number of variables in the model is that the resultant model is more likely to be numerically stable, and is more easily generalized" (p. 92). Following this, a final polytomous logistic regression was conducted. Finally, to verify the model, another polytomous logistic regression was conducted, using all the variables (both non-significant and significant) initially included in the analyses.

Since these analyses indicated that the selected factors did not distinguish between the adoption of a coercive and a non-persuasive strategy, the only category of dependent variable for which the fit of the model was assessed was the adoption of a manipulative strategy. To assess the fit of the model, we used Hosmer and Lemeshow's goodness-of-fit statistic, which we obtained by conducting a dichotomous logistic regression. To assess multicollinearity and singularity, coefficient stability for each independent variable was also measured each time a new block was included in the model.

In order to find the best cut-off point to classify cases, the Receiving Operating Characteristics (ROC) curve was determined. This curve plots the probability of detecting true (sensitivity) and false (1-specificity) signals over the entire range of possible cut-off points (Hosmer and Lemeshow, 2000). This procedure also generates the area under the ROC curve (AUC), which provides a measure of the final model's discriminatory power.

Bivariate Analyses

As depicted in Table 1, participants who adopted a manipulative strategy (77.2%) or a coercive strategy (71.4%) had higher prior offending achievement than those who used a non-persuasive strategy (56.6%) (χ^2 (2) = 9.71, p = .008). The age (F (5.81), p = .003) and gender (χ^2 (2) = 7.21, p = .027) of the victim were both significantly related to the type of strategy. A manipulative strategy was more often adopted with older victims (mean age of 9.4 years, SD = 2.8), and a coercive or a non-persuasive strategy was more frequently observed with female victims (78.6% and 74.5%, respectively).

Table 1: Bivariate Analyses of Manipulative (M), Coercive (C) and Non-Persuasive Strategy (NP)[1,2]

	M	C	NP	χ^2	F	p
Offender characteristics						
School diploma (grade school)	79.3%	67.9%	67.0%	4.03		.133
Offender criminal activity characteristics						
Prior sexual offence(s)	50.0%	32.1%	41.5%	3.21		.201
Prior offending achievement	77.2%	71.4%	56.6%	9.71		.008**
Victim characteristics						
Age of the victim[3]	9.4 (2.8)	8.6 (3.2)	7.9 (3.2)		5.81	.003**
Gender of the victim (female)	58.7%	78.6%	74.5%	7.21		.027*
Situational factors						
Time of day				5.53		.237
Night	22.8%	25.0%	35.8%			
Day and night	58.7%	53.6%	43.4%			
Offender-victim relationship (extrafamilial)	44.6%	28.6%	34.9%	3.17		.205
Premeditation	31.5%	17.9%	12.3%	11.26		.004**
Deviant sexual fantasies (48 hours before the crime)	47.8%	25.0%	19.8%	18.50		.000**

Note: *p<0.05, ** p<0.01 (2-tailed).
[1.]There was no multicollinearity in this study.
[2.]Only the variables with a p-value lower than 0.25 are presented.
[3.]Mean and standard deviation are presented. Linearity was verified and Levene test was used to identify problems of homogeneity of variance (sig. =.255).

Two situational variables were related to the type of strategy adopted by the offender: premeditation (χ^2 (2) = 11.26, p = .004) and deviant sexual fantasies 48 hours before the crime (χ^2 (2) = 18.50, p = .000). Participants who adopted a manipulative strategy were more likely to have premeditated their crime (31.5%) and to have had deviant sexual fantasies 48 hours prior the offence (47.8%).

Hierarchical Polytomous Logistic Regression Analyses

As shown in Table 2, the Hosmer and Lemeshow' goodness-of-fit statistic indicates that the model fits well (χ^2 (8) = 9.98, p = .267) for the prediction of adopting a manipulative strategy. No residual was greater than 3, and 74% of the area was under the ROC curve. Thus, the capacity of the model to discriminate between offenders who adopted a manipulative strategy from those who used a non-persuasive strategy is considered acceptable (Hosmer and Lemeshow, 2000). However, the comparison between offenders who adopted a coercive strategy and those who used a non-persuasive strategy was not significant.

In block 2, the introduction of prior offending achievement predicted the type of strategy (χ^2 (2) = 10.00, p = .007). Participants having a higher prior offending achievement were 2.6 times (Ψ (OR) = 2.63) more likely to adopt a manipulative than a non-persuasive strategy. The inclusion of the age of the victim in block 3 (χ^2 (2) = 10.00, p = .007) also proved to be a relevant predictor. Results showed that participants who adopted a manipulative strategy distinguished themselves from those who used a non-persuasive strategy by abusing an older victim. Consequently, for each one-unit increase of the victim's age (0 to 13 years old), the likelihood that a manipulative strategy will be used as opposed to a non-persuasive strategy increases 1.2 times (Ψ = 1.17). Furthermore, adding block 4, situational factors, contributed to the prediction of the type of strategy. Among the block 4 factors, the presence of deviant sexual fantasies 48 hours before the crime (χ^2 (2) = 7.04, p = .030) was statistically significant. Participants with deviant sexual fantasies 48 hours prior to the crime were 2.4 times (Ψ = 2.48) more likely to adopt a manipulative, rather than a non-persuasive strategy.

Following this, an analysis using the significant variables was performed. Prior offending achievement, victim age, and deviant sexual fantasies 48 hours prior to the crime, all remained significant. Lastly, another polytomous logistic regression with all the variables (non-significant and

Table 2: Hierarchical Polytomous Logistic Regression Analysis of Manipulative versus Non-persuasive and Coercive versus Non-persuasive Strategy

χ²	df	p	Predictors	Manipulative (n = 92) p	Ψ	Conf. int.	Coercive (n = 28) p	Ψ	Conf. int.
			Block 1						
4.13	2	.127	School diploma (grade school)	.053	1.89	(1.0–3.6)	.930	1.04	(.43–2.5)
			Block 2						
–	–	–	School diploma (grade school)						
3.42	2	.180	Prior sexual offence(s)	.201	1.46	(.82–2.6)	.399	.683	(.28–1.7)
10.00	2	.007*	Prior offending achievement	.002	2.63	(1.4–4.9)	.169	1.89	(.76–4.7)
			Block 3						
–	–	–	School diploma (grade school)						
–	–	–	Prior sexual offence(s)						
6.40	2	.041*	Prior offending achievement	.018	2.18	(1.1–4.2)	.145	2.00	(.79–5.0)
10.00	2	.007**	Age of the victim	.002	1.17	(1.1–1.3)	.335	1.07	(.93–1.2)
5.03	2	.081	Gender of the victim	.078	.563	(.30–1.1)	.496	1.43	(.51–4.0)
			Block 4						
–	–	–	School diploma (grade school)						
–	–	–	Prior sexual offence(s)						
7.39	2	.025*	Prior offending achievement	.010	2.43	(1.2–4.8)	.147	1.98	(.79–5.0)
10.30	2	.006**	Age of the victim	.002	1.19	(1.1–1.3)	.159	1.11	(.96–1.3)
–	–	–	Gender of the victim						
4.42	4	.352	Time of day						
			Night	.057	.488	(.23–1.0)	.289	.572	(.20–1.6)
			Day and night	.830	.907	(.37–2.2)	.850	1.12	(.35–3.6)
1.03	2	.597	Offender-victim relationship	.927	.967	(.48–2.0)	.334	.602	(.22–1.7)
5.77	2	.056	Premeditation	.018	2.74	(1.2–6.3)	.340	1.80	(.54–6.1)
7.04	2	.030*	Deviant sexual fantasies (48 hours before the crime)	.012	2.48	(1.2–5.0)	.832	1.12	(.39–3.2)
			Final analyses						
6.99	2	.030*	Prior offending achievement	.012	2.32	(1.2–4.5)	.180	1.86	(.75–4.6)
8.67	2	.013*	Age of the victim	.004	1.16	(1.0–1.3)	.336	1.07	(.93–1.2)
15.41	2	.000**	Deviant sexual fantasies (48 hours before the crime)	.000	3.45	(1.8–6.6)	.620	1.28	(.48–3.4)

	χ²	df	p	χ²	df	p
Goodness-of-fit χ² (Hosmer-Lemeshow)	9.98	8	.267	–	–	–

	χ²	df	p
Final model	35.20	6	.000**

Final cutpoint	.50
Area under the curve (ROC)	.74
Residual > 3	0

Note: * $p<0.05$, ** $p<0.01$ (2-tailed).

significant) initially included in the analyses was conducted, to verify the model. This analysis confirmed the model.

Despite the fact that the statistical analysis did not distinguish between adopting a coercive and a non-persuasive strategy, some results are worthy of attention. In fact, as Table 2 indicates, the odds ratios (Ψ) for the significant predictors of the final model (i.e., prior offending achievement, victim age and deviant sexual fantasies) were also positive in this analysis (1.86, 1.07, and 1.28, respectively). As it is the case for the use of a manipulative strategy, this means that offenders who have a higher prior offending achievement, who sexually abused an older victim and who have deviant sexual fantasies could be also more likely to adopt a coercive, rather than a non-persuasive strategy. However, in that regard, other studies are warranted.

DISCUSSION

The main goal of the present study was to determine whether offenders who adopted a manipulative or a coercive strategy to involve their victim in sexual activity could be distinguished from those who adopted a non-persuasive strategy. Polytomous logistic regression revealed that prior offending achievement, victim age, and the presence of deviant sexual fantasies 48 hours prior to the assault are important predictors of the type of strategy (manipulative vs. non-persuasive) that the offenders adopted to involve their victim in sexual activity. However, the characteristics included in this study did not allow offenders who adopted a coercive strategy to be statistically distinguished from those who adopted a non-persuasive strategy.

Prior Offending Achievement

Although our measure of prior offending achievement may have some limitations, our results showed that offenders considered to have a high probability of successfully re-offending were more prone to use a manipulative than a non-persuasive strategy. These results could mean that the adoption of manipulative strategies improves the success of offending. For instance, the gradual introduction of sexual contacts day after day following touching allows sexual offenders to assess, after each criminal event, the risks of being reported by the child. This minimizes the risks of being apprehended (Kaufman et al., 1998; see also Young, 1997) and facilitates the long-term abuse of the same victim.

The above sophisticated process is characteristic of sexual offenders who work with children. To reduce the risks of apprehension and facilitate repeat offending, many of these offenders maintain their victims' silence about the abuse through very subtle threats involving the withdrawal of love, rather than the use or threat of violence (Leclerc et al., 2005). In fact, Leclerc et al. (2005) found that the most frequent strategy (34.7%; n = 8) adopted by these offenders was to claim that they would go to jail if their victim told anyone about the abuse; none used actual or threatened violence. Manipulative strategies reflect a more sophisticated modus operandi (Kaufman et al., 1996) which provides benefits for the offender. This is consistent with the rational choice perspective, which stipulates that crimes are committed with the intention of benefiting the offender (Clarke and Cornish, 2001).

The fact that offenders who have a high probability of successfully re-offending, on the basis of their prior offending achievement, were more likely to use a manipulative rather a non-persuasive strategy, may be a consequence of a process of behavioural change resulting from differential reinforcement. "Differential reinforcement refers to the balance of anticipated or actual rewards and punishments that follow or are consequences of behavior" (Akers, 1998, pp. 66–67). Further, criminal behaviour and criminal techniques are shaped according to the principles of operant conditioning. Therefore, offenders who adopt manipulative strategies may be more experienced offenders who have learned that these strategies are more effective in providing benefits and reducing the risks of apprehension.

The Age of the Victim

Our results showed that offenders who sexually abused older victim were more likely to use a manipulative, rather than a non-persuasive strategy. But why exactly would manipulative offenders be likely to abuse older children, when younger children are more vulnerable? Erickson et al. (1988) found that the sexual contacts offenders have with older victims are more intrusive than those with younger ones. Further, they stated that, albeit unwilling, older children have more chances of being treated like sexual partners than younger children. The rational choice perspective (Clarke and Cornish, 2001) would indicate that sexual offenders try to obtain the maximum sexual gratification. Thus, a possible explanation for the fact that offenders who abuse older victims adopt manipulative strategies is that these offenders are probably fixated offenders with emotional and sexual preferences for children and who thus try to obtain the maximum sexual gratification possible. Over the course of their "careers," these offenders have developed effective strategies to satisfy their emotional and sexual needs with children.

Our results also showed that adult offenders may not need to use a manipulative or a coercive strategy with younger victims. The younger the victim, the more successful non-persuasive strategies are likely to be in involving a victim in sexual activity. Thus, the sophistication of strategies may also reflect the age of the victim. In fact, apart from their experience, offenders may alter their methods on the basis of the degree of vulnerability of their target (see Reppetto, 1976).

Deviant Sexual Fantasies

Proulx et al. (1999a) found that the presence of deviant sexual fantasies was related to the adoption of a non-coercive (i.e., manipulative) pathway. This pathway also matched the positive affect pathway found by Ward et al. (1995) related to the presence of deviant sexual fantasies prior to the offence (regarding the role of sexual fantasies in the commission of sexual offences involving adult women, see Beauregard et al., 2005). The results of the present study are consistent with these findings: offenders with deviant sexual fantasies 48 hours prior to their offence were significantly more prone to use a manipulative, rather than a non-persuasive strategy.

Results obtained by Proulx et al. (1995) and Proulx et al. (1999b) provide us some explanation of why offenders who adopt manipulative strategies have deviant sexual fantasies. These authors found that offenders who were more likely to adopt non-coercive strategies and have deviant sexual fantasies had avoidant and dependent personalities. An offender with this personality profile has low self-esteem and thinks that adults reject him. Consequently, he avoids adults and turns to children, most often male children, to satisfy the emotional and sexual needs he is unable to satisfy with adults. The presence of deviant sexual fantasies is a consequence of this emotional and sexual investment in children, whereas the adoption of manipulative strategies is a result of their experience in successfully satisfying these needs. Thus, psychological factors, like the personality attributes of the offender, may also need to be taken into account in understanding the choices he makes when offending (Trasler, 1993). The presence of deviant sexual fantasies and the use of manipulative strategies are influenced by the personality of the offender.

CONCLUSION

This research suffered from certain limitations. The study sample included only a small number of offenders who had adopted a coercive strategy. This is probably the reason the analyses did not distinguish between offenders who had adopted a coercive strategy and those who had used a non-persuasive strategy. Furthermore, our sample included only incarcerated offenders. It is possible that the modus operandi of these sexual offenders was different (either less or more sophisticated) from those used by offenders who have not been apprehended. Moreover, data were only collected for the main type of strategy adopted by the offenders (manipulative, coercive or non-persuasive). In other words, we do not have specific information about whether an offender had tried another type of strategy before adopting the strategy that actually allowed him to involve his victim in sexual activity.

The population of sexual offenders against children appears to include both offenders who adopt relatively sophisticated strategies and those who adopt no particular strategy at all (i.e., use non-persuasive strategies). This result is relevant for crime prevention. Although speculative, prevention measures can be suggested. For instance, sexual offenders who work with children use manipulative strategies to gain the trust of their victims and gradually involve them in sexual activity. It should therefore be possible to design situational measures that block offenders while they are in the process of committing their crimes, that is, before they sexually abuse a child (Leclerc et al., 2005; see also Cornish, 1998). One such measure might be restriction to or monitoring of access to unsupervised areas. For instance, sports coaches could be prohibited from going to competitions or on trips alone with groups of children, or from using the same changing room and shower. This should also be the case for school teachers and other employees who are in a position of trust (Leclerc et al., 2005).

To prevent child sexual abuse, parents should be aware of how sexual offenders behave in the company of children. Moreover, selected administrators of youth-oriented organisations (e.g., Boy Scouts) should be trained to understand the pattern of behaviour of offenders. This would allow parents and youth-oriented organisations to more easily identify potential offenders. Thereafter, this information could be used as early-warning signs whose presence would indicate a need for further investigation of the personal and social lives of these individuals (Leclerc et al., 2005; van Dam, 2001). However, parents and youth-oriented organisations should also be aware that some offenders do not use any particular strategies (i.e., non-persuasive strategy) with younger children. In those cases, effective supervision remains the most efficient measure to reduce offending opportunities. As Smallbone and Wortley (2000) have pointed out, public education programs can also be employed to provide information to parents and guardians about the need for effective supervision and protection of children. According to these authors, public campaigns need to be expanded to include the recognition of the danger that exists for children at home and among their friends. Finally, the issue of reporting the abuse should also be addressed in these campaigns (Smallbone and Wortley, 2000).

Where offenders do not engage in prior grooming behaviour, it is not possible to intervene with situational prevention measures at this point, at least on the basis of their pattern of behaviours. In those cases, the intervention points are more limited and the emphasis must be on stages such as the preparation phase in which restriction of access to and use of child pornography are possible prevention measures (Cornish, 1998). It should also be noted that for these offenders, a single opportunity at a particular moment is enough for them to sexually offend. For instance, a child left alone in a park provides an opportunity for those offenders. Thus, capable guardianship could be extended to parks, video arcades, playgrounds, swimming pool and, even, apartment buildings.

A larger sample size could enable researchers to distinguish offenders who adopted a coercive strategy from those who adopted a non-persuasive strategy. The personality of offenders and victims are also characteristics that should be studied. In fact, Proulx et al. (1995) and Proulx et al. (1999b) found that the personality of the offender may influence the offending process, including the modus operandi. Following these results, Proulx et al. (1995) suggested that offender profiles could be developed and used when treating offenders, in order to help them identify their own offending process and prevent recidivism. As for the personality of the victim, Berliner and Conte (1990) found that many victims came from dysfunctional families, and that the sexual abuse relationship filled a deficit in their life. Parents could benefit from understanding the characteristics of vulnerable children that attract sexual offenders, and should pay special attention to the protection of vulnerable children (Conte et al., 1989). The presentation of information on the process of victimization to children who have already been abused may also help prevent future aggression (Berliner and Conte, 1990).

Most importantly, there is a need for detailed information on each stage of the modus operandi. This would improve the identification of particular crime scripts and, by extension, the development of situational crime prevention strategies (Cornish, 1994a, 1994b, 1998) specific to each stage of the modus operandi. For this purpose, it would be relevant to analyse the crime-commission process for different types of sexual offenders (e.g., sexual offenders who work with children). Moreover, according to Cornish (1994b), identifying crime scripts provides designers of situational measures with a wide range of intervention points. For instance, it makes it possible to disrupt the preparation phase (e.g., by restricting access and use of child pornography) and the preconditions (e.g., by providing capable guardianship in settings where potential victims could be easily identified by offenders) necessary for the crime to occur. Further, since crime scripts offer the possibility of examining alternative pathways that offenders might follow if they meet obstacles in the crime-commission process, designers of situational measures could anticipate the types of "displacement" that may result from particular situational strategies (Cornish, 1994b). This would provide even more intervention points at which the crime could be disrupted. For instance, an offender may try to abuse children in parks if the children he knows are too well supervised by their parents. In this situation capable guardianship in parks could be a measure to block the offending process. Thus, identifying crime scripts provides the possibility of maximizing prevention strategies.

Address correspondence to: Benoit Leclerc, Institut Philippe Pinel de Montréal, Centre de recherche Philippe Pinel de Montréal, 10 905 boul. Henri-Bourassa est, Montréal, Québec, Canada, H1C 1H1; e-mail: benoit. leclerc4@sympatico.ca.

Acknowledgments: The authors wish to thank Derek Cornish, Richard Wortley and the anonymous reviewers for thoughtful comments made on an earlier version of this paper.

NOTES

1. The term *non-coercive* used in these studies refers to the same strategies that are termed *manipulative* in the present study. We believe this term is more precise and less misleading when the term coercive is also used in the same study.

2. Prior offending achievement refers to the probability, on the basis of the history of convictions, of successfully re-offending. For each subject, the number of previous convictions was determined and a ratio of the number of previous convictions to the total number of crimes committed was calculated. A dichotomous variable was then constructed on the basis of this ratio. Subjects whose ratio was less than 0.50 were considered to have a high probability of successfully re-offending, as they had been convicted of less than half of their previous crimes.

REFERENCES

Akers, R.L. (1998). *Social Learning and Social Structure: A General Theory of Crime and Deviance.* Boston, MA: Northeastern University Press.

Beauregard, E., P. Lussier and J. Proulx (2005). "The Role of Sexual Interests and Situational Factors on Rapists' Modus Operandi: Implications for Offender Profiling." *Legal and Criminological Psychology* 10:265–278.

Berliner, L. and J.R. Conte (1990). "The Process of Victimization: The Victim's Perspective." *Child Abuse and Neglect* 14:29–40.

Clarke, R.V. and D.B. Cornish (2001). "Rational Choice." In: R. Paternoster and R. Bachman (eds.), *Explaining Criminals and Crime: Essays in Contemporary Criminological Theory* (pp. 23–42). Los Angeles, CA: Roxbury Publishing Company.

Cohen, J. and P. Cohen (1983). *Applied Multiple Regression/Correlation Analysis for the Behavioural Sciences.* Second edition. Lawrence Erlbaum Associates, Publishers.

Conte, J.R., S. Wolf and T. Smith (1989). "What Sexual Offenders Tell Us About Prevention Strategies." *Child Abuse and Neglect* 13:293–301.

Cornish, D.B. (1998). "Regulating Lifestyles: A Rational Choice Perspective." Paper presented at the 7th International Seminar on Environmental Criminology and Crime Analysis, Barcelona.

Cornish, D.B. (1994a). "Crimes as Scripts." In: D. Zahm and P. Cromwell (eds.), *Proceedings of the International Seminar on Environmental Criminology and Crime Analysis* (pp. 30–45). University of Miami, Coral Gables, Florida, 1993. Tallahassee, FL: FL Statistical Analysis Center, FL Criminal Justice Executive Institute, Florida Dept of Law Enforcement.

Cornish, D.B. (1994b). "The Procedural Analysis of Offending and Its Relevance for Situational Prevention." In: R.V. Clarke (ed.), *Crime Prevention Studies* (vol. 3, pp. 151–196). Monsey, NY: Criminal Justice Press.

Cornish, D.B. and R.V. Clarke (1986). "Introduction." In: D.B. Cornish and R.V. Clarke (eds.), *The Reasoning Criminal: Rational Choice Perspectives on Offending* (pp. 1–16). New York: Springer-Verlag.

Elliott, M., K. Browne and J. Kilcoyne (1995). "Child Sexual Abuse Prevention: What Offenders Tell Us." *Child Abuse and Neglect* 19:579–594.

Erickson, W.D., N.H. Walbeck and R.K. Seely (1988). "Behavior Patterns of Child Molesters." *Archives of Sexual Behaviour* 17:77–87.

Hosmer, D.W. and S. Lemeshow (2000). *Applied Logistic Regression* (2nd ed.). New York: John Wiley & Sons.

Johnson, E. and J. Payne (1986). "The Decision to Commit a Crime: An Information-Processing Analysis." In: D.B. Cornish and R.V. Clarke (eds.), *The Reasoning Criminal: Rational Choice Perspectives on Offending* (pp. 170–185). New York: Springer-Verlag.

Kaufman, K.L. (1991). *Modus Operandi Questionnaire*. Columbus, OH: Author (Children's Hospital).

Kaufman, K. L., J. Holmberg, K. A. Orts, F. McCrady, A.L. Rotzien, E.L. Daleiden and D. Hilliker (1998). "Factors Influencing Sexual Offenders' Modus Operandi: An Examination of Victim-Offender Relatedness and Age." *Child Maltreatment* 3:349–361.

Kaufman, K.L., K. Orts, J. Holmberg, F. McCrady, E.L. Daleiden and D. Hilliker (1996). "Contrasting Adult and Adolescent Sexual Offenders' Modus Operandi: A Developmental Process?" Paper presented at the 15th Annual Conference of the Association for the Treatment of Sexual Abusers, Chicago, IL.

Leclerc, B., J. Proulx and A. McKibben (2005). "Modus Operandi of Sexual Offenders Working or Doing Voluntary Work with Children and Adolescents." *Journal of Sexual Aggression* 2:187–195.

Proulx, J., M. Ouimet and N. Lachaîne (1995). "Criminologie De L'acte Et Pédophilie." *Revue Internationale de Criminologie et de Police Technique* 48:294–310.

Proulx, J., C. Perreault and M. Ouimet (1999a). "Pathways in the Offending Process of Extrafamilial Sexual Child Molesters." *Sexual Abuse: A Journal of Research and Treatment* 11:117–129.

Proulx, J., C. Perreault, M. Ouimet and J.P. Guay (1999b). "Les Agresseurs Sexuels D'enfants: Scénarios Délictuels Et Troubles De La Personnalité." In: J. Proulx, M. Cusson and M. Ouimet (eds.), *Les Violences Criminelles* (pp. 187–216). Saint-Nicholas, Quebec: Les Presses de l'Université Laval.

Reppetto, T.A. (1976). "Crime Prevention and the Displacement Phenomenon." *Crime & Delinquency* 22:166–177.

Repucci, N.D. and J.J. Haugaard (1989). "Prevention of Child Sexual Abuse: Myth or Reality." *American Psychologist* 44:1266–1275.

Smallbone, S. and R. Wortley (2000). *Child Sexual Abuse in Queensland: Offender Characteristics and Modus Operandi* (full report). Brisbane, Australia: Queensland Crime Commission.

Trasler, G. (1993). "Conscience, Opportunity, Rational Choice and Crime." In: R.V. Clarke and M. Felson (eds.), *Routine Activity and Rational Choice* (pp. 305–322). (Advances in Criminological Theory, vol. 5.) New Brunswick, NJ: Transaction Publishers.

van Dam, C. (2001). *Identifying Child Molesters: Preventing Child Sexual Abuse by Recognizing the Patterns of the Offenders*. New York: Haworth Maltreatment and Trauma Press.

Ward, T., K. Louden, S.M. Hudson and W.L. Marshall (1995). "A Descriptive Model of the Offense Chain for Child Molesters." *Journal of Interpersonal Violence* 10:452–472.

Young, S. (1997). "The Use of Normalization as a Strategy in the Sexual Exploitation of Children by Adult Offenders." *Canadian Journal of Human Sexuality* 6:285–295.